MICHIGAN PROFICIENCY PRACTICE TESTS for the ECPE

Diane Flanel Piniaris

REVISED EDITION 2013

Australia • Brazil • Japan • Korea • Mexico • Singapore • Spain • United Kingdom • United States

Michigan Proficiency Practice Tests for the Michigan ECPE
Student's Book Revised edition (2013)
Diane Flanel Piniaris

Development Editor: Kayleigh Buller
Head of Production: Alissa McWhinnie
Manufacturing Buyer: Eyvett Davis
Marketing Manager: Michelle Cresswell
Project Editor: Tom Relf
Publisher: Gavin McLean
Compositor: MPS Limited

Acknowledgements

Every effort has been made to trace copyright holders. If any have been inadvertently overlooked, the publishers will be pleased to make the necessary acknowledgments at the first opportunity.

Illustrations by George Alexandris

British Library Cataloguing-in-Publication Data
A catalogue record for this book is available from the British Library.

ISBN: 978-1-4080-9261-3

Cengage Learning EMEA
Cheriton House, North Way, Andover, Hampshire, SP10 5BE
United Kingdom

Cengage Learning products are represented in Canada by Nelson Education Ltd.

For your lifelong learning solutions, visit **www.cengage.co.uk**

Purchase your next print book, e-book or e-chapter at **www.cengagebrain.com**

Printed in China by RR Donnelley
Print Number: 08 Print Year: 2019

Contents

ACKNOWLEDGMENTS

Thanks everyone! We couldn't have done it without you!

I would like to extend my heartfelt thanks to all the people behind the scenes who have aided me over the years in keeping this volume of ECPE practice tests up to date. Special mention goes to Sue Trory, Kayleigh Buller and Tania Psatha at Cengage for helping to make this new edition a reality; to Margaret Brooks for her invaluable work on the Speaking Tests; and to Matthew Banks for his help with the revised Extra Cloze passages. My appreciation also goes to Anita Cooper Tsamakis, Dorothy Adams Metaxopoulou, Gwen Moidinis and Rachel Finnie for their help with the Model Compositions; and "extra credit" goes to Dorothy's venerable English teacher for leaving us his legacy of the "Tell them" writing formula that features so prominently in the Writing Tutorial.

Thanks are also due to all the private language schools in Volos, Greece, that helped pilot the composition topics; to Maria Kandarakia and her students in Skiathos for coming up with the idea of putting a rose in their time capsule; and to my former students who served as eager "guinea pigs" in the piloting stages of the first edition. I am also grateful for the warm reception and loyal support that I have received from members of the ELT community in Greece since the mid-1990s. Their insightful comments and feedback have been the springboard for many of the improvements I have been able to make to the series over the years.

Finally, this page would not be complete without acknowledging the initial vision of Sophia Zaphiropoulos and Carl Wantenaar, founders of New Editions, the original publishers of my ECPE and ECCE titles. Without their support and friendship, this series would never have seen the light of day.

Diane Flanel Piniaris

ABOUT THE AUTHOR

Diane Flanel Piniaris is a native New Yorker who has been teaching EFL since 1980. After graduating from Cornell University in Ithaca, New York, with a Bachelor of Arts *summa cum laude* in English Literature, she spent nine years working as a book editor for publishing houses in New York City and London. In 1980, after studying TEFL methodology at the International Teacher Training Institute in Hastings, England, she moved to Thessaloniki, where she began her teaching career in EFL while studying Modern Greek in the program for foreigners at Aristotle University. From 1983 through 1992, she lived in Germany, where she wrote curriculum materials and taught courses in reading, writing and ESL for soldiers in the U.S. Army and their foreign-born spouses. In 1992, she returned to Greece, where she taught English and launched her ELT writing career. Since 2001, she has resided in New York City, where she continues to write and edit ELT textbooks.

Among her other ECPE and ECCE publications (all published by Cengage) are:

For the ECPE
Michigan Proficiency First Steps
Michigan Proficiency Skills Builder
Michigan Proficiency Listening and Speaking
Michigan Proficiency Final Countdown Practice Tests
Michigan Proficiency All-Star ECPE Practice Tests

For the ECCE
Michigan ECCE All-Star Extra Practice Tests, volume 1
Michigan ECCE All-Star Extra Practice Tests, volume 2

INTRODUCTION

The 2013 revised edition of *Michigan Proficiency Practice Tests* consists of eight complete practice tests plus supporting exercises, activities and test-taking advice for the most recent version of the ECPE (Examination for the Certificate of Proficiency in English).

What's New in this Revision?

In keeping with minor changes made to the format of several sections of the ECPE since 2009, the 2013 revised edition includes changes in the following three areas:

- **Listening Part III:** Printed questions now appear above the answer choices.
- **Cloze sections:** Two 10-item passages now replace the single 20-item passage in each GCVR, and all new passages have been provided in the Extra Cloze Practice section.
- **Grammar sections:** These have been updated to reflect the movement away from conversational grammar items based on short dialogues. All grammar items are now based on a single gapped sentence followed by four answer choices.

Unique Features

1. Thematic content and continuity with other books in the author's ECPE series

The practice tests in this volume are specially designed to provide students with exposure to the kind of material that frequently appears on the ECPE exam. Anyone who has followed the evolution of the ECPE over the years will be aware that certain topics appear in the Cloze, Reading and Listening sections with almost surprising regularity. Chief among these topics are **plants and animals, health and medicine, the environment** and **technology** – all topics which students who have used the author's *Michigan Proficiency First Steps* and/or *Michigan Proficiency Skills Builder* have been systematically exposed to. Students who have used one or both of these books will especially benefit from using the practice tests in this book. This is because the texts that appear in the Cloze, Reading and Listening sections have been carefully chosen to reinforce and build on the topic-related material that students have already encountered. In addition, the tests also include a sprinkling of other, more general topics that occasionally appear on the ECPE (eg, American history and the social sciences), ensuring that students build their confidence by dealing with a broad range of subjects.

2. Special emphasis on vocabulary reinforcement

- **ITEM SELECTION** – Another major feature of the tests is that the large majority of the words tested in the Vocabulary sections come from a master list compiled by the author from ECPE testing materials (eg, Preliminary and Final Tests) made available over the years by the developers of the ECPE. This ensures that students have the opportunity to expand their vocabulary with words at the appropriate level of difficulty. Additionally, it is important to note that students who have used the author's *Michigan Proficiency First Steps* and/or *Michigan Proficiency Skills Builder* will already have encountered many of the words in the Reading, Cloze and Vocabulary tasks in those books. The Vocabulary sections included in this volume will thus serve as a valuable tool for recycling, reviewing and reinforcing lexical items that have previously been introduced.

- **VOCABULARY CONSOLIDATION EXERCISES** – To ensure immediate reinforcement of the words that are encountered, each practice test is followed by a four-page Vocabulary Consolidation section. The Consolidations after Practice Tests 1–3 and 5–7 contain exercises that allow students to focus on the meanings and usage of most of the 160 verbs, nouns, adjectives and adverbs encountered in the corresponding Vocabulary sections. For variety, the Consolidations after Practice Tests 4 and 8 highlight prepositions, idioms, phrasal verbs and adverbial collocations that students have seen in previous units.

- **RECYCLING IN FINAL TESTS 4 AND 8** – The Vocabulary sections in Practice Tests 4 and 8 introduce no new material. Instead, they intentionally recycle words that have already been introduced in the previous three units so that students can catch their breath and consolidate what they already know. To aid consolidation, teachers should encourage students to undertake a complete revision of the appropriate practice tests before attempting the Vocabulary sections in Practice Tests 4 and 8.

3. Special emphasis on composition writing

One of the major hurdles that every candidate encounters when taking the ECPE is the 30-minute time limit for writing the composition in the Writing section. When students begin Proficiency-level work, it is logical for teachers to focus their efforts on making students aware of different composition types and on teaching them strategies for organizing and developing their ideas. As exam time nears, however, another element needs to be added, and that is helping students develop the "lightning reflexes" they need to succeed on the Writing section. *Michigan Proficiency Practice Tests* addresses this by including two unique features.

- **WRITING TUTORIAL** *(Student's Book / Teacher's Book)* – Prefaced by a fun parable introducing the three-part "tell them" paragraph plan and a chart summarizing the four main composition types, the Writing Tutorial contains 16 optional mini-lessons that correspond to the 16 topics that occur in the Writing sections of Practice Tests 1–8. Each tutorial is broken into two parts:

  Before you begin – which contains discussion and brainstorming activities designed to provide younger students with the raw material they need to develop competent compositions; and

  Suggestions for development – which includes step-by-step guidance (eg, **sample topic sentences** and **sequences of linking words**) for building up each paragraph.

  How teachers use these mini-lessons depends, of course, on how much time is available and how good the students' composition skills already are. Teachers may want to rely heavily on the tasks in the first month of preparation and then gradually allow students to work more independently once the main message of using clear topic sentences and linking devices has been driven home. The main objective, of course, is to provide students with a sure-fire method for organizing and developing each composition type so they know exactly how to approach the 30-minute writing task on the day of the exam.

- **MODEL COMPOSITIONS** *(Teacher's Book only)* – Supporting the 16 mini-lessons in the Writing Tutorial are 16 annotated models that demonstrate how the step-by-step guidance provided in the mini-lessons can be put into practice. The models are intended to be used as follow-ups to be shared and discussed with the class after students have attempted one or both of the compositions in each test.

Other Key Features

- A section entitled: *Tips and Strategies for the Day of the Exam*, which provides valuable tips on how students should approach each section of the exam;
- A section entitled *Extra Cloze Practice*, providing 16 additional passages to help students sharpen their Cloze skills;
- An audio program (available on CDs) containing eight Listening Comprehension Tests; and
- A separate Teacher's Book containing answers, examiner scripts for the Speaking Tests, 16 model compositions and an audioscript.

Relation to Other Books in the Author's ECPE Series

Michigan Proficiency Practice Tests is designed to be used in the final stages of a student's preparation for the Michigan ECPE – either on its own or in addition to one or both of the other books of full-length practice tests in the author's ECPE series: *Michigan Proficiency All-Star ECPE Practice Tests* and *Michigan Proficiency Final Countdown Practice Tests*. As the tests in all three of these books review and recycle the thematic, lexical, grammatical and skills content of *Michigan Proficiency First Steps*, *Michigan Proficiency Skills Builder* and *Michigan Proficiency Listening and Speaking*, they are an invaluable tool for the final months of preparation for both first-time candidates and re-takers alike.

It is our sincere hope that the material in these tests will go a long way towards making our students competent test-takers and more confident users of the language.

THE ECPE: OVERVIEW*

The Examination for the Certificate of Proficiency in English (ECPE) is administered in many countries around the world at test centers authorized by Cambridge Michigan Language Assessments (CaMLA).

As of spring 2013, the ECPE consists of the following four sections administered in the order below. For a summary of how the Writing and Speaking sections are graded, see Scoring Criteria for Writing and Speaking on page 9.

1 **Writing** (30 minutes)
Candidates must choose one out of two topics and write an argumentative or expository composition (about 250–300 words).

2 **Listening** (approximately 35–40 minutes) – Audio CD
50 multiple-choice items divided into three parts:
- Part 1 – Interpret short dialogues (17 items)
- Part 2 – Choose the appropriate response to a question (18 items)
- Part 3 – Answer questions about three extended listening passages (15 items)

3 **Grammar, Cloze, Vocabulary, Reading (GCVR)** (75 minutes)
40 multiple-choice Grammar items
20 multiple-choice Cloze items, based on two passages of ten items each
40 multiple-choice Vocabulary items
20 multiple-choice Reading items, based on four passages of five items each

4 **Speaking** (usually 25–35 minutes)
Two or three candidates participate in a decision-making task that allows candidates to demonstrate the full range of their speaking ability while performing a multi-stage semistructured task consisting of the following: introduction and small talk; summarizing and recommending; reaching a consensus; presenting and convincing; justifying and defending. Two examiners will be present during the Speaking Test. In the rare event that three candidates are examined together, the test will last 35–45 minutes. For more information, see page 206.

All examinees will receive an Examination Report that shows their overall performance in one of three categories: Honors, Pass, or Fail.

Additionally, examinees are provided with their results for each section. The five levels of performance, from highest to lowest, are:

Honors (H)
Pass (P)
Low Pass (LP)
Borderline Fail (BF)
Fail (F)

Examinees' scores on the four sections of the examine are taken into consideration in determining who passes the exam and receives a certificate. Here are the guidelines:

- Examinees who receive scores in the Low Pass or higher on all four sections are awarded a certificate.
- Examinees who receive scores in the Low Pass band or higher on three sections and a Borderline Fail on one section are also awarded a certificate.
- Examinees who receive one or more section scores in the Fail band are not awarded a certificate.

* Adapted from the Cambridge Michigan Language Assessments website, retrieved August 13, 2013 from: http://www.cambridgemichigan.org

SCORING CRITERIA FOR WRITING AND SPEAKING*

Writing

The Writing section is graded by CaMLA-trained and certified raters who assign grades according to a five-band scale:

A (Honors) **B** (Pass) **C** (Low Pass) **D** (Borderline Pass) **E** (Fail)

In general, candidates are rated on four main criteria:

- **Rhetoric**: organization, topic development, linking
- **Grammar and syntax**
- **Vocabulary**
- **Mechanics**: punctuation, spelling

A candidate who receives a C displays the following characteristics:

Rhetoric	Grammar and Syntax	Vocabulary	Mechanics
• Topic clearly developed, but not always completely or with acknowledgment of its complexity. • Organization generally controlled; connection sometimes absent or unsuccessful.	• Both simple and complex syntax present. For some, syntax is cautious but accurate, while others are more fluent but less accurate. • Morphological control may be inconsistent.	• Adequate vocabulary, but may sometimes be inappropriately used.	• Spelling and punctuation errors sometimes are distracting.

Speaking

The Speaking Test is rated by two local examiners, following guidelines established by the CaMLA. Candidates are rated on a five-band rating scale as follows:

A (Expert) **B** (Consistent) **C** (Effective) **D** (Dependent) **E** (Limited)

In general, candidates are rated on three main criteria:

- **Discourse and interaction**: production of independent, spontaneous speech; contribution to extended interaction; ability to comprehend what is said in order to engage effectively in conversation
- **Linguistic resources**: range and accuracy of vocabulary and grammar
- **Deliverability and intelligibility**: fluency of delivery, rate of speech, register, ability to be understood

A candidate who receives a C displays the following characteristics:

Discourse and Interaction	Linguistic Resources	Deliverability and Intelligibility
• Summarizes concisely and accurately; may sometimes rely on written material. • Elaborates, often without prompting, and offers coherent explanations. • Often presents decisions clearly; is occasionally limited in extending discourse. • Often contributes to development of interaction; aware of listener. • Usually understands information in order to engage in interaction.	• Uses moderate range of vocabulary accurately and appropriately. • Sometimes uses incorrect collocations that may lead to vagueness. • Often uses a variety of basic and complex grammatical structures accurately and effectively. • Gaps and/or errors in vocabulary and grammar, sometimes self-corrected, usually do not hinder communication.	• Often fluent, usually articulate; may require some listener effort. • Fluency may decline with more challenging speech events, but this does not stop the flow of discourse. • Pace usually consistent, may occasionally be relatively slower. • An increase in rate of delivery may occasionally lead to decrease in clarity of speech or ability to be understood.

* Adapted from the Cambridge Michigan Language Assessments website, retrieved August 13, 2013 from: http://www.cambridgemichigan.org

TIPS AND STRATEGIES FOR THE DAY OF THE EXAM

Here is a section-by-section rundown offering tips and strategies for the day of the exam. The sections are presented in the order that you will encounter them on the exam.

WRITING (30 minutes)

- In the days before the exam, read over the Writing Tutorial (pages 188–205) and make a careful study of your own work and any models your teacher has given you. Pay careful attention to advice on organizing and developing and on using clear topic sentences and linking devices.
- Review the Scoring Criteria for Writing on page 9. Remember that you are being graded on four main criteria: rhetoric, grammar and syntax, vocabulary and mechanics. Keep these in mind as you plan your composition.
- Although handwriting is *not* one of the grading criteria, do your best to write neatly and legibly. You may write with pen or pencil. If you tend to change your mind a lot, use pencil and a clean eraser!
- Remember that you have only got 30 minutes, which means that you cannot possibly delve into every single aspect of a subject. What you *can* do in that time is to treat a topic by mentioning and developing two or three points in each paragraph … and that limit should be uppermost in your mind as you begin to work. Here is what we recommend:

Focus → → → → → → → *How to handle the 30-minute composition*

1. **Study the two topics** and decide which one you can develop more effectively.
2. **Read the question carefully**. Make sure you are clear on what it asks you to do and what type of composition it is (see *Summary of Main Composition Types*, page 189).
3. **Take 5–10 minutes to plan out the composition on scrap paper**. Jot down a quick paragraph plan and make brief notes about points to include in the Introduction, each paragraph of the Main Body and the Conclusion. Also jot down any impressive vocabulary or phrases that you might like to fit in. All this may seem like a waste of time, but it could be a life-saver if your mind goes blank while you're writing.
4. **Remember to start each paragraph with a clear topic sentence.**
5. **Use linking devices wherever possible** as you develop your ideas with reasons and examples.
6. **Take a few minutes to read over your work.** When you have finished, proofread what you have written, looking for omitted words and obvious errors in grammar, spelling and punctuation.

Composition Checklist

- Introduction – Main Body – Conclusion
- Clear topic sentences
- Linking words for logical development
- General ideas supported with reasons / examples
- Good range of vocabulary and grammar

LISTENING (approximately 35–40 minutes)

- Keep in mind that items are *not* repeated on the ECPE. You will hear each part only *once*!
- Try to stay cool, even if a question goes by you too quickly. If you allow yourself to panic, you might miss the next question as well!
- Finally, pray that the exam room has a good sound system *and* good acoustics ... and that there are no dogs barking or workers drilling outside the window! If anything irregular occurs (eg, if the volume is distorted or needs adjusting), immediately raise your hand and bring it to the examiners' attention.

Tackling the radio-program segments in Part III

Use the months before the exam to experiment with both of the methods below. On the day of the exam, use the one you feel most comfortable with.

Method 1 – The Traditional Way: Taking Notes

The instructions to Part III suggest that you may want to make notes in your test booklet. This is fine if you are an experienced note-taker in English, but if you aren't, you may find it unhelpful. Needless to say, the purpose of note-taking is defeated if writing down one thing causes you to miss the next thing the speaker says. The only way to know if note-taking will work for you is to try it. You'll undoubtedly improve with practice, but – if you're like many of our past students – you'll probably find that you listen better if you don't write! If that's the case, forget note-taking and try Method 2.

Method 2 – Previewing the Questions and Listening for the Choices in the Test Booklet

A method that many students have success with is to (a) underline key words in the questions in the test booklet before listening, and then (b) focus on the choices while listening. With practice, you should get better at these steps. Remember, too, that the questions almost always follow the order of the information in the text. Here is a closer look:

1. Before the segment begins, underline the key words in each question. (This helps you know what to listen for and gives you a better idea of the content of the segment.)
2. As the segment begins, reread the first two questions and focus on the first set of choices. When you hear something that repeats or, more likely, paraphrases a choice, put a mark next to the choice and move on. If you hear something that relates to the second question, quickly shift your focus to the next set of choices. (You'll have 10 seconds at the end to reconsider each question, so don't panic if you can't answer one or more questions as you listen.)
3. Do the same for the others, always keeping in mind the next item in case you miss an answer.
4. At the end, as the narrator reads each question, check your answer and transfer it to the separate answer sheet. If you left anything blank, carefully consider the choices again, **guess** if you have to, and mark the answer sheet. Remember that you are not penalized for wrong answers.

THE GCVR: GRAMMAR – CLOZE – VOCABULARY – READING (75 minutes)

USE YOUR TIME WISELY – A word about overall strategy

The GCVR is the last, longest and most demanding section. Even native speakers of English have trouble finishing it in 75 minutes! To maximize your score, you **must** use your time wisely.

We recommend that you spend as much time as you can on Grammar, Cloze and Reading and proportionately less time on Vocabulary. Our reasons are as follows:

- If you slow down on Grammar and read each item carefully, you will avoid making careless mistakes and you'll accumulate a solid base of points. There are few surprises here, so a few more seconds per question means fewer mistakes! (13 minutes is ideal.)
- Spending more time on Vocabulary will *not* improve your score. Go through the questions as quickly as possible *without* wasting time on items you don't know. This will give you a few more minutes for the Cloze and Reading passages. (10–12 minutes for Vocabulary is ideal.)
- The more time you have for Cloze and Reading passages, the more time you have to work through the passages and find the answers. Staying within the above limits leaves you with 50 minutes for the two Cloze passages and four Reading passages. That gives you five minutes for each Cloze and ten minutes for each Reading, which is tight but achievable.

GRAMMAR

- Remember that every question tests one or more specific grammar topics (eg, conditionals, wishes, modals, tenses, subject-verb agreement, word order, inversion, reported speech and the subjunctive). Use the list in the box as a basis for review.
- Watch out for "avoidable errors" on question types that you've seen a thousand times before. To do this, open your eyes (it really does help!), read the entire question stem and consider all four choices carefully.
- Expect six to eight "killer" questions. These questions often test emphatic phrases, complex sentence structure or fine points of grammar that you may not have seen. How to cope? Admit you don't know, **guess**, then cut and run! Staring at the question means you're taking valuable time away from the Cloze and Reading passages.

Commonly-Tested Grammar Topics

subject-verb agreement
verb tenses
active vs. passive voice
reported speech
embedded questions
tag questions
wishes
conditionals
constructions of probability
modal verbs + functions
inversion
word order
subjunctive mood
causative form
infinitives vs. gerunds
verbs + dependent prepositions
word forms and derivatives
participles/participial phrases
countable/uncountable nouns
relative clauses
connectors and conjunctions
adjective and adverb forms
compound adjectives
so/such vs. too/enough

CLOZE

Remember that to do well on Cloze passages, it's vital that you understand that the examiners are testing you on two different levels:

- **The sentence level**, where you focus on a single sentence to

  a) determine what its structure is and what is missing grammatically; or
  b) check whether or not the missing item is part of a phrasal verb or other collocation.

- **The text (or discourse) level**, where you must consider the overall meaning, organization and development of a passage. Unlike sentence-level questions, text-level questions cannot be answered by focusing on single sentences. They require you to understand **what** the writer is saying and **how** he unfolds his ideas sentence by sentence from one paragraph to the next. Text-level questions often ask you to:

  a) choose appropriate vocabulary, as determined by the context;
  b) supply pronouns or other referent words that refer to other parts of the text;
  c) choose appropriate linking words and discourse markers.

Here is a suggested approach that will help you answer Cloze questions at both levels.

Focus → → → → → → → → → → *How to handle a Cloze passage*

1. **Read the passage quickly <u>without</u> looking at the choices.**

   This will give you a feel for what the text is about, which in turn will make it easier for you to recognize and answer questions concerning vocabulary, referent words and overall meaning.

2. **Glance quickly at the verbs in each paragraph and get a feel for the tenses.**

   Does one tense dominate or are a variety of tenses used? Are the verbs active or passive voice? This will help you make choices about sentence-level grammar-based questions.

3. **Notice the <u>function</u> of each paragraph.**

   Some paragraphs contain a topic statement supported by reasons and examples, while others may contain a procedure or sequence of events, a list of reasons, or ideas in contrast to each other. You will be better able to answer questions related to linking words and discourse markers if you are more sensitive to the kind of information in each paragraph and to how a sentence relates to the ones before and after it.

4. **Work through the passage, item by item and choice by choice.**

   As you come to each blank, decide whether the item is testing you at sentence level or at text level by quickly studying the choices. Do they suggest that a verb or part of a collocation is missing at sentence level? Or are you being asked to supply a linking word, vocabulary item or pronoun that depends on your understanding of the wider context? Whatever the question type, remember to consider all four choices and use process of elimination to narrow down the choices.

5. **Remember that the clock is ticking.**

   Don't spend too much time on any one question. If you're not sure of an answer, guess and move on. You should plan to spend about five minutes on each ten-item passage.

6. **When you have completed all the items, read the passage again as a final check to see if your answers make sense.**

VOCABULARY

This is the "Achilles' heel" of students taking the ECPE. No matter how many thousands of words you know, chances are there will be words on the exam that you haven't seen. But don't despair! Believe it or not, there is plenty of "room for error" on the Vocabulary section of the GCVR. If you get a good base of points on Grammar (say, 30 out of 40) and do fairly well on both the Cloze (say, 13 out of 20) and the Reading sections (say, 13 out of 20), then all you need is 22 out of 40 on Vocabulary to achieve a Low Pass on the GCVR.

You have a good chance of achieving this if you follow these simple tips:

- **Don't panic**! Expect to encounter unknown words and remember that there is room for error. Don't allow yourself to lose even a second worrying about 5 or 10 or even 15 questions that you don't know. The math is still on your side!
- **Remember that your goal is to do this section as quickly as possible**. Don't waste time staring at the test booklet when you encounter trouble. Read each sentence carefully, rule out the choices that you know are wrong, **guess** and move on. Answer all 40 questions and do not leave blanks. The time you save by "being done" with Vocabulary can be used to much better advantage on the Cloze and Reading sections.
- **Don't lose points on words you do know**! Here's a few things to keep in mind so you don't make silly errors in the heat of the moment:
  - **Make sure you read the main sentence all the way to the end** so you have a clear idea of the meaning before making your choice.
  - **Check to see if a preposition or particle follows the blank** and make sure your choice agrees with it. Test-makers often include questions with prepositions or particles to try and catch you off guard. Don't fall into the trap of choosing the synonym of a phrasal verb when it's the main part of a phrasal verb that's missing!
- **As a final review, go over the Vocabulary sections and Vocabulary Consolidations** in this book to keep the words you've encountered fresh in your mind.

A little knowledge is a great thing … Don't give up because you don't know one of the choices!

When all seems lost, remember to use process of elimination. This may seem obvious, but you'd be amazed at how many times we've seen students throw up their hands and say they're not sure of the answer to a question when three of the four choices are words they surely know! The fact that the remaining choice is unknown does not mean that you should feel unsure. If you know enough about the other three choices to know they are clearly wrong, then you've brought hard-earned knowledge to the exam and deserve to be awarded a point for it!

Remember: The more choices you can rule out based on the knowledge you have, the more you increase your chance of getting the correct answer. This is not wild guessing; it's educated guessing … and there's a world of difference.

I know 3 out of the 4 words but none of them fit!
No sweat! The 4th is the answer. Move on and stop worrying!
M

READING

If you follow the suggested time guidelines for Grammar, Cloze and Vocabulary, you'll have 40 minutes to work on Reading. Bear in mind that ten minutes per passage isn't a lot (especially as you'll be nearing exhaustion by the end of the exam!), but if you work carefully and efficiently, you'll still be able to pick up a good number of the available 20 points. Here are some suggestions to help you cope.

Before you begin

- Glance at all four passages. If one seems overly technical or difficult, consider leaving it for the end. This will let you get the most out of the passages that seem easy to you. Plan on doing these to your satisfaction (take an extra minute or two if you wish), and then go on to the one you left. Do what you can in the time remaining, and **guess** at any questions you can't figure out or don't have time for.

As you work through the questions

- Remember that you will be pressed for time on this part. Your goal is to work accurately and efficiently, which means not getting hung up on any one question. If need be, **guess** and move on. You need to "mine" this section for all the right answers you can … and there may be several easier questions just ahead. Don't let the time run out without giving yourself a chance to answer them!

- Don't panic if you see technical terms. Remember that such terms are usually explained the first time they are used. If you find yourself getting "hung up" because of the technical nature of a passage, skim the questions to see which parts of the text you need to focus on. If that fails as well, **guess** and move on!

- Remember that ECPE Reading questions tend **not** to be in the order that facts are presented in the text.

- Expect most questions to be straightforward. If you can't justify an answer by pointing to specific details in the text, don't let that work against you. As soon as you feel you're in trouble, shift gears and start eliminating choices that are clearly wrong. If all else fails, **guess** and move on.

- Keep your eyes open for common **distractors**, such as:

  Truth statements: choices that are true but do not answer the question posed in the stem.

  Opposite statements: choices that look like exact paraphrases of details in the text but may include a word or phrase that makes them exactly the opposite of the expected answer.

  Absolute statements: choices that contain words like *always* or *never* that subtly conflict with text phrases such as *sometimes, most of the time, in the majority of cases, hardly ever.*

Tip

Learn to approach each question as if it were four "True or False" statements. This is one of the wisest pieces of advice that we have ever come across in test-taking strategies books. We strongly advise you to try it out, as it might be just the strategy you need to turn you into a "world-class" test-taker!

The logic behind the technique is simple but elegant! If you test the "truth" of each of the four choices, you will end up with one statement that is "True" and three statements that are "False." This ensures that you carefully consider all four choices until you have ruled out the three that are false and are left with the one that is true.

Try it! It may feel like slow-going at first, but you'll soon pick up speed **and** accuracy!

TIPS AND STRATEGIES FOR THE DAY OF THE EXAM

SPEAKING

Here are a few pointers for handling the Speaking Test.

Several Days before the Test

- Read over the introduction to the Speaking Tests section on pages 206-207 so you know exactly what to expect. Go over the Speaking Criteria on page 9 and the "Fluency Builders" chart on page 208 so they're fresh in your mind.
- Review the Speaking Tests at the back of the book to remind yourself of the kinds of information that might be included in the options.
- If you feel you'd benefit from extra practice, invite one or more of your classmates to a practice session and redo some of the tasks that you're already familiar with.

During the Test

- **Take advantage of the friendly atmosphere that the examiners try to establish**. Those butterflies in your stomach will fly away if you take a few deep breaths and try to relax.
- **Try not to be too dominant or too passive**. Remember that you're being tested on your ability to participate in an extended interaction. Being a good listener and building on what your partner says are important, but so are sensing when to give up your turn and inviting your partner to speak.
- **Remember to maintain eye contact with your partner and the lead examiner**. It's all right to refer occasionally to your information sheet as you're speaking, but try not to rely on it. If you do, you'll wind up speaking to it and not to your partner and the examiner.
- **Don't be afraid to ask your partner to repeat or clarify**. If you do, you're demonstrating that you have the skills you need to keep the interaction moving. If you don't, communication may break down.
- **Speak clearly, confidently and naturally, and don't panic if you make an occasional mistake in verb tense, structure or vocabulary**. Fluency and overall intelligibility (ie, how well you make yourself understood) are more important than 100% accuracy.

SPEAKING TIPS

- Smile – Breathe – Relax!
- Be an active participant.
- Speak – Know when to give up your turn – Listen!
- Don't worry about minor mistakes.

FINAL CHECKLIST: Before you leave home . . .

Use this checklist to make sure you have everything you need.

✓ Your official "Receipt / Testing Program"
(sent to you or your school by the official test center before the examination)

✓ Your identity card, passport or equivalent document

✓ A good supply of pencils, erasers, and pens

✓ A watch (Your teacher has only one, and she can't lend it to everybody!)

And, finally, make sure you're familiar with the ECPE Answer Sheet *(see pages 17–18)*.

SIDE 1

PRINT YOUR NAME IN THE BLOCKS PROVIDED, BLACKEN THE CORRESPONDING CIRCLE.

LAST NAME	FIRST	MI

USE A #2 (SOFT) PENCIL ONLY

BIRTHDATE			SEX	LANG.	CENTER NO.	REG. NO.	SPKG	FORM
Jan, Feb, Mar, Apr, May, Jun, Jul, Aug, Sep, Oct, Nov, Dec	DAY	YEAR	M MALE, F FEMALE				A B C D E	A B C D E F G H

EXAMINATION FOR THE CERTIFICATE OF PROFICIENCY IN ENGLISH

FULL NAME (PRINT) ____________ YOUR SIGNATURE ____________

(PRINT IN BOXED IN AREA ONLY)

TEST CENTER ____________ NATIVE LANGUAGE ____________ TODAY'S DATE ____________

EXAMPLES

WRONG 1

WRONG 2

WRONG 3

RIGHT 4

IMPORTANT DIRECTIONS FOR MARKING ANSWERS

- Use a #2 (soft) pencil only.
- Do NOT use ink or ballpoint pens.
- Make heavy black marks that fill the circle completely.
- Erase cleanly any answer you wish to change.
- Make no stray marks on the answer sheet.
- Do not fold or crease the answer sheet.
- The examiner will tell you how to grid in the identification section.

LISTENING

1 A B C	11 A B C	21 A B C	31 A B C	36 A B C	46 A B C
2 A B C	12 A B C	22 A B C	32 A B C	37 A B C	47 A B C
3 A B C	13 A B C	23 A B C	33 A B C	38 A B C	48 A B C
4 A B C	14 A B C	24 A B C	34 A B C	39 A B C	49 A B C
5 A B C	15 A B C	25 A B C	35 A B C	40 A B C	50 A B C
6 A B C	16 A B C	26 A B C		41 A B C	
7 A B C	17 A B C	27 A B C		42 A B C	
8 A B C	18 A B C	28 A B C		43 A B C	
9 A B C	19 A B C	29 A B C		44 A B C	
10 A B C	20 A B C	30 A B C		45 A B C	

Adapted from the Cambridge Michigan Language Assessments website, retrieved August 13, 2013 from: http://www.cambridgemichigan.org

DO NOT WRITE IN THIS AREA

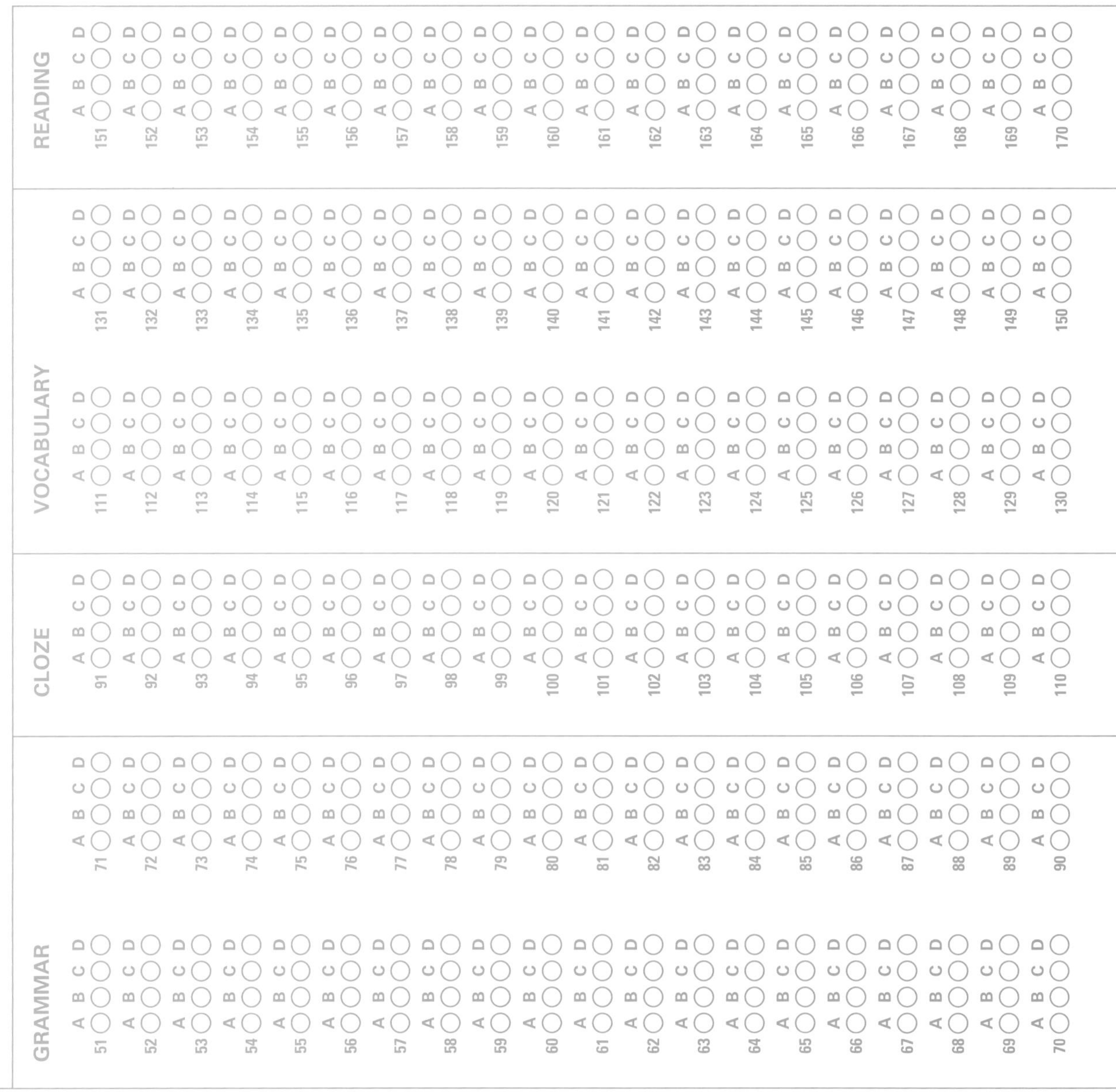
SIDE 2

GRAMMAR		CLOZE	VOCABULARY		READING
51 A B C D	71 A B C D	91 A B C D	111 A B C D	131 A B C D	151 A B C D
52 A B C D	72 A B C D	92 A B C D	112 A B C D	132 A B C D	152 A B C D
53 A B C D	73 A B C D	93 A B C D	113 A B C D	133 A B C D	153 A B C D
54 A B C D	74 A B C D	94 A B C D	114 A B C D	134 A B C D	154 A B C D
55 A B C D	75 A B C D	95 A B C D	115 A B C D	135 A B C D	155 A B C D
56 A B C D	76 A B C D	96 A B C D	116 A B C D	136 A B C D	156 A B C D
57 A B C D	77 A B C D	97 A B C D	117 A B C D	137 A B C D	157 A B C D
58 A B C D	78 A B C D	98 A B C D	118 A B C D	138 A B C D	158 A B C D
59 A B C D	79 A B C D	99 A B C D	119 A B C D	139 A B C D	159 A B C D
60 A B C D	80 A B C D	100 A B C D	120 A B C D	140 A B C D	160 A B C D
61 A B C D	81 A B C D	101 A B C D	121 A B C D	141 A B C D	161 A B C D
62 A B C D	82 A B C D	102 A B C D	122 A B C D	142 A B C D	162 A B C D
63 A B C D	83 A B C D	103 A B C D	123 A B C D	143 A B C D	163 A B C D
64 A B C D	84 A B C D	104 A B C D	124 A B C D	144 A B C D	164 A B C D
65 A B C D	85 A B C D	105 A B C D	125 A B C D	145 A B C D	165 A B C D
66 A B C D	86 A B C D	106 A B C D	126 A B C D	146 A B C D	166 A B C D
67 A B C D	87 A B C D	107 A B C D	127 A B C D	147 A B C D	167 A B C D
68 A B C D	88 A B C D	108 A B C D	128 A B C D	148 A B C D	168 A B C D
69 A B C D	89 A B C D	109 A B C D	129 A B C D	149 A B C D	169 A B C D
70 A B C D	90 A B C D	110 A B C D	130 A B C D	150 A B C D	170 A B C D

Adapted from the Cambridge Michigan Language Assessments website, retrieved August 13, 2013 from: http://www.cambridgemichigan.org

MICHIGAN PROFICIENCY

PRACTICE TESTS

for the ECPE

Practice Test 1

Writing

(30 minutes)

Write on one of the topics given below. If you write about something else, your paper will not be graded. If you do not understand the topics, ask the examiner to explain or translate them. You will be graded on the clarity of your writing and the linguistic range and accuracy you show. Write $1\frac{1}{2}$ to 2 pages. You may make any corrections or other changes in the body of the composition.

TOPICS

1. As the second millennium drew to a close, many people made their own personal time capsules – that is, they put items they believed were typical of their life and times into a waterproof container, which they buried in hopes that it would be found by future generations. If you were to make such a time capsule today, what two items would you include? Give reasons for your choices.

2. As medical science improves, the number of elderly people in the population continues to grow. In many ways this is a mixed blessing. Discuss the positive and negative implications of this for the older person and for society in general.

For help in writing these compositions, see *Writing Tutorial*, pages 190–191.

Listening Comprehension Test

(35–40 minutes)

This part of the examination is a listening test that will assess your understanding of spoken English. The listening test has three parts. There are 50 questions. Mark all your answers on the separate answer sheet. Do not make any stray marks on the answer sheet. If you change your mind about an answer, erase your first answer completely.

PART 1 – In this part of the test, you will hear a short conversation. From the three answer choices given, choose the answer which means the same thing as you hear, or that is true based on what you hear.

For problems **1–17**, mark your answers on the separate answer sheet. No problem can be repeated. Please listen carefully. Do you have any questions?

1. a. She thought the movie wasn't scary.
b. He hasn't heard anything about the movie.
c. He's planning on seeing the movie.

2. a. She needs to study more.
b. She's finished studying.
c. He thinks the test is going to be easy.

3. a. He's going to be late for class.
b. He's tired of waiting.
c. He doesn't like buying tickets online.

4. a. It wasn't the food that bothered them.
b. They didn't like the noisy atmosphere.
c. They'll never go there again.

5. a. She approves of the marriage.
b. She thinks marriage is a bad idea.
c. She has doubts about the marriage.

6. a. He's frightened for Peter.
b. He doesn't know the answer to her question.
c. He doesn't know where Peter is.

7. a. He thinks she should have it repaired.
b. He thinks he might be able to fix it for her.
c. He thinks she should return it.

8. a. She's too embarrassed to talk to him.
b. She'll talk to him in a few days.
c. She's angry at him for what he did.

9. a. She's glad he did what she asked.
b. She's upset with him.
c. She thinks he's a good friend.

10. a. He thinks she's exaggerating.
b. He thinks things will get worse.
c. He thinks the situation will improve.

11. a. He'll be too busy to do a lot of sight-seeing.
b. He doesn't like sight-seeing in crowded places.
c. He doesn't like mixing business and pleasure.

12. a. She's planning to buy a new car soon.
b. She can't afford to buy a new car right now.
c. She'll buy a car when she finds a new job.

13. a. They couldn't hear the lecture.
b. They disagreed with what the lecturer said.
c. They couldn't understand the lecture.

14. a. She's willing to give the young woman advice.
b. She doesn't think her help will be needed.
c. She thinks he's made a bad choice.

15. a. He's not used to living in an expensive house.
b. Rents are higher in the city.
c. He prefers living in the suburbs.

16. a. He's not going to graduate from college.
b. He'll probably go to grad school after his trip.
c. He doesn't intend to go to grad school.

17. a. She's thinking about quitting her job.
b. She's been given a promotion.
c. She doesn't like her current position.

PART II – In this part of the test, you will hear a question. From the three answer choices given, choose the one which best answers the question.

For problems **18–35**, mark your answers on the separate answer sheet. No problem can be repeated. Please listen carefully. Do you have any questions?

18. a. Somebody moved it.
b. Not yet.
c. Never again.

19. a. You aren't listening.
b. He isn't speaking to you.
c. You don't ever listen.

20. a. I couldn't afford anything else.
b. This was the cheapest they had.
c. The shop was out of stock.

21. a. He doesn't like working.
b. I'm sorry about that.
c. He's always going on like that.

22. a. I won't forget.
b. I thought you were going to.
c. I may not have the time.

23. a. Sorry. I've been meaning to tell you.
b. Yes, I know. I'll see you there.
c. Yes, tomorrow's fine.

24. a. I'm working on it.
b. I hope not.
c. In a little while.

25. a. She said she'd think about it.
b. Possibly. She's quite generous.
c. I'd like to believe she wouldn't.

26. a. If he can find the time.
b. I'd better show you myself.
c. Suit yourself.

27. a. No, I've got plans later on.
b. No, I just got here.
c. Yes, would you like to come, too?

28. a. I wish you'd slow down.
b. Because you usually go too fast.
c. Because you don't have the time.

29. a. OK, let's look into it.
b. Smells good, doesn't it?
c. I hate it when you pick at your food.

30. a. Sorry, what did you say?
b. Do you always make so much noise?
c. I'd rather you didn't.

31. a. Not until 7 p.m.
b. Take a right at Ninth Street.
c. The hotel, I believe.

32. a. I've been working out.
b. I lost weight and my clothes are too big.
c. You're right. It's much too small now.

33. a. Possibly even worse.
b. He hasn't been there very long.
c. No, he never exaggerates.

34. a. What shall I say?
b. It would be a pleasure.
c. Good idea. I'm always getting lost.

35. a. I can't come any earlier.
b. I'll call you before I leave.
c. You should have seen the traffic.

PART III – In this part, you will hear three short segments from a radio program. The program is called "Learning from the Experts." Each talk lasts about two minutes. As you listen, you may want to take notes to help you remember information given in the talk. After each talk, you will be asked some questions about what was said. From the three answer choices given, you should choose the one which best answers the question according to the information you heard.

Remember, no problems can be repeated. For problems **36–50**, mark your answers on the separate answer sheet. Do you have any questions?

SEGMENT 1

36. What is the main theme of the program?
- a. The pros and cons of using animals in scientific research
- b. The influence of the animal rights movement on animal experimentation
- c. The immorality of animal experimentation

37. What is true about the number of animals now used in laboratory research?
- a. It is about the same as it always was.
- b. It is slightly larger than it used to be.
- c. It has decreased.

38. How did the public respond to animal rights' protests in the 1970s and '80s?
- a. They reacted sympathetically when they saw the protests were justified.
- b. They remained apathetic to reports in the media.
- c. They were shocked by the activists' violent methods.

39. What is true of the Laboratory Animal Welfare Act?
- a. Animal rights groups are still not satisfied with it.
- b. It forbids federally-funded research facilities to use animals in their experiments.
- c. It has been changed in response to pressure from animal rights groups.

40. What is so "humane" about the in-vitro method of testing animals?
- a. It employs sophisticated computer simulations rather than live animals.
- b. It experiments with cell and tissue samples rather than whole animals.
- c. It requires fewer animals than traditional methods.

SEGMENT 2

41. What is the main idea of the segment?
- a. Thrill-seekers have stronger genes than other people.
- b. Being a thrill-seeker is largely determined by one's genes.
- c. Thrill-seekers suffer from an abnormality of the blood.

42. What is true of thrill-seekers and the levels of dopamine in their brains?
- a. They normally produce and absorb more dopamine than others.
- b. They only produce and absorb dopamine when engaging in high-sensation activities.
- c. They normally produce and absorb less dopamine than others.

43. According to scientists, how many people carry the genes for thrill-seeking?
- a. A large majority
- b. Almost one in three
- c. Not even 20 percent

44. What is true about people who have the thrill-seeking genes?
- a. Most are in danger of becoming drug addicts and alcoholics.
- b. They long for new sensations all the time.
- c. They may satisfy their cravings in various ways.

45. Why does the speaker mention Columbus, Wall Street and putting a man on the moon?
- a. To emphasize the positive side of adventure-seeking
- b. To point out the exceptions to the rule
- c. To illustrate the need to control a thrill-seeker's self-destructive urges

SEGMENT 3

46. What was wrong with the young man's right eye?
    a. He had no vision in it.
    b. The shape of the pupil had been affected.
    c. The lens had been pushed backward.

47. What was the first thing doctors tried to correct the problem?
    a. They inserted wires to pull the lens into place.
    b. They replaced the old lens with a new one.
    c. They used eye drops to widen the man's pupil.

48. How successful was their attempt?
    a. It had no effect on the problem.
    b. It partially corrected the problem.
    c. It made the problem worse.

49. In Dr. Thiel's opinion, what was it about the roller coaster ride that corrected the problem?
    a. The patient's excited emotional state
    b. The extreme gravitational force
    c. The combined effect of both of these

50. What is the underlying message of the radio program?
    a. Patients with eye implants should probably avoid roller coasters.
    b. Doctors are not sure what effect rollers coasters will have on eye implants.
    c. Patients with eye implants should be careful when riding roller coasters.

Grammar – Cloze – Vocabulary – Reading

(75 minutes)

This part of the examination contains 120 problems, numbered **51–170**. There are 40 grammar, 20 cloze, 40 vocabulary and 20 reading comprehension problems. The examiner will not explain any test problems. If you do not understand how to do the problems, raise your hand and a proctor will explain the examples to you.

Do not spend too much time on any one problem. Each problem counts the same. If you do not know the answer to a problem, you may make a reasonable guess. Each problem has only one correct answer. Work fast but carefully. You have 75 minutes to answer all 120 problems.

GRAMMAR

51. The dress was exactly what she'd been looking for, but it was ..... expensive for her.
   a. too way
   b. much too
   c. quite too
   d. too so

52. This year's laptop computer sales have far exceeded ..... of last year.
   a. them
   b. this
   c. those
   d. the ones

53. The couple's friends were impressed ..... they had redecorated the house.
   a. from the tastiness
   b. by the tastefulness
   c. at how tastefully
   d. with the taste of

54. ..... called to remind him, he would have forgotten his wife's birthday.
   a. If his mother didn't
   b. Were it not his mother
   c. If only his mother had
   d. Had his mother not

55. What a lovely outfit you're wearing! It really ..... you.
   a. is becoming
   b has become
   c. becomes
   d. became

56. To alleviate her son's fears, she promised ..... as soon as her plane landed.
   a. calling him
   b. would call him
   c. to call him
   d. that she'll call

57. Police officers on patrol caught the burglar red-handed ..... through the window.
   a. from coming
   b. just as he came
   c. once coming
   d. by having come

58. By the time she arrived, he ..... on the street corner for thirty minutes.
   a. waited
   b. would be waiting
   c. has been waiting
   d. had been waiting

59. ..... was how we were going to get the job done in such a short time.
   a. It was unclear
   b. The unclear
   c. Being unclear
   d. What was unclear

60. I've ..... to meet a more efficient secretary than Mrs. Smith.
   a. hardly
   b. never
   c. even
   d. yet

61. ..... the whole incident, he couldn't give us a detailed account.
   a. As not seeing
   b. Not having seen
   c. So as not to have seen
   d. Because not seeing

62. ..... moved away, none of his friends know what he's up to.
   a. Because of his
   b. Ever since
   c. Now that he's
   d. Even though he

Practice Test 1

63. The critics agreed that the director's new film was ..... her best.
    a. far and away
    b. as far as
    c. far away from
    d. from afar

64. If ..... to mow the lawn right now, why not leave it till tomorrow?
    a. you're not feeling moody
    b. your mood isn't good
    c. you don't have a mood
    d. you aren't in the mood

65. Jane and Sue are good with children, but ..... wants to be a teacher.
    a. both of whom
    b. neither of whom
    c. both of them
    d. neither of them

66. John is usually willing to work overtime, but only if you ask him ..... in advance.
    a. very
    b. well
    c. quite
    d. too

67. He is hoping ..... to medical school in the next few months.
    a. he will accept
    b. to be accepted
    c. he was accepted
    d. to have accepted

68. ..... the mayor's "to do" list today is the opening ceremony of the new orphanage.
    a. The topping on
    b. The top of
    c. Topping
    d. At top of

69. All things ..... , the couple is intending to spend a quiet evening at home.
    a. that are equal
    b. are equal
    c. equal
    d. being equal

70. ..... hard he tries, he will never be good at speaking French.
    a. No matter
    b. However
    c. Even though
    d. As

71. He said he was intending to join us this evening, but I'd better ..... forgotten.
    a. him to call if it's
    b. call him in case he's
    c. him call so it's
    d. to call so he won't be

72. It wouldn't surprise me if that ..... table turned out to be a valuable antique.
    a. oval, old, dining-room, useless
    b. old, useless, oval, dining-room
    c. dining-room, oval, old, useless
    d. useless, old, oval, dining-room

73. We warned him he was making a mistake, and he ..... listened.
    a. ought to have
    b. must have
    c. should have to
    d. had better have

74. Only when she heard his side of the story ..... how wrong she had been.
    a. she had realized
    b. had she realized
    c. did she realize
    d. was she realizing

75. It's often difficult for young musicians to understand ..... practice.
    a. how important is the
    b. the importance of
    c. how important is it to
    d. importance of the

76. Nowadays it's rare for girls in their mid-teens to consider themselves of ..... age.
    a. married
    b. marry
    c. marriageable
    d. marriage

77. Shawn is the one ..... John shared an apartment with in college.
   a. which
   b. with who
   c. of whom
   d. that

78. My supervisor approved of my idea, and ..... did as well.
   a. most of others
   b. the most of others
   c. the most of the others
   d. most of the others

79. The more sleep he gets at night, ... he feels the next day.
   a. it's the best
   b. it's better that
   c. the better
   d. so much better

80. They've resigned ..... they may never see their homeland again.
   a. themselves to the thought that
   b. to thinking
   c. from the thought which
   d. by thinking that

81. It was kind ..... him to let us know about his change of plans.
   a. for
   b. about
   c. from
   d. of

82. ..... our high expectations, we found the performance rather dull and uninspired.
   a. In contrast of
   b. The opposite of
   c. Contrary to
   d. In opposition to

83. Believe it or not, that strange contraption is used ..... cans.
   a. for opening
   b. to opening
   c. in the opening
   d. while it opens

84. It is urgent that the doctor ..... of any change in the patient's condition.
   a. should notify
   b. be notified
   c. notifies
   d. is to be notified

85. When I make my decision, I promise you'll be the first ..... .
   a. I'll let you know
   b. knowing
   c. that is known
   d. to know

86. They set out on their journey just as the sun ..... up over the distant hills.
   a. raised
   b. arose
   c. aroused
   d. rose

87. From what everyone is saying, the writer's new novel is ..... .
   a. a most enjoyable read
   b. mostly enjoyed to be read
   c. more enjoyable than reading
   d. more enjoying reading

88. His proposal is interesting, but I haven't had a chance ..... yet.
   a. of reading details
   b. to read it in detail
   c. for reading the details
   d. reading about the detail

89. As she turned the corner, she saw two masked men ..... into the bank.
   a. who run
   b. run
   c. who are running
   d. to have run

90. ..... are saying, I wasn't alone in thinking that the test was challenging.
   a. Though others who
   b. Judging that others
   c. From what others
   d. If all the others

CLOZE

Passage 1 is about chimpanzees.

Although chimpanzees have a largely plant-based diet, there are times when their habitat teems with termites, ants and caterpillars, and their diet changes accordingly. This is when they display a remarkable behavior called termiting. When a chimpanzee finds a thriving termite hill, it will go in ....(91).... of a suitable termiting tool. A rather thin, straight twig is best, and it may ....(92).... quite a while ....(93).... the chimp to choose a suitable one. Once the choice is made, ...(94).... extraneous side branches and leaves must ....(95).... cleared off. The chimp may even select and prepare ....(96).... at a time, carrying them all back to the termite hill firmly held in the closed palm of the hand while it ....(97).... on its knuckles. The chimp will then lie down on its side next to the hill and skillfully ....(98).... the twig into an open tunnel. The ....(99).... is wiggled and then slowly withdrawn. If it has termites on it, the chimp licks them off and repeats the ....(100).... . The task may look simple, but it takes skill to maneuver the stick through a twisting tunnel.

91. a. search b. aid c. need d. view
92. a. have b. be c. take d. make
93. a. and b. for c. before d. that
94. a. then b. and c. so d. while
95. a. have b. take c. not d. be
96. a. them b. several c. more d. few
97. a. chews b. sits c. walks d. holds
98. a. pull b. cut c. drop d. insert
99. a. stick b. termite c. tunnel d. chimp
100. a. proceedings b. procession c. procedure d. proceeds

Passage 2 is about bows and arrows.

It's a simple truth that American military men and women no longer go off to war fearing fatal injuries from bows and arrows. But up until the late 1800s, soldiers in the U.S. Army had to be exceedingly brave to confront Native Americans ....(101).... with bows and arrows. Even though those basic weapons seem ....(102).... today, 19th-century army surgeons had ....(103).... a challenge on their hands. ....(104).... arrowheads from open, gaping wounds ....(105).... skill, strength and ingenuity.

American soldiers first dealt with arrows and arrowhead wounds in the East, of course, ...(106).... the Eastern Indians got their hands on firearms soon enough. Among the Western tribes, firearms ....(107).... by trade and war. At times, guns proved decisive when groups of Native Americans had them and their enemies ....(108).... not. But because guns were at times hard to ....(109).... by and ammunition was ....(110).... , the Plains Indians continued to use bows and arrows in battle well into the second half of the 19th century.

101. a. carrying b. armed c. dressed d. fought
102. a. antiquated b. antique c. anachronism d. untimely
103. a. such b. only c. quite d. just
104. a. The b. Operating c. Removing d. When
105. a. required b. had c. meant d. with
106. a. and b. since c. although d. if
107. a. scattered b. expanded c. sold d. spread
108. a. had b. did c. were d. would
109. a. come b. go c. get d. find
110. a. scarce b. seldom c. little d. infrequent

VOCABULARY

111. Absent-minded people are often ..... to what goes on around them.
   a. reluctant
   b. oblivious
   c. inferior
   d. redundant

112. There are more important issues at stake here. Let's not ..... about petty details.
   a. quibble
   b. conspire
   c. gloat
   d. collaborate

113. Her ..... is beginning to get on my nerves. Who does she think she is?
   a. personnel
   b. resumption
   c. conception
   d. arrogance

114. The judge ordered the witness to stick to the facts and not make any ..... comments.
   a. extraneous
   b. superficial
   c. illegible
   d. simultaneous

115. The dinner guests were shocked by the child's rude ..... .
   a. conduct
   b. intersection
   c. urbanity
   d. breakthrough

116. Rather than buy a new computer, she decided to ..... her old one.
   a. upgrade
   b. uplift
   c. upstage
   d. upend

117. Scientists are still trying to work out the mechanics of the ..... chemical reaction.
   a. provisional
   b. conspicuous
   c. defective
   d. complex

118. The accident victim was ..... to the hospital in serious condition.
   a. entranced
   b. imported
   c. registered
   d. admitted

119. John didn't really win the lottery. He was just ..... .
   a. racking his brains
   b. twisting your arm
   c. pulling your leg
   d. picking your brains

120. Financial analysts are concerned at how ..... the economy has been performing lately.
   a. sullenly
   b. spontaneously
   c. alternately
   d. sluggishly

121. He's always buying things on ...... No wonder he's broke at the end of every month.
   a. impulse
   b. purpose
   c. condition
   d. whim

122. Health officials have assured the residents that the city's water supply is not ..... .
   a. contingent
   b. intoxicated
   c. potable
   d. contaminated

123. Thanks to improved standards of public health, the infant ..... rate continues to decline.
   a. mortality
   b. fatality
   c. propagation
   d. preservation

124. They bought a huge German Shepherd in hopes of ..... off burglars.
   a. warding
   b. provoking
   c. suppressing
   d. deferring

125. The students resent the way the teacher ..... over them when they take a test.
   a. hovers
   b. floats
   c. stumbles
   d. languishes

126. The massive explosion left a ..... hole in one side of the building.
   a. glaring
   b. vacant
   c. gaping
   d. prestigious

127. He found it hard to ..... all the information in the professor's lectures.
   a. abort
   b. preserve
   c. consume
   d. assimilate

128. She apologized profusely for having ..... left her cousin's name off the guest list.
   a. inadvertently
   b. vigorously
   c. supposedly
   d. coincidentally

129. He's always trying to ..... accepting responsibility for his own mistakes.
   a. put the blame on
   b. wriggle out of
   c. do away with
   d. put an end to

130. Young children are ..... to a wide range of minor ailments.
   a. partial
   b. overexposed
   c. superfluous
   d. susceptible

131. Health officials are attempting to contain the disease before it reaches ..... proportions.
   a. magnanimous
   b. epidemic
   c. contagious
   d. deathly

132. We couldn't resist the mouth-watering ..... of cakes and pies in the bakery window.
   a. variation
   b. array
   c. affinity
   d. disarray

133. The children ..... with delight when they saw the mountain of gifts under the Christmas tree.
   a. shriveled
   b. shrieked
   c. barked
   d. writhed

134. The incriminating letter was all the ..... the prosecutor needed to assure a conviction.
   a. documentary
   b. ammunition
   c. eviction
   d. temptation

135. The telephone connection was so bad that her voice was barely ..... .
   a. eligible
   b. compatible
   c. conceivable
   d. audible

136. Given the unfair treatment he had received, he had every right to feel ..... .
   a. indignant
   b. undignified
   c. indigent
   d. indigenous

137. ..... of sweat ran down his face as he cycled up the steep hill.
   a. Ripples
   b. Rivulets
   c. Ruffles
   d. Remnants

138. Hundreds of workers were laid off when the company was forced to ..... .
   a. downsize
   b. downplay
   c. download
   d. downgrade

139. Diplomatic efforts have been intensified in hopes of averting a military ..... .
   a. controversy
   b. alteration
   c. conflict
   d. antagonism

140. Suddenly, the sky went black and it began to rain ..... .
   a. cats and mice
   b. with a vengeance
   c. head over heels
   d. like a storm in a teacup

141. Most of the guests arrived ..... , within minutes of the hour stated on the invitation.
   a. timely
   b. consistently
   c. concisely
   d. punctually

142. The tiny kitten was fascinated by the ..... of images on the television screen.
   a. flicker
   b. glimmer
   c. shiver
   d. simmer

143. His behavior was not only unacceptable but ..... rude.
   a. merely
   b. downright
   c. down and out
   d. upright

144. Few men ..... the thought of having to spend the weekend with their in-laws.
   a. perish
   b. cherish
   c. dread
   d. divulge

145. The coroner's ..... determined that the death was not a suicide.
   a. influx
   b. inmate
   c. input
   d. inquest

146. Despite his youth, he is a remarkably ..... musician.
   a. accomplished
   b. imminent
   c. deficient
   d. prevalent

147. Both parties must ..... to the terms of the contract.
   a. sympathize
   b. compile
   c. adhere
   d. harmonize

148. She dislikes people who display a(n) .... sense of their own self-importance.
   a. abrupt
   b. escalated
   c. exaggerated
   d. hyperactive

149. The students were asked to ..... and discuss the various causes of the war.
   a. enumerate
   b. alleviate
   c. congregate
   d. ventilate

150. He lives in a quiet residential neighborhood on the ..... of town.
   a. outreach
   b. outlay
   c. outskirts
   d. outcomes

READING

Passage 1 is about inventors.

We picture inventors as heroes with the genius to recognize and solve a society's problems. In reality, the greatest inventors have been tinkerers who loved tinkering for its own sake and who then had to figure out what, if anything, their devices might be good for. The prime example is Thomas Edison, whose phonograph is widely considered to be his most brilliant invention. When he built his first one, in 1877, it was not in response to a national clamor for hearing Beethoven at home. Having built it, he wasn't sure what to do with it, so he drew up a list of ten uses, like recording the last words of dying people, announcing the time and teaching spelling. When entrepreneurs used his invention to play music, Edison considered it a debasement of his idea.

Our widespread misunderstanding of inventors as setting out to solve society's problems causes us to say that necessity is the mother of invention. Actually, invention is the mother of necessity, by creating needs that we never felt before. (Be honest: did people really feel a need for the Walkman CD player long before it existed?) Far from welcoming solutions to its supposed needs, society's entrenched interests commonly resist inventions. In Gutenberg's time, no one pleaded for a new way to churn out books: there were hordes of copyists whose desire not to be put out of business led to local bans on printing. The first internal-combustion engine was built in 1867, but no cars came along for decades, because the public was content with horses and railroads. Transistors were invented in the United States, but the country's electronics industry ignored them to protect its investment in vacuum-tube products; it was left to Sony in postwar Japan to adapt them to consumer electronics.

All too often we fail to realize that neither the solutions to the most difficult problems of technology nor the potential uses of most basic research discoveries have been predictable in advance. Instead, penicillin, X-rays and other modern wonders were discovered accidentally – by tinkerers driven by curiosity.

151. What common idea does the writer set out to disprove?

a. Many scientific discoveries are accidental.
b. Necessity is the mother of invention.
c. Great inventors are creative geniuses.
d. Given enough time, inventors will find solutions to most of society's problems.

152. According to the writer, what is the Walkman CD player an example of?

a. an invention that responded to a specific social need
b. an invention that society was slow to accept
c. an invention that people didn't know they needed
d. an invention that created a demand that previously did not exist

153. What is true about the invention of the phonograph?

a. Edison originally resented the idea that it be used to play music.
b. Edison realized it was an impractical device.
c. Edison had no idea what it should be used for.
d. It created an unexpected market for classical music.

154. Why did Gutenberg's invention lead to bans on printing in some places?

a. Copyists were unwilling to learn how to use the new technology.
b. People were not willing to pay high prices for printed material.
c. It threatened the financial interests of copyists.
d. There was no need for books to be mass produced.

155. What point does the writer make about great inventors and scientists?

a. They are brilliant, but impractical people.
b. They are unaware of society's needs.
c. They have a highly unpredictable nature.
d. Their discoveries are often unexpected.

Passage 2 is about tsunamis.

Though it's true that tsunamis are ocean waves, calling them by the same name as the ordinary wind-driven variety is a bit like referring to firecrackers and atomic warheads as both "explosives." Toss a stone in a pond and you create a series of concentric ripples. A tsunami is just like those ripples, except the disturbance that sets them in motion is of a much greater magnitude. Triggered by volcanic eruptions, landslides, earthquakes and even impacts by asteroids or comets, a tsunami represents a vast volume of seawater in motion. On the open ocean, tsunami waves approach speeds of 500 mph, almost fast enough to keep pace with a jetliner. In deep water, tsunami waves spread out and hunch down, with hundreds of miles between crests that may be just a few feet high. Passengers on a ship would scarcely detect their passing. In fact, the tsunami crest is just the tip of a vast mass of moving water. Though wind-driven waves and swells are confined to a shallow layer near the ocean surface, a tsunami extends thousands of feet deep into the ocean.

As the waves in the tsunami reach shore, they slow down due to the shallowing sea floor, and the loss in speed is often accompanied by a dramatic increase in wave height. Depending on the geometry of the seafloor warping that first generated the waves, tsunami attacks can take different forms. In certain cases, the sea can seem at first to draw a breath and empty harbors, leaving fish flopping on the mud. This sometimes draws the curious to the shoreline and to their deaths, since the withdrawing of the sea is inevitably followed by the arrival of the crest of a tsunami wave. Tsunamis also flood in suddenly without warning. Survivors of tsunami attacks describe them as dark "walls" of water. Impelled by the mass of water behind them, the waves bulldoze onto shore and inundate the coast, snapping trees like twigs, toppling stone walls and lighthouses, and smashing houses and buildings into kindling.

156. Which phrase best describes a tsunami?

a. a series of concentric ripples on a pond
b. a wind-driven wave
c. an atomic warhead
d. a vast mass of moving seawater

157. What is true of tsunamis on the open ocean?

a. They cannot be distinguished from wind-driven waves.
b. They are so high that they overwhelm any ships in their path.
c. They move so fast that jets cannot keep up with them.
d. They extend thousands of feet in all directions.

158. What happens as a tsunami reaches the shore?

a. It accelerates.
b. It decelerates and rises impressively.
c. It causes changes in the shape of the sea floor.
d. It suddenly reverses itself.

159. What sometimes signals the approach of a tsunami?

a. a wall of dark water
b. curious onlookers being drawn towards the beach
c. the sea receding and fish being stranded on the beach
d. the uprooting of trees and the collapse of stone walls and buildings

160. What impression are readers left with at the end of the passage?

a. what a tsunami looks like
b. how unpredictable tsunamis are
c. how a tsunami is formed
d. how devastating a tsunami is

Passage 3 is about spontaneous generation.

Until the mid-19th century, it was generally accepted that some life forms – such as maggots*, insects and mice – arose spontaneously from nonliving matter. Such "spontaneous generation" appeared to occur primarily in decaying matter, such as rotting meat. The first serious attack on the idea was made in 1668 by Francesco Redi, who believed that maggots developed from eggs laid by flies. To test his hypothesis, he set out meat in a variety of flasks, some open, some sealed completely and others covered with gauze. As he expected, maggots appeared only in the open flasks in which flies could reach the meat and lay their eggs.

In 1745 John Needham proposed another experiment. As everyone knew that boiling killed microorganisms, he proposed to test whether or not microorganisms appeared spontaneously after boiling. He boiled chicken broth, put it into a flask, sealed it and waited. Sure enough, microorganisms grew and Needham claimed victory for spontaneous generation. Unconvinced, an Italian named Spallanzani suggested that microorganisms had entered the broth from the air after the broth was boiled but before it was sealed. To test this, he placed chicken broth in a flask, sealed the flask, drew off the air, then boiled the broth. No microorganisms grew. This time proponents of spontaneous generation argued that Spallanzani had only proven that spontaneous generation could not occur without air.

The idea was finally laid to rest in 1859 by Louis Pasteur. He boiled meat broth in a flask, heated the flask's neck until it became pliable and bent it into an S shape. Air could enter the flask, but airborne microorganisms would settle by gravity in the neck. As Pasteur expected, no microorganisms grew. When he tilted the flask so that the broth reached the point where airborne particles would have settled, the broth rapidly became cloudy with life. Pasteur had both refuted the theory of spontaneous generation and demonstrated that microorganisms are everywhere – even in the air.

***maggot** – small worm-like creatures that are the young of flies and other insects.

161. Which phrase best defines "spontaneous generation"?
   a. the process by which microscopic life forms cause matter to decay
   b. the sudden death of microscopic life forms that occurs during boiling
   c. the process of sudden decay that takes place when something dies
   d. the idea that life forms out of nowhere in decaying matter

162. Whose experiment supported the idea of spontaneous generation?
   a. Redi's
   b. Needham's
   c. Spallanzani's
   d. Pasteur's

163. What flaw did Spallanzani uncover in Needham's experiment?
   a. The flask had not been sealed tightly enough.
   b. The broth had not been boiled long enough.
   c. The broth had been exposed to air after boiling.
   d. The flask should not have been sealed.

164. Why did Pasteur bend the neck of the flask?
   a. to isolate microorganisms from the air that reaches the broth
   b. to prevent the broth from being exposed to air
   c. to let microorganisms settle to the bottom of the broth
   d. to prevent microorganisms from entering the flask

165. What is true of Pasteur's experiment?
   a. It proved that spontaneous generation did actually occur after boiling.
   b. It employed an air-tight flask.
   c. It was designed to show that microorganisms could grow in boiled broth.
   d. It was an effective adaptation of previous experiments.

Passage 4 is about the ecosystem of a cave.

In 1986 engineers drilling an exploratory hole at a possible construction site in southeastern Romania, near the Black Sea, discovered a cave 80 feet below ground. Taking advantage of the chance find, explorers from the Emil Racovita Speleological Institute of Bucharest soon clambered down the hole. They were stunned by what they saw: the cave was crawling with spiders, scorpions, leeches, millipedes: a rich variety of invertebrate animals, all thriving in total darkness and isolation. Over the years, further research has revealed just how extraordinary the cave is: it has been recognized as the first known ecosystem on land that does not derive its energy from sunlight through photosynthesis.

The base of the food web, the researchers discovered, was a thick scum of bacteria floating on five feet of water at the bottom of the cave. The bacteria practice chemosynthesis: that is, they use hydrogen sulfide in the cave air, rather than sunlight, as a source of energy to make carbohydrates. The scientists found that all the animals in the cave either fed on bacteria directly or ate animals that did. Hot springs on the ocean floor support much the same kind of food chain, and the source of the hydrogen sulfide in the cave is probably geothermal as well; the water is relatively warm. The ecosystem is also an ancient one, having been sealed by some geological event some 5.5 million years ago. Since then, trapped animals have developed the typical appearance of many cave creatures, turning blind and pale and small. They've also evolved into a number of new species: 33 of the roughly 50 species that now live in the cave are found nowhere else. Meanwhile, the bacteria may have done more than provide food: they may have enlarged the habitat. The sulfuric acid they excrete gnaws away at the cave's limestone walls much faster than water alone would.

166. What is true about the cave?
- a. Experts had been searching for it for years.
- b. Researchers were astounded by its lack of biodiversity.
- c. It is the only known ecosystem not to be supported by energy from photosynthesis.
- d. Its importance as a unique habitat was not immediately recognized by researchers.

167. What is the probable source of hydrogen sulfide in the cave?
- a. hot springs on the ocean floor
- b. underground springs heated by energy from the earth's core
- c. bacterial chemosynthesis
- d. carbohydrates

168. What role does chemosynthesis play?
- a. It is the way all life forms in the cave manufacture energy.
- b. Without it, the bacteria would not produce enough hydrogen sulfide.
- c. It has resulted in the typical appearance of many cave creatures.
- d. It enables bacteria in the cave to produce carbohydrates.

169. According to the passage, what have more than five million years of darkness and isolation resulted in?
- a. the preservation of rare prehistoric species
- b. species that have been seriously weakened and disabled
- c. the extinction of many species that once lived in the cave
- d. the evolution of new species uniquely adapted to their environment

170. What is **not** true of bacteria in the cave?
- a. They grow in a thick layer at the bottom of a pool of water.
- b. They give off an acidic substance that slowly disintegrates the walls of the caves.
- c. All animals in the cave depend on them as a direct or indirect food source.
- d. They do not use photosynthesis as a source of energy.

VOCABULARY CONSOLIDATION 1

VEXING VERBS

A Common collocations – Complete each phrase with a word from the box.

abort	adhere	collaborate	compile	conspire	divulge	quibble	writhe

1. .... in pain
2. .... a secret
3. .... over minor details
4. .... on a project
5. .... a mission
6. .... statistics
7. .... to assassinate the president
8. .... to the rules

B Fine-tuning your knowledge – The numbers below refer to the questions in the Vocabulary section of Practice Test 1. Review the words, then fill each blank with the correct form of the appropriate verb.

116. **upstage** **uplift** **upgrade** **upend**

a. Let the boss have the last word. He doesn't like anyone .... him.
b. The rousing performance of Handel's *Messiah* .... the audience.
c. You can .... your computer by adding more memory to it.
d. The naughty child extended his foot and .... the poor teacher!

124. **ward off** **provoke** **suppress** **defer**

a. Government troops had to be called in to .... the rebellion.
b. The Senate will .... voting on the bill until after the elections.
c. Is it true that vitamin C will .... a cold?
d. What .... you to do such a foolish thing?
e. You've been doing this for years. I'll .... to your experience.

127. **abort** **preserve** **consume** **assimilate**

a. The immigrant children were eager to .... into American society.
b. Sumo wrestlers .... enormous amounts of food.
c. If neither side agrees to compromise, the talks will have to be ....
d. The ancient Egyptians were experts at .... dead bodies.

133. **shrivel** **shriek** **bark** **writhe**

a. The woman .... when she saw a mouse scamper across the kitchen.
b. The sergeant .... out orders to his men.
c. After months of neglect, the plants on her balcony had .... and died.
d. The dancers .... and stretched as if their bodies were made of elastic.

138. **downsize** **downplay** **download** **downgrade**

a. Not wanting to upset him, she .... the damage she had done to the car.
b. If the company .... , several hundred employees will be laid off.
c. He spent the evening .... pages from the Internet.
d. If his work does not improve, he will be .... to assistant manager.

144. **perish** **cherish** **dread** **divulge**

a. The airline announced that everyone aboard had .... in the crash.
b. He was executed for .... classified information to a foreign power.
c. The anxious student .... the thought of her upcoming exams.
d. Knowing their father was dying, they .... every moment with him.
e What if the Cold War had turned into World War III? .... the thought!

149. **enumerate** **alleviate** **congregate** **ventilate**

a. A group of angry protesters have .... in front of the Town Hall.
b. We can .... the room by opening the windows a bit.
c. The new peripheral road has greatly .... traffic in the downtown area.
d. How many causes of World War II can you .... ?

NOTORIOUS NOUNS

A Amusing associations – Find the word in the box that is suggested by each prompt.

ammunition	eviction	mortality	ripples	ruffles	temptation	urbanity	whims

1. .... - Eve gave in to this when she bit into the apple.
2. .... - It afflicts tenants who don't pay their rent.
3. .... - It keeps a funeral director in business.
4. .... - You see these when you throw a stone into a quiet lake.
5. .... - Little girls either love them or hate them.
6. .... - Spontaneous women are never without them – note the pun!
7. .... - A refined city-dweller has this, but not a country bumpkin.
8. .... - Without this, a gun's a not-so-deadly weapon.

B Fine-tuning your knowledge – The numbers below refer to the questions in the Vocabulary section of Practice Test 1. After reviewing the words, fill in the blanks with the appropriate words.

115. conduct, intersection, urbanity, breakthrough

a. The discovery of the structure of DNA was a great scientific ....
b. Another word for refinement and sophistication is ....
c. He is a noisy, unruly child whose .... leaves a lot to be desired.
d. The accident occurred at the .... of Main Street and Vine.

132. variation, array, affinity, disarray

a. After her son's birthday party, the house was in total ....
b. She has always felt a strong .... with the objectives of Greenpeace.
c. The children were dressed in their best ....
d. I didn't say he's lying. I said his story is an interesting .... on the truth.

137. ripple, rivulet, ruffle, remnant

a. Girls who are tomboys wouldn't be caught dead in dresses with ....s.
b. During the storm ....s of water ran through the streets.
c. The villagers gazed in horror at the charred ....s of their homes.
d. A .... of laughter went through the crowd as the comic fell onto the stage.

139. controversy, alteration, conflict, antagonism

a. They divorced years ago, but the .... between them is still intense.
b. Women executives feel a strong .... between their careers and families.
c. Decades after abortion was legalized in the USA, the .... still rages.
d. The tailor assured him that the suit would fit perfectly after a few ....s.

145. influx, inmate, input, inquest

a. The prison guards feared that the ....s were about to stage a rebellion.
b. The new teacher valued the .... of her more experienced colleagues.
c. Islanders are busy preparing for the summer .... of tourists.
d. The police commissioner has ordered an .... to investigate the scandal.

150. outreach, outlay, outskirts, outcome

a. Would anyone like to place a wager on the .... of the match?
b. Residents are opposed to building an industrial zone on the .... of town.
c. Educating your children requires a substantial .... of money.
d. The community has launched an .... program for troubled youths.

ADDLING ADJECTIVES

A Common collocations – Complete each phrase with a word from the box.

abrupt **accomplished** **defective** **gaping** **glaring** **imminent** **indigenous** **prestigious** **prevalent**

1. an .... musician	4. .... merchandise	7. a .... hole
2. a .... omission	5. a .... award	8. an .... halt
3. an .... species	6. a .... belief	9. an .... crisis

B Fine-tuning your knowledge – The numbers below refer to the questions in the Vocabulary section in Practice Test 1. After reviewing the words, fill in the blanks with the appropriate words.

114. **extraneous** / **superficial** / **illegible** / **simultaneous**

a. Who signed this letter? The name is totally ....
b. If you remove the .... information, the report will be easier to follow.
c. The student's essay was extremely .... and lacking in detail.
d. The terrorists set off .... explosions at several points in the city.

117. **provisional** / **conspicuous** / **defective** / **complex**

a. The store replaced the .... stereo as the product was under warranty.
b. The problem was highly .... and difficult to solve.
c. If you must cheat, do you have to be so .... about it?
d. The appointment is .... , but if your work is satisfactory you will be offered a permanent position.

122. **contingent** / **intoxicated** / **potable** / **contaminated**

a. No one was willing to risk fishing in the .... lake.
b. The driver had his license revoked for driving while ....
c. Only a very small percentage of the earth's water supply is ....
d. Needless to say, our picnic plans are .... on the weather.

126. **glaring** / **vacant** / **gaping** / **prestigious**

a. Harvard and Yale are among the most .... universities in the USA.
b. The bullet had left a .... wound in the victim's leg.
c. The article contained several .... errors.
d. The apartment has been .... for several months.

130. **partial** / **overexposed** / **superfluous** / **susceptible**

a. If you point the camera into the sun, the photo will be ....
b. The patient may never walk again; a .... recovery is all we can hope for.
c. As a child, he was highly .... to colds and respiratory infections.
d. It was clear that the couple wanted to be alone; so, feeling .... , I left.
e. He's always been .... to fast cars and beautiful women.

135. **eligible** / **compatible** / **conceivable** / **audible**

a. The printer will work with all IBM-............................... computers.
b The patient was so weak that his voice was barely ....
c Desperate for work, she applied for every job she was .... for.
d It is highly .... that the politician's phone had been bugged.

136. **indignant** / **undignified** / **indigent** / **indigenous**

a. Massive deforestation in the area has endangered many .... species.
b. Rude salesclerks make for .... customers – and vice versa!
c. How dare he ruin her party with his bad manners and .... behavior! The hostess had every right to be ....
d. When the stock market crashed in 1929, many families were left ....

AUDACIOUS ADVERBS

Fine-tuning your knowledge – The numbers below refer to the questions in the Vocabulary section in Practice Test 1. After reviewing the words, fill in the blanks with the appropriate words. One word is an adjective. Can you find it? (..............)

120.

sullenly	a. Most people react .... when they are told they no longer have a job.
spontaneously	b. After a few drinks, the three friends .... burst into song.
alternately	c. Her crying was .... mixed with sniffling and sobs.
sluggishly	d. I've never seen you move so .... Are you coming down with the flu?

128.

inadvertently	a. Many a break-in occurs when home-owners .... leave a window open.
vigorously	b. .... we bought identical jackets at the same shop last week.
supposedly	c. It was a brilliant performance, which the audience .... applauded.
coincidentally	d. The necklace is .... valued at over a million dollars.

141.

timely	a. The boy was saved, thanks to the .... arrival of the fireman.
consistently	b. The boss insists that everyone be here .... , so don't be late.
concisely	c. There is little space for the article, so write it as .... as possible.
punctually	d. The employee was dismissed as his work was .... below standard.

FINE LINES AND DELICATE DIFFERENCES

Below are groups of words that are easily confused. At least one of the words in each group has appeared in the Vocabulary section of Practice Test 1. Discuss each group, and then fill in the blanks with the appropriate words.

1.

alteration	a. The bartender's black eye was the result of an .... with a drunk customer.
altercation	b. When the scandal broke, the politician had no other .... but to resign.
alternative	c. Animal migration patterns tend to follow the .... of the seasons.
alternation	d. After a few minor ....s, the contract was signed by both parties.

2.

fatality	a. Many religions are based on a belief in the .... of the soul.
mortality	b. The head-on car collision ended in four ....s.
morality	c. The 20th century witnessed a dramatic decrease in infant ....
immortality	d. "How dare you question the .... of my actions!" she said indignantly.

3.

resumption	a. Reducing energy .... is a high priority in the 21st century.
presumption	b. The article, to my mind, is based upon several false ....s / ....s.
assumption	c. The peace talks came to an abrupt halt with the .... of hostilities.
consumption	d. I'm sick and tired of his arrogant .... Just who does he think he is?
	e. In the old days, the disease tuberculosis was also referred to as ....

4.

eviction	a. Is it true that the company has a .... in the Personnel Department?
evacuation	b. Months behind in his rent, the tenant knew he was facing imminent ....
vacancy	c. The police assisted the firemen in the .... of the burning building.
vaccination	d. The children lined up to receive their polio ....s.

5.

illegible	a. The roast was so overdone that it was ....
ineligible	b. Their meeting had made an .... impression on him.
inedible	c. The dying woman was so weak that her voice was virtually ....
indelible	d. His composition was so .... that the teacher refused to read it.
inaudible	e. His lack of experience makes him .... for the job.

PRACTICE TEST 2

Writing

(30 minutes)

Write on one of the topics given below. If you write about something else, your paper will not be graded. If you do not understand the topics, ask the examiner to explain or translate them. You will be graded on the clarity of your writing and the linguistic range and accuracy you show. Write $1\frac{1}{2}$ to 2 pages. You may make any corrections or other changes in the body of the composition.

TOPICS

1. In recent years people have become increasingly aware that the key to living a long, healthy life is to adopt a "proactive" lifestyle – that is, a lifestyle in which you actively work to promote and maintain your health so that you don't become ill. What **two** ingredients do you regard as the keys to such a lifestyle?

2. How different do you think life will be in the second half of the 21st century? Discuss in relation to any **two** of the following areas:

   - transportation
   - energy consumption
   - houses of the future
   - education
   - leisure pursuits
   - medical care

For help in writing these compositions, see *Writing Tutorial*, pages 192–193.

Listening Comprehension Test

(35–40 minutes)

This part of the examination is a listening test that will assess your understanding of spoken English. The listening test has three parts. There are 50 questions. Mark all your answers on the separate answer sheet. Do not make any stray marks on the answer sheet. If you change your mind about an answer, erase your first answer completely.

PART 1 – In this part of the test, you will hear a short conversation. From the three answer choices given, choose the answer which means the same thing as you hear, or that is true based on what you hear.

For problems **1–17**, mark your answers on the separate answer sheet. No problem can be repeated. Please listen carefully. Do you have any questions?

1. a. She agrees to let him read the letters.
   b. She doesn't want him to read the letters.
   c. She's upset that he wants to read the letters.

2. a. She thinks the house is ugly.
   b. She thinks he doesn't want her to come.
   c. The house makes her feel uneasy.

3. a. The CD's success surprised them both.
   b. The group's music has changed a lot.
   c. The group's CD is very bad.

4. a. Mark has never traveled before.
   b. It was Mark's first trip out of the country.
   c. Mark doesn't like to travel very far.

5. a. They hadn't planned to see each other.
   b. They've had an accident.
   c. He thinks she's strange.

6. a. He wants to own his own business.
   b. She thinks he deserves a promotion.
   c. He can't afford to quit his job.

7. a. She's happy to help him.
   b. She's worried he'll change his mind.
   c. She's agreed to go out with him.

8. a. They'll include Sue in the group photo.
   b. They'll tell Sue what happened.
   c. They'll invite Sue to the movies.

9. a. They'll look for a better place tomorrow.
   b. They'll call Ed to ask what they should do.
   c. They'll try to get the room for half price.

10. a. He wants to know if the store is still open.
    b. He wants to know if the store is closed.
    c. He wants to confirm the store's hours.

11. a. He recently ordered a new car.
    b. He'll probably wait before ordering a new car.
    c. He won't order the car until he test drives it.

12. a. The boss left in the middle of the meeting.
    b. They held the meeting without the boss.
    c. They decided to postpone the meeting.

13. a. He and Frank will buy the gift together.
    b. Frank has already bought the gift.
    c. Frank may not have bought the gift yet.

14. a. He didn't like the restaurant.
    b. He liked the Italian restaurant more.
    c. He prefers this restaurant to the Italian one.

15. a. He hates shopping at malls.
    b. It's cheaper to shop on-line than at malls.
    c. He prefers shopping on-line.

16. a. She'll go if she can find the time.
    b. She's definitely not going.
    c. She doesn't want to go.

17. a. It may rain again next weekend.
    b. He wants her to go camping with him.
    c. He's got other plans for next weekend.

PART II – In this part of the test, you will hear a question. From the three answer choices given, choose the one which best answers the question.

For problems **18–35**, mark your answers on the separate answer sheet. No problem can be repeated. Please listen carefully. Do you have any questions?

18. a. Not until the movie's over.
b. But I'm still not sleepy.
c. I'm not going anywhere.

19. a. Louis will be holding the reins.
b. It's going to cost an awful lot.
c. I'll be gone for about a week.

20. a. Don't mention it.
b. She isn't.
c. What, again?

21. a. He got his reward.
b. I might give him a raise.
c. I suppose it's possible.

22. a. You won't tell me if you leave.
b. You go out too much.
c. You haven't been out for a while.

23. a. I'll get a funny feeling.
b. I just sort of know.
c. I heard the weather report.

24. a. You always come clean.
b. You'll be sorry.
c. You asked for it.

25. a. It just isn't permitted.
b. No, we can allow you in.
c. Yes, you'll have to go home.

26. a. I'm going to go soon.
b. I'd rather not.
c. I doubt if I'll be on time.

27. a. No, that's about it.
b. No, there was nobody else.
c. If you find out, please let me know.

28. a. You're right. He ought to see a doctor.
b. He's obviously having a tough day.
c. I've always liked the service here.

29. a. It's finally under control.
b. No, so be careful how you turn it.
c. Don't worry. I'm a big believer in recycling.

30. a. She's looking all over for them.
b. I advised her against them, but yes.
c. I thought she'd never get rid of them.

31. a. No, I want to watch TV.
b. That's not a bad idea.
c. I didn't mind a bit.

32. a. There's a nice place over that way.
b. Vegetables are always a healthy choice.
c. The prices are just too high.

33. a. No, it's confidential.
b. Sorry, I can't make out anything.
c. No, but I've been meaning to.

34. a. Do you think I should?
b. I've already been to one.
c. It's everyone's dream, isn't it?

35. a. All next week.
b. I told you a month ago.
c. I came back last week.

PART III – In this part, you will hear three short segments from a radio program. The program is called "Learning from the Experts." Each talk lasts about two minutes. As you listen, you may want to take notes to help you remember information given in the talk. After each talk, you will be asked some questions about what was said. From the three answer choices given, you should choose the one which best answers the question according to the information you heard.

Remember, no problems can be repeated. For problems **36–50**, mark your answers on the separate answer sheet. Do you have any questions?

SEGMENT 1

36. What is the speaker's main point?
- a. The earth's water supply will dry up in the 21st century.
- b. Future water shortages can be averted with sounder management.
- c. Water mismanagement has already caused irreparable damage to the planet.

37. What is true about traditional irrigation methods?
- a. They are surprisingly efficient.
- b. Despite being primitive, they deliver water exactly where and when it is needed.
- c. They lead to over-irrigation, which may cause soil damage.

38. What is "salinization"?
- a. A problem associated with over-irrigation
- b. A method of removing salt from seawater
- c. A new method of irrigation

39. Which is NOT mentioned as a possible solution for the future?
- a. Large-scale hydro-engineering projects
- b. Processing municipal sewage into water for irrigation
- c. Removing salt from seawater

40. What does the speaker say about the possibility of removing salt from sea water?
- a. More and more countries are turning to it as a solution.
- b. Current technology limits its widespread use.
- c. It is only used in countries that have cheap and efficient solar power.

SEGMENT 2

41. What is the main finding of the Scottish study?
- a. A higher percentage of Scots die of coronary heart disease on Monday than in other countries.
- b. A majority of Scottish heart attack victims die on Monday.
- c. More Scots die of coronary heart disease on Monday than on any other day.

42. What does the study reveal about people who are already being treated for heart disease?
- a. They are at less risk of dying on Monday than other groups.
- b. They have a greater risk of dying on Monday than other groups.
- c. They have the same risk of dying on Monday as other groups.

43. What is true about the results of the study?
- a. They seem to be a uniquely Scottish phenomenon.
- b. They are more worrisome than findings in other countries.
- c. They are similar to findings in other countries.

44. Why is the weekend a dangerous time for people?
- a. It is a peak period for emergency admissions for heart-related problems.
- b. It is a time when many people drink much more alcohol than during the week.
- c. It is a period when people are likely to go into alcoholic withdrawal.

45. What else it true about the "Morbid Monday effect"?
- a. It seems to affect workers who do not relax during the weekend.
- b. It seems to be related to job stress at the start of a new week.
- c. It seems to affect employees who work over the weekend.

SEGMENT 3

46. What happened in the high school chemistry lab in Genoa, Illinois?
    a. Several students were killed.
    b. Several students were injured.
    c. A girl suffered burns over 20% of her body.

47. Why do experts fear that the problem will increase?
    a. Teachers are becoming more careless.
    b. More students are studying chemistry than ever before.
    c. Students are spending more time in science labs.

48. Why is the state of Iowa mentioned?
    a. It has had many more lab accidents than other states.
    b. It has wisely refused to adopt the new science standards.
    c. It has kept records that clearly document the problem.

49. What is true of the accidents that have occurred?
    a. Most of them could have been avoided.
    b. Most of them have resulted in law suits.
    c. Most of them were caused by students.

50. Which is NOT mentioned as a way of correcting the situation?
    a. Enforcing laws requiring labs to undergo regular safety inspections
    b. Dropping the tough new science standards that have caused the problem
    c. Setting up a centralized agency that will monitor the problem

Grammar – Cloze – Vocabulary – Reading

(75 minutes)

This part of the examination contains 120 problems, numbered **51–170**. There are 40 grammar, 20 cloze, 40 vocabulary and 20 reading comprehension problems. The examiner will not explain any test problems. If you do not understand how to do the problems, raise your hand and a proctor will explain the examples to you.

Do not spend too much time on any one problem. Each problem counts the same. If you do not know the answer to a problem, you may make a reasonable guess. Each problem has only one correct answer. Work fast but carefully. You have 75 minutes to answer all 120 problems.

GRAMMAR

51. There was so much work to do that they didn't know where ..... .

a. they began
b. to begin
c. should they begin
d. it had begun

52. John isn't usually late, so I'm assuming he ...... held up at the office.

a. must have got
b. had to get
c. should have got
d. must get

53. ...... in a small town, he finds city life much too fast paced.

a. He grew up
b. Grown up
c. Having grown up
d. To grow up

54. Given that there's nothing good on TV tonight, ... go to bed early.

a. we'd be better off
b. we might as well
c. we had better
d. we should have to

55. ..... you ran out of gas on a deserted road, would you know what to do?

a. If only
b. Provided
c. On condition that
d. Supposing

56. ..... the fact that the death rate from the disease has risen sharply over the past decade.

a. Alarmingly,
b. Alarmed at
c. It is alarming that
d. Even more alarming is

57. ..... a quick-thinking doctor who happened to witness the accident, it all turned out OK.

a. Thanking
b. We should thank
c. Thanks to
d. Thank

58. Many of her friends like opera, but she finds it not to her ..... .

a. liking
b. likelihood
c. likeness
d. likes

59. She might have got the job, ... such a bad case of nerves at the interview.

a. did she not have
b. unless she would have had
c. had she not had
d. if she hasn't had

60. Should you ever need help, please ..... to give me a call.

a. not to hesitate
b. don't hesitate
c. you wouldn't hesitate
d. you aren't hesitating

61. Construction on the new highway has been ..... progress for several months.

a. under
b. in
c. on
d. about

62. I told you that I'll let you know ..... anything from him.

a. once I will hear
b. no sooner than I hear
c. the minute I've heard
d. when do I hear

63. An eye-witness claims she saw a masked man ..... out of the bedroom window.
    a. to climb
    b. who he was climbing
    c. climbing
    d. climbed

64. My car's making strange noises, so I guess it needs ..... again.
    a. to be servicing
    b. to being serviced
    c. to be serviced
    d. to have serviced

65. An impatient person by nature, George ..... on other people's conversations.
    a. is breaking always in
    b. is breaking in always
    c. always is breaking in
    d. is always breaking in

66. Would you mind ..... I get the children ready for bed?
    a. the clear table so
    b. to clear the table when
    c. clearing the table while
    d. that you clear the table until

67. He pointed out that there were ..... such factories in the area.
    a. quite
    b. few
    c. little
    d. almost none

68. Fifty years ago, ... anyone realize the environment would be in such bad shape.
    a. little did
    b. never
    c. not only did
    d. did hardly

69. Relatively ..... , winter temperatures are milder than they used to be.
    a. telling
    b. talking
    c. saying
    d. speaking

70. In the old days, his family was so poor they couldn't afford bus fares ..... a car.
    a. much less
    b. not even
    c. apart from
    d. rather than

71. In medieval morality plays, good always triumphs ..... evil.
    a. above
    b. to
    c. over
    d. from

72. This article on the causes and consequences of global warming is ..... I've ever read.
    a. more convinced than
    b. most convincing
    c. one of most convinced
    d. among the most convincing

73. Her papers are often quite superficial, but this time she seems ..... a thorough job.
    a. that she did
    b. to have done
    c. to do
    d. like doing

74. The football team has won seven ..... its last ten games.
    a. from
    b. in
    c. out of
    d. among

75. The mailman ..... entered the yard than he was bitten by the dog.
    a. had no sooner
    b. had just
    c. did hardly
    d. no sooner had

76. They had no idea ..... brilliant a painter their next-door neighbor was.
    a. how
    b. what a
    c. so
    d. such a

77. After the long hike, the children wolfed down their dinner as if ..... weeks.
    a. they had to eat for
    b. they hadn't eaten in
    c. they wouldn't eat for
    d. they didn't eat in

78. Some people were shocked by the news, but, ... , the manager deserved to be fired.
    a. as far as I'm concerned
    b. according to me
    c. to my opinion
    d. for my point of view

79. ..... most action sports, sea kayaking poses certain risks to those who participate in it.
    a. Similar to the case in
    b. As is the case with
    c. Taking the case of
    d. In cases like

80. The couple enjoys entertaining friends in the ..... of their own home.
    a. private
    b. privation
    c. privacy
    d. privatization

81. On calling to inquire about my order, I was told ..... later this morning.
    a. they deliver it
    b. to deliver it
    c. it would be delivered
    d. it would have been delivered

82. She's ..... sensitive child that she's always bursting into tears.
    a. so
    b. too
    c. a very
    d. such a

83. Other than his cousin Joyce, I had met virtually everyone at the party at ..... .
    a. a time
    b. this time or the other
    c. time and time again
    d. one time or another

84. He declined their invitation to watch the sunrise, using the excuse that he ..... so early.
    a. didn't use to be up
    b. hadn't usually been up
    c. wasn't used to being up
    d. never got used to be up

85. After weeks of discussing the proposal, the council was finally ready to ..... .
    a. vote it
    b. put it to a vote
    c. cast vote
    d. make it a vote

86. If you find yourself ..... a loose end, give me a call.
    a. from
    b. on
    c. at
    d. with

87. As he hasn't studied all year, ... pass the final exam, it will be a miracle.
    a. so for him to
    b. if he does
    c. it's doubtful he will
    d. it means that to

88. I left an urgent voice mail for my manager ..... contact me as soon as possible.
    a. requesting that he
    b. with request that he will
    c. to request him
    d. which requested to

89. The escaped convict has been ..... for several weeks now.
    a. on the run
    b. in the running
    c. at a run
    d. in the long run

90. She's managing to attend night school without allowing ..... with her day job.
    a. that it interferes
    b. it to interfere
    c. the interference
    d. interfering

Practice Test 2

CLOZE

Passage 1 is about penicillin.
Most school children are familiar with the story of Alexander Fleming and the discovery of a bacteria-killing mold he called penicillin. What they may not know is that, ...(91).... found the mold in 1928, he didn't do much of anything with it. It was ....(92).... until 1938 ....(93).... two Oxford University scientists, Howard Florey and Ernst Chain, went back to Fleming's mold, ...(94).... found a way to produce penicillin and, by 1942, showed that it could be used to ....(95).... infections. ....(96).... purified and available in usable quantities, penicillin was an instant success. It became an important weapon for the Allies in the last years of World War II, ...(97).... thousands of soldiers who ....(98).... would have died from infected wounds.

....(99).... the war, penicillin and other new "wonder drugs" were finally available to use against such life-threatening diseases as pneumonia, tuberculosis and bacterial meningitis. Antibiotics gave ....(100).... the opportunity to intervene in these infectious diseases for the first time. It was an advance that transformed medicine.

91. a. having b. when c. he d. while

92. a. only b. still c. just d. not

93. a. before b. did c. the d. that

94. a. had b. eventually c. and d. they

95. a. spread b. diagnose c. treat d. cause

96. a. It b. Unless c. Once d. They

97. a. so b. saving c. survived d. when

98. a. otherwise b. unless c. never d. they

99. a. Ending b. Since c. Because d. After

100. a. physicists b. physicians c. naturalists d. doctorates

---

Passage 2 is about new research on weight loss.
Why do some people gain weight relentlessly, while others who eat the same amount stay slim? The answer, ...(101).... on the results of a recent study, may have something to do with ....(102).... researchers call "the fidget factor." For their study, researchers chose 16 people who ....(103).... to stuff themselves with an extra 1,000 calories a day for eight weeks. Those chosen had ....(104).... jobs, like office work, and did not ....(105).... in regular physical workouts. To determine their exact energy expenditure, they wore monitors and ....(106).... special blood chemistry tests.

The result showed that it wasn't the big movements, such as walking or climbing stairs, ...(107).... made the difference. ....(108).... , it was the small, fidgeting movements that separated the weight gainers from ....(109).... who stayed slim. The people who burned a lot of extra calories were doing so in the activities of daily life, such as fidgeting, standing up, stretching or just ....(110).... the effort to maintain good posture. It appears that each such muscle movement burns calories and uses some of the excess energy that might otherwise be stored as fat.

101. a. depending b. judging c. based d. relied

102. a. that b. what c. the d whose

103. a. asked b. refused c. told d. agreed

104. a. sedative b. sedentary c. sedated d. sedate

105. a. engage b. succeed c. undergo d. involve

106. a. made b. passed c. underwent d. conducted

107. a. but b. who c. and d. that

108. a. Instead b. However c. Comparatively d. Additionally

109. a. these b. ones c. they d. those

110. a. making b. taking c. doing d. trying

VOCABULARY

111. It was ..... that the frightened young child had wandered away from his parents.
    a. blatant
    b. obvious
    c. ominous
    d. transparent

112. She loves reading murder mysteries with ..... plots.
    a. intricate
    b. suspended
    c. subversive
    d. recurrent

113. After the controversial program, the television station was ..... with complaints.
    a. endowed
    b. invaded
    c. inundated
    d. interrogated

114. He's a prudent businessman who knows the importance of not making ..... decisions.
    a. snap
    b. crisp
    c. crucial
    d. prompt

115. A marriage counselor can help couples resolve their ..... problems.
    a. martial
    b. material
    c. marital
    d. wedded

116. Photocopying books without the publisher's permission is a clear ..... of copyright law.
    a. inference
    b. infliction
    c. infringement
    d. interference

117. It is natural for a person to feel ..... after the death of a spouse.
    a. despondent
    b. pretentious
    c. destitute
    d. precarious

118. Mike can always be depended on to ..... when a friend needs help.
    a. keep a stiff upper lip
    b. go out of his way
    c. be a fair-weather friend
    d. pass the buck

119. The personnel manager was favorably impressed with the ..... young woman.
    a. intelligible
    b. confidential
    c. tenuous
    d. self-assured

120. He ..... gave his daughter permission to go to the rock concert.
    a. callously
    b. grudgingly
    c. unanimously
    d. indefinitely

121. The Congressman from Virginia is a leading ..... of educational reform.
    a. proponent
    b. denomination
    c. proprietor
    d. entrepreneur

122. Bomb experts found .... of plastic explosive in the wreckage of the plane.
    a. imprints
    b. rudiments
    c. fractions
    d. traces

123. An effective manager is one who knows how to ..... responsibility to his subordinates.
    a. attribute
    b. donate
    c. delegate
    d. divert

124. His driver's license was ..... for driving under the influence of alcohol.
    a. abolished
    b. revoked
    c. repealed
    d. confiscated

125. When all the delegates had ..... in the auditorium, the meeting was called to order.
   a. intervened
   b. congested
   c. assembled
   d. conspired

126. Several hours passed before people realized the ..... of the disaster.
   a. magnitude
   b. extension
   c. legacy
   d. accuracy

127. The passengers and crew had to ..... after an explosion ripped a hole in the ship's hold.
   a. weigh anchor
   b. run aground
   c. abandon ship
   d. swab the decks

128. The mayor ..... a warm welcome to the group of visiting diplomats.
   a. suspended
   b. extended
   c. amended
   d. pretended

129. It's natural for teachers to .... on students who constantly disrupt their classes.
   a. focus
   b. frown
   c. infringe
   d. discipline

130. His unwillingness to accept criticism does nothing but ..... the problem.
   a. complicate
   b. enhance
   c. formulate
   d. elaborate

131. As a token of ..... for all their help, she invited them to dinner at her home.
   a. hospitality
   b. apprehension
   c. appreciation
   d. gratification

132. Hypothermia may result from prolonged ..... to severe cold.
   a. exhibition
   b. exemption
   c. exposure
   d. expedition

133. The dentist assured her that the numbness from the anaesthetic would ..... in a few hours.
   a. break down
   b. churn out
   c. phase out
   d. wear off

134. After an extensive manhunt, the escaped convict was finally ..... .
   a. captivated
   b. apprehended
   c. acquitted
   d. surrendered

135. She knew her father ..... when he threatened to ground her if she failed the test.
   a. was begging the question
   b. hit the nail on the head
   c. meant business
   d. was a glutton for punishment

136. The shrewd politician had mastered the art of making ..... statements to the press.
   a. ambiguous
   b. discernible
   c. raucous
   d. negotiable

137. I ..... remember locking the front door. Is it possible we've been burgled?
   a. evidently
   b. obviously
   c. distinctly
   d. profoundly

138. The ..... point of the meeting was the company's fall advertising campaign.
   a. hypothetical
   b. vocal
   c. verbal
   d. focal

139. The citizens were ..... opposed to the government's plans to build a nuclear reactor.
 a. formerly
 b. vehemently
 c. unwillingly
 d. exclusively

140. After playing in the snow, the children's faces were ..... with a healthy glow.
 a. blushed
 b. flushed
 c. rushed
 d. hushed

141. She's an opinionated woman who always tries to ..... her ideas on others.
 a. persuade
 b. inscribe
 c. impose
 d. invest

142. Budget cuts will have a(n) ..... effect on the government's welfare program.
 a. reversible
 b. perpetual
 c. adverse
 d. convertible

143. Scurvy is a blood disease that is caused by a(n) ..... of vitamin C.
 a. deficit
 b. insufficiency
 c. discrepancy
 d. deficiency

144. He found it difficult to ..... his parents' high expectations.
 a. make up for
 b. live up to
 c. catch up to
 d. keep pace with

145. Children from poor families have to overcome many ..... in life.
 a. hurdles
 b. fences
 c. obstructions
 d. barricades

146. His parents are pressuring him to study medicine, but he has no ..... to do so.
 a. implication
 b. initiation
 c. inclination
 d. inhibition

147. She found it hard to choose from among the ..... of smartphones on the market.
 a. consensus
 b. variability
 c. profusion
 d. affluence

148. The factory was fined for not being in ..... with safety regulations.
 a. conjunction
 b. agreement
 c. compliance
 d. tandem

149. Initial reports had ..... underestimated the damage wreaked by the hurricane.
 a. grossly
 b. meticulously
 c. arbitrarily
 d. progressively

150. It is ..... that freshmen students take a course in academic writing.
 a. impertinent
 b. compulsive
 c. mandatory
 d. repulsive

READING

Passage 1 is about microdiamonds.

Though valued as gemstones for 3,000 years, diamonds have recently proved to be ideal for industrial use. An incredibly pure composition of more than 99 percent carbon, diamond is the hardest substance known, making it suitable for use in abrasives and in cutting, grinding and polishing tools. It also has high thermal conductivity – more than three times that of copper – and is thus optimal for spreading and dissipating heat in electronic devices such as semiconductor lasers. Because most applications can be accomplished with tiny crystals, interest has begun to focus on microdiamonds, samples that measure less than half a millimeter in any dimension. Previously, microdiamonds were ignored, mainly because of their minimal size and the complex and expensive procedure required to mine them. But as extraction techniques improve and industrial demand grows, microdiamonds are becoming increasingly attractive.

Scientists believe that commercial-sized stones, or macrodiamonds, form in the earth's mantle and are transported to the surface by volcanoes. The origins of microdiamonds, however, remain a mystery, but scientists now believe that the tiny particles may have origins distinct from those of macrodiamonds. One hypothesis asserts that some form within ascending magma, where growth conditions and processes limit the size to which carbon crystals can grow. Another theory contends that magma is merely the delivery mechanism and that microdiamonds are products of the earth's mantle. Complicating the issue, researchers have discovered microdiamonds that they believe were formed in the earth's crust from the collision of tectonic plates. Tiny diamonds have been found in meteorites as well as in craters known to have been formed by meteor impacts.

With continuing work, scientists may one day resolve how microdiamonds are related to their larger siblings. This knowledge will lead to a greater understanding of the carbon substance, perhaps resulting in more effective techniques for mining the mineral and growing it synthetically.

151. Why were microdiamonds largely ignored in the past?
    a. Their tiny size made them unsuitable for use as abrasives and conductors.
    b. They were not as pure as large diamonds.
    c. They were difficult and expensive to mine.
    d. Their size was so minimal that their existence went unnoticed.

152. What factor accounts for the sudden interest in microdiamonds?
    a. recent discoveries of them in meteorites and in meteor craters
    b. the desire to unravel the mystery of how they are formed
    c. increased industrial demand
    d. their microscopic size

153. What does thermal conductivity refer to?
    a. a substance's hardness
    b. a substance's ability to distribute heat
    c. a substance's melting point
    d. a substance's purity

154. The passage suggests that microdiamonds ...
    a. are the only crystals suitable for use in semiconductor lasers.
    b. are formed in the same distinctive way as macrodiamonds.
    c. come from deep within the earth's core.
    d. may originate in more than one way.

155. According to the passage, which is **not** a goal of continuing scientific research?
    a. to develop ways of growing synthetic diamonds
    b. to find ways to purify the carbon from which diamonds are made
    c. to improve the way in which microdiamonds are extracted from the ground
    d. to explore the relationship between macrodiamonds and microdiamonds

Passage 2 is about the Fertile Crescent.

The Fertile Crescent was the arena of numerous firsts in human history: the first farmers, cities and writing systems, to name but a few. But such achievements also brought unanticipated dangers as society began to alter the environment in ways not possible among its hunting and gathering ancestors.

Between 7,000 and 6,000 B.C., inhabitants were gradually forced to desert every known farming village in the Jordan Valley and Israel, probably because of human damage wreaked on local ecology. 'Ain Ghazal, near Jordan's capital of Amman, is the world's largest Neolithic site, and recent research there has revealed one of the principal factors in the disruption of farming settlements. House construction in the area routinely used lime for solid, waterproof plaster floors and as whitewash to brighten house interiors. Lime had to be manufactured, requiring at least six trees as fuel to produce more than three tons of lime for each structure. Additionally, four trees were used as posts to support the roof, and once a generation an important family member was buried beneath the floor, consuming six trees for a new floor every twenty or thirty years.

The population grew rapidly and new houses were required at an accelerating rate. By 7,000 B.C. more than 36,000 trees had been removed, representing a deforested area of some 2,000 hectares in the surrounding countryside. Population growth was due not only to the stable supply of agricultural produce but also to the supply of meat from goat herds. Goats prefer woody plants, including seedlings of trees that would normally have replaced at least part of the deforested area. The growing deforestation exposed the topsoil to persistent erosion by wind and rain, and field productivity constantly declined. After 7,000 B.C. the population began to diminish, and by 6,000 B.C. a town that had survived for more than two millennia was abandoned to periodic visits by nomadic pastoralists, whose flocks grazed over the deserted fields and hillsides.

156. What factor(s) precipitated the ecological disaster that is mentioned in the passage?

a. ancient burial customs
b. the housing requirements of a rapidly expanding population
c. an increased demand for goat meat
d. a combination of all of the above factors

157. What did massive deforestation lead to?

a. a steady decrease in crop yields
b. a reduction in soil erosion
c. a decline in the manufacture of lime
d. a change in the grazing habits of goat flocks

158. What happened in the area after 7,000 B.C.?

a. Agriculture flourished.
b. People began to abandon the communities.
c. The population grew at an unprecedented rate.
d. Goats were banned from grazing in the deforested area.

159. Why is lime mentioned?

a. Its use soon disrupted life in the settlements.
b. It was unknown before Neolithic times.
c. A huge supply of trees was required to manufacture it.
d. It was widely used to paint the outside of houses.

160. The writer clearly suggests that ...

a. new trees should have been replanted to prevent erosion.
b. the inhabitants were wrong to have abandoned the farming settlements.
c. the inhabitants should not have attempted to modify their environment.
d. such ecological devastation would not have been possible in earlier times.

Passage 3 is about human-factors engineering.

The basis of human-factors engineering – the consideration of information about human users in the design of tools, machines, jobs and work environments – has always been present. One of the oldest and most efficient of human implements, the scythe, shows a remarkable degree of human-factors engineering, undoubtedly reflecting modifications made over many centuries: the adroitly curved handle and blade and the peg grasp for the left hand. All of this contrasts sharply with the conventional snow shovel, a modern implement of generally poor design that has been blamed for many a wintertime back strain.

The designing of a much more complicated device, such as a space suit, presents more intricate problems. A space suit is a complete miniature world, a self-contained environment that must supply everything needed for an astronaut's life as well as his comfort. The suit must provide a pressurized interior, without which an astronaut's blood would boil in the vacuum of space. The consequent pressure differential between the inside and the outside of the suit is so great that, when inflated, the suit becomes a distended, rigid capsule. Even the engineering of special joints has not been able to provide as much flexibility of movement as is desirable, so to compensate for that lack, attention has been directed towards the human-factors design of the tools and devices that an astronaut must use.

In addition, a space suit must provide oxygen and a system for removing excess carbon dioxide and water vapor. It must also offer protection against extreme heat, cold and radiation and facilities for speech communication and the temporary storage of body wastes. This is such an imposing list of requirements that an entire technology has been developed to deal with them and, indeed, with the provision of simulated environments and procedures for testing and evaluating space suits.

161. What is true about human factors engineering?
   a. It is a relatively recent innovation.
   b. It is present only in the most sophisticated devices and work environments.
   c. It is responsible for the revolution in modern technology.
   d. It refers to the designing of products with the human user in mind.

162. What do the scythe and the space suit have in common?
   a. They are highly sophisticated technological achievements.
   b. They are self-contained work environments.
   c. They are devices embodying successful human-factors engineering.
   d. They are devices that entail modifications made over many centuries.

163. What have space-suit designers **not** succeeded in providing astronauts with?
   a. a means of storing body wastes
   b. the ability to move easily
   c. an adequate breathing system
   d. protection against extremes of temperature

164. What is **not** true of the air pressure within a space suit?
   a. It enhances the astronaut's ability to bend and move about.
   b. It is greater than the surrounding pressure in space.
   c. It has necessitated the development of special joints and tools.
   d. Without it the astronaut's blood would overheat.

165. What does the passage imply about human factors engineering?
   a. It should be used to redesign a new snow shovel.
   b. It would be incapable of solving problems more intricate than designing a space suit.
   c. It can be seen in every aspect of the space suit's design and development.
   d. It may someday be applied in the testing and evaluation of space-suit design.

Passage 4 is about a battle of the American Civil War.

At New Market, Virginia, on May 15, 1864, a small force of Confederates handed a dramatic defeat to a larger army of Yankee invaders.* A small portion of the Rebel command – just 226 men – was the cadet corps of the Virginia Military Institute (VMI). In the battle's final moments, the Confederates advanced. Major General Breckinridge's Southern ranks were so thinly stretched that he had no choice but to put the cadets, some no more than 15 years old, into a gap in his line. By chance, their route of advance took them directly toward the 30th New York Light Artillery Battery, commanded by Captain Alfred von Kleiser. With the rest of his line collapsing around him, von Kleiser gave up his position well before the cadets reached him, but he was forced to abandon one cannon on the field. Moments later the VMI boys surged over the gun, exulting in their prize.

Those are the facts. Yet within days, Southern newspapers had the boys engaged in hand-to-hand fighting, of which there was virtually none on that part of the battlefield. Not one contemporary account mentioned that the gun had been abandoned and only by chance in the boys' line of march. In 1867 one of the cadets wrote to another recalling the day "we took the battery" at New Market. Suddenly one gun had become all six. In saying "battery," of course, he might have meant the position occupied by the battery. But such distinctions were lost on the generation after the war, and by the 1880s the impression was firmly planted that the cadets had held a vital place in the Confederate line under intense hand-to-hand fighting and in surging forward, virtually alone, had captured a whole battery and single-handedly given the South a victory. Only in the last few decades have the facts been re-established, thanks in considerable part to the Virginia Military Institute.

* The battle referred to occurred during the American Civil War (1861–1865), in which Southerners (known as Confederates or Rebels) fought against Northerners (or Yankees).

166. What happened in the final moments of the battle?
- a. The outnumbered Confederates surrendered to the Yankees.
- b. A group of young cadets fought troops in hand-to-hand combat.
- c. Yankees attacked the Southerners' thinly stretched ranks.
- d. Troops from New York retreated, leaving a cannon behind.

167. What does the passage imply about why Breckinridge sent the boys into battle?
- a. He did it as a test to see how well trained they were.
- b. He did it as a last resort.
- c. He did it without thinking.
- d. He did it only when he saw that they would not be in danger.

168. According to the passage, what is true of contemporary newspaper accounts?
- a. They were critical of the general's decision to send the boys into battle.
- b. They intentionally downplayed the cadets' role.
- c. They failed to report the event accurately.
- d. They mentioned that the boys had captured the gun by chance.

169. What happened in the years immediately following the war?
- a. The cadets continued to be seen as the battle's main heroes.
- b. The cadets did whatever they could to hide the truth.
- c. The cadets continued to exaggerate the role they played.
- d. The battle was soon forgotten by those in the next generation.

170. What is one of the main purposes of the passage?
- a. to give long overdue praise to the cadets and the Virginia Military Institute
- b. to show how tall tales and legends grow unintentionally from a tiny grain of truth
- c. to praise the press for creating false impressions
- d. to show how unwilling people are to believe lies in newspapers

VOCABULARY CONSOLIDATION 2

VEXING VERBS

A Common collocations – Complete each phrase with a word from the box.

abolish	apprehend	blush	confiscate	conspire	delegate

1. .... against the government
2. .... slavery
3. .... responsibility
4. .... with embarrassment
5. .... stolen goods
6. .... a criminal

divert	donate	impose	invade	invest	revoke

7. .... a driver's license
8. .... a fine
9. .... in the stock market
10. .... traffic
11. .... blood
12. .... a person's privacy

B Fine-tuning your knowledge – The numbers below refer to the questions in the Vocabulary section of Practice Test 2. Review the words, then fill each blank with the correct form of the appropriate verb.

113.
endow
invade
inundate
interrogate

a. While being .... , the suspect broke down and confessed.
b. It's clear that the child is .... with extraordinary musical talent.
c. After the dam burst, the area was .... for miles around.
d. Iraqi forces .... Kuwait in the summer of 1990.
e. The wealthy businessman has .... the hospital with a new wing.

125.
intervene
congest
assemble
conspire

a. The pneumonia patient's lungs were .... with fluid.
b. Several generals have been arrested for .... against the government.
c. To .... the model ship, you'll need glue – and a lot of patience!
d. Had the police not .... , the protest would have turned into a riot.
e. During recess, all the students .... in the school yard.

128.
suspend
extend
amend
pretend

a. He .... his arm as far as he could but still couldn't reach the apple.
b. The president will veto the new law unless the Senate .... it.
c. The principal threatened to .... anyone caught vandalizing the school.
d. He claims he's ill, but I think he's only ....

129.
focus
frown
infringe
discipline

a. He's a moral man who .... on intolerance and prejudice.
b. Anyone who .... the regulations will be severely ....
c. I'm .... because you're being noisy and I can't .... on my work.
d. Do you agree that smoking in public .... on the rights of non-smokers?

130.
complicate
enhance
formulate
elaborate

a. The patient's condition was .... by his refusal to stop smoking.
b. Going to university will greatly .... your prospects for the future.
c. Images sent to earth by the Hubble Telescope are .... by computer.
d. His book .... on the theory that he .... in an article last year.

134.
captivate
apprehend
acquit
surrender

a. Police are confident that the robbers will be .... shortly.
b. The audience was .... by the singer's exquisite performance.
c. Do you think the jury will .... the defendants?
d. Realizing that the battle was lost, the soldiers ....

NOTORIOUS NOUNS

A Ridiculous riddles – Find the phrase or nonsense word in the box that is suggested by each prompt.

X-hibitions discreet discrepancies hen apprehension fractious fractions intrepid entrepreneurs proficiency deficiency af-FLU-ence proper proprietors rudiments of rudeness

What do you call ... ?

1. the state of not yet having the Michigan ECPE? ....
2. museum shows not suitable for children? ....
3. bad-tempered 1/2s and 1/4s? ....
4. a virus that poor people wouldn't mind catching? ....
5. shop owners with good manners? ....
6. differences that are barely noticeable ? ....
7. a primer on bad manners? ....
8. brave businessmen? ....
9. the clinical term for "fear of chickens"? ....

B Fine-tuning your knowledge – The numbers below refer to the questions in the Vocabulary section of Practice Test 2. After reviewing the words, fill in the blanks with the appropriate words.

116. **inference, infliction, infringement, interference**

a. You were fired because your actions were a clear .... of company policy.
b. Children should be protected against the .... of pain and suffering.
c. Your .... is unwelcome. Please mind your own business.
d. The evidence speaks for itself. There is only one .... to be drawn.

126. **magnitude, extension, legacy, accuracy**

a. Applications must be submitted by 1 May. No ....s will be granted.
b. Her essay displayed a remarkable degree of fluency and ....
c. It was only later that he realized the .... of his mistake.
d. She was left a .... of $10,000 in her grandmother's will.

132. **exhibition, exemption, exposure, expedition**

a. The more children you have, the more tax ....s you can claim.
b. She wears sunscreen to minimize her .... to the sun's UV rays.
c. I have never seen such an embarrassing .... of bad manners.
d. Trapped by a blizzard, the climbers on the .... died of ....

145. **hurdle, fence, obstruction, barricade**

a. The runners jumped over the last .... and made for the finish line.
b. The soldiers easily made their way over the hastily constructed ....s.
c. He had to undergo surgery to remove a(n) .... in his intestines.
d. The house was surrounded by a wooden ....

146. **implication, initiation, inclination, inhibition**

a. He became a member of the organization at a secret .... ceremony.
b. If your .... is that I'm lying, you're barking up the wrong tree.
c. He rudely replied that he had neither the time nor the .... to help us.
d. Ann is a shy child with many ....s.

147. **consensus, variability, profusion, affluence**

a. It's difficult to choose among the .... of textbooks on the market.
b. The United States is a nation of both .... and poverty.
c. The .... of the child's performance greatly concerns his teachers.
d. After meeting for several hours, the group has still not reached a ....

ADDLING ADJECTIVES

A Common collocations – Complete each phrase with a word from the appropriate box.

adverse	marital	material	martial	ominous	perpetual

1. .... law
2. .... bliss / strife
3. .... possessions / goods
4. .... conditions
5. .... black clouds
6. .... motion

compulsive	convertible	crisp	repulsive	snap	tenuous

7. a .... judgment
8. a .... odor
9. a .... liar
10. a .... sofa-bed / car
11. a .... head of lettuce
12. a .... hold on life / reality

B Fine-tuning your knowledge – The numbers below refer to the questions in the Vocabulary section of Practice Test 2. After reviewing the words, fill in the blanks with the appropriate words.

112.

intricate suspended subversive recurrent	a. This isn't the first time you've been late; it's a .... problem. b. She enjoys reading long spy novels with .... plots. c. The extremist group is said to be involved in .... activities. d. Since it was his first offense, the judge gave him a .... sentence.

114.

snap crisp crucial prompt	a. The boss has asked that we all be .... ; lateness will not be tolerated. b. It is .... that the boss be given the message as soon as possible. c. The couple enjoys going for walks on .... fall days. d. Think carefully before acting; .... decisions will get you in trouble.

117.

despondent pretentious destitute precarious	a. I've never met anyone so arrogant and .... Who does he think he is? b. The torrential rain made the long drive home extremely .... c. Imagine being completely .... , without job or home. d. What can I do to cheer you up? I hate to see you so ....

136.

ambiguous discernible raucous negotiable	a. After a few months the students saw a(n) .... improvement in their skills. b. The writer rewrote the chapter to make his ideas clearer and less .... c. He's hoping to get $3,000 for the car, but I'm sure the price is .... d. When the teacher fell off her chair, the class burst into .... laughter.

138.

hypothetical vocal verbal focal	a. She enjoys .... music, which is why she's such an opera lover. b. His ideas are still .... ; he'll know more when he analyzes the data. c. If a .... agreement isn't good enough for you, let's put it in writing. d. The .... point of the meeting will be the proposed tax reform. e. He is an extremely .... critic of the government's new tax reforms.

150.

impertinent compulsive mandatory repulsive	a. Some women like men with bulging muscles; others find them .... b. You did a good job of insulting her with your .... remarks. c. Attendance at the meeting is .... ; no one will be excused. d. I stayed up all night reading the novel; it's absolutely .... reading.

AUDACIOUS ADVERBS

Fine-tuning your knowledge – The numbers below refer to the questions in the Vocabulary section of Practice Test 2. After reviewing the words, fill in the blanks with the appropriate words.

120. **callously, grudgingly, unanimously, indefinitely**

a. The workers voted .... to strike for higher wages. No one disagreed.
b. Are you ever getting married, or do you plan to stay engaged .... ?
c. She .... agreed to help him paint the house even though she didn't want to do it.
d. They .... refused to listen to his side of the story.

139. **formerly, vehemently, unwillingly, exclusively**

a. The African nation of Zimbabwe was .... known as Rhodesia.
b. This product is available .... at Radio Shack stores.
c. She .... denies having any knowledge of her husband's crimes.
d. Can't you be more enthusiastic? You always seem to agree so ....

149. **grossly, meticulously, arbitrarily, progressively**

a. As the days went by, the patient grew .... stronger.
b. He can't give you a reason because he decided ....
c. His latest biography was, as always, ... researched.
d. They .... underestimated the cost of the repairs.

LOOK-ALIKES ... UP TO A POINT

Below are groups of words that look so much alike that it's easy to confuse them. At least one of the words in each group has appeared in the Vocabulary Section of Practice Test 2. Discuss each group, then fill in the blanks with the appropriate words.

1. **intelligible, intellectual, intelligent**

a. John's an .... person, but in no way is he interested in .... pursuits such as reading literature or listening to opera.
b. Why is it that people with great .... ability have so much difficulty in expressing themselves in an .... manner? Half the time I have no idea what they're saying!

2. **proprietor, propriety, proponent, proposition**

a. The author is best known as a .... of animals rights.
b. When put to a vote, the .... turned out to be highly unpopular.
c. The .... of the shop runs his business with great ....
d. Your business .... is interesting, but I need some time to consider it.

3. **deficit, deficiency, deference, defiance**

a. Children should show .... to their elders.
b. Beriberi is a nerve disease caused by a .... of vitamin B1.
c. The government's goal is to cut spending and reduce the national ....
d. His parents hoped that his .... of authority was just a passing phase.

4. **negligible, negligent, neglected**

a. "Golf widows" feel .... when their husbands play golf all weekend.
b. .... parents fail to provide a proper home for their children.
c. There is a .... difference between the values 0.0001 and 0.00011.

5. **repeal, repel, repulse**

a. This spray .... mosquitoes; it's a must when you go camping.
b. When lawmakers don't like a law, they .... it.
c. Opposite magnetic poles attract; similar poles .... each other.
d. When something disgusts you, it .... / .... you.

PRACTICE TEST 3

Writing

(30 minutes)

Write on one of the topics given below. If you write about something else, your paper will not be graded. If you do not understand the topics, ask the examiner to explain or translate them. You will be graded on the clarity of your writing and the linguistic range and accuracy you show. Write $1\frac{1}{2}$ to 2 pages. You may make any corrections or other changes in the body of the composition.

TOPICS

1. From Christmas and birthdays to baptisms and weddings, we live in a society that revolves around giving gifts. Some people say this is true to such an extent that the meaning has gone out of gift-giving. Do you agree? Think back on gifts you have received and discuss **two** that stand out – one because it had special meaning and another because it was totally inappropriate. What did these gifts teach you about giving gifts?

2. As a result of increasing divorce rates and changing social values, more and more children are growing up in single-parent families. Discuss some of the main problems that the children of single parents might confront and how these problems might be overcome.

For help in writing these compositions, see *Writing Tutorial*, pages 194–195.

Listening Comprehension Test

(35–40 minutes)

This part of the examination is a listening test that will assess your understanding of spoken English. The listening test has three parts. There are 50 questions. Mark all your answers on the separate answer sheet. Do not make any stray marks on the answer sheet. If you change your mind about an answer, erase your first answer completely.

PART 1 – In this part of the test, you will hear a short conversation. From the three answer choices given, choose the answer which means the same thing as you hear, or that is true based on what you hear.

For problems **1–17**, mark your answers on the separate answer sheet. No problem can be repeated. Please listen carefully. Do you have any questions?

1. a. She isn't able to do something.
b. She thinks the price is too high.
c. He wants her to give her something.

2. a. She can go in if she shows him some ID.
b. She'll have to wait, like everyone else.
c. He'd like to get to know her better.

3. a. Jim has promised to come, but won't.
b. Jim is sure he can't come.
c. Jim doesn't know if he can come yet.

4. a. She's had plenty of farm experience.
b. She worked in a field ten years ago.
c. She's sure she's properly qualified.

5. a. They're not in any immediate danger.
b. They're swimming further out to sea.
c. They're worried they may not make it.

6. a. He can't find his formal clothes.
b. He's dressed inappropriately.
c. He'll borrow a friend's tuxedo.

7. a. He's relieved the boss isn't angry.
b. He's had a disagreement with the boss.
c. He's convinced the boss will fire him.

8. a. If it rains, they won't go to a restaurant.
b. She'll pay for the meal on Friday.
c. She'd like to join him another time.

9. a. One of them is ill and may die tomorrow.
b. Some of them may lose their jobs tomorrow.
c. Something must be finished by tomorrow.

10. a. She doesn't know what to tell her friend.
b. She absolutely refuses to do what he asks.
c. She's too nervous to do what he asks.

11. a. She knows she would hate the film he saw.
b. She hated the film they saw.
c. She's about to see a film.

12. a. He's forgotten something at the office.
b. He admits he's not working very hard.
c. He often comes home in a bad mood.

13. a. Everything is under control.
b. The car service is delayed in traffic.
c. She'll arrange to take a later flight.

14. a. She doesn't like having to drive to work.
b. Business travel no longer appeals to her.
c. She may have to quit because of her age.

15. a. He'll finish the paper later today.
b. He's on his way to submit the paper now.
c. He's rushing because he left the paper at home.

16. a. He wishes he had her motivation.
b. He's much less fit than she is.
c. He never goes to the gym.

17. a. A few people left before she could tell them.
b. She's already told everyone she knows.
c. He's always the last person she tells.

PART II – In this part of the test, you will hear a question. From the three answer choices given, choose the one which best answers the question.

For problems **18–35**, mark your answers on the separate answer sheet. No problem can be repeated. Please listen carefully. Do you have any questions?

18.
a. It was better than I imagined.
b. It will be very exciting.
c. It's not what I expected.

19.
a. Soon, I hope.
b. The doors open at ten.
c. Over there, just around the corner.

20.
a. I definitely won't. They have rights.
b. Well, I was planning to.
c. No, I always say that.

21.
a. No, I'm not.
b. Yes, I'll see.
c. Sure, why not?

22.
a. Well, it's never happened before.
b. I know, I heard you the first time.
c. Sorry, I always forget.

23.
a. They prefer to go outside.
b. They're just lazy, that's all.
c. They can't make up their minds.

24.
a. Eventually, I guess.
b. I'm sorry you feel that way.
c. There's too much to do right now.

25.
a. Why did you come by car?
b. I suppose Jim could give you a lift.
c. There's a stop right in front of my house.

26.
a. Maybe some other time.
b. Don't mention it.
c. My pleasure.

27.
a. Actually, we got a letter last week.
b. To be honest, she does get on my nerves.
c. Perhaps she's moved.

28.
a. One day, for sure.
b. Me, for one.
c. Actually, he should be back by now.

29.
a. I swear, I won't say a thing.
b. I suppose I should have.
c. I don't know who to tell.

30.
a. They won't be admitted.
b. They shouldn't have come back.
c. They can try again after the concert.

31.
a. Not a lot, really. Only $50.
b. I think it's lovely. And not very expensive.
c. I asked, but nobody knew.

32.
a. He's always been athletic.
b. Over two hundred dollars.
c. It was cut off last week.

33.
a. Don't worry. Everything works fine.
b. I hope so. I'd hate to see them break up.
c. They've worked there for a while.

34.
a. I didn't realize you were leaving.
b. Actually I would. You look a bit tired.
c. I'd rather you didn't. There's too much to do.

35.
a. Not yet, but I'll make time after dinner.
b. No, I stayed home all evening.
c. I might have. What about you?

PART III – In this part, you will hear three short segments from a radio program. The program is called "Learning from the Experts." Each talk lasts about two minutes. As you listen, you may want to take notes to help you remember information given in the talk. After each talk, you will be asked some questions about what was said. From the three answer choices given, you should choose the one which best answers the question according to the information you heard.

Remember, no problems can be repeated. For problems **36–50**, mark your answers on the separate answer sheet. Do you have any questions?

SEGMENT 1

36. What has recent research shown about mice and exercise?

a. Mice that run are slimmer and have stronger hearts.
b. Mice that run have larger brains than those who don't.
c. Mice that don't run learn more slowly and have fewer new brain cells.

37. Which function is NOT associated with the hippocampus?

a. Learning
b. Controlling cell growth
c. Remembering

38. Which of the following best describes the experiment?

a. Mice with running wheels learned the water maze faster than mice without running wheels.
b. Mice that swam voluntarily learned the water maze faster than mice that ran voluntarily.
c. Mice that were forced to run did not learn the water maze as fast as mice that ran voluntarily.

39. What is LTP?

a. A chemical in the brain that promotes learning
b. A technical term for any electrical impulse in the brain
c. A strengthening of the electrical activity between brain cells

40. What is true about mice that were forced to swim the water maze?

a. They produced the same amount of new brain cells as sedentary mice.
b. They produced just as many brain cells as mice that voluntarily used running wheels.
c. They produced more new brain cells than mice that swam the maze voluntarily.

SEGMENT 2

41. What is the main point of the study described by the health columnist?

a. Weather conditions can trigger migraines.
b. The Chinook winds bring welcome relief to migraine sufferers.
c. The Chinook winds seem to set off migraines in some people.

42. Which symptom is NOT associated with migraine headaches?

a. Temporary loss of vision
b. Nausea
c. Sensitivity to light

43. What was true of the older migraine sufferers who were studied?

a. They are particularly at risk in the days before the arrival of the Chinooks.
b. They tend to suffer more than other groups when the winds are strongest.
c. They continue to suffer for days after the winds die down.

44. Which is mentioned as a possible explanation for the phenomenon?

a. The drop in temperature
b. The increase in atmospheric pressure
c. The rise of positive ions in the atmosphere

45. Why are researchers optimistic about their findings?

a. They believe their findings will help them find a cure for migraines.
b. They believe their findings may lead to the development of a seasonal treatment.
c. They believe their research will help females who suffer during their monthly periods.

SEGMENT 3

46. When did the inventor get the initial idea for the Java Log?
    a. While he was on a search-and-rescue mission
    b. While he was researching another substance
    c. While he was living above a café in Paris

47. How long did it take the inventor to develop a successful formula for the Java Log?
    a. A few months
    b. Several years
    c. More than ten years

48. Where does the inventor hope to get his supply of coffee grounds once production increases?
    a. From an instant-coffee manufacturer
    b. From landfills all over North America
    c. From a large chain of coffee houses

49. What is the major advantage of the Java log over sawdust logs and other alternatives?
    a. It produces more heat.
    b. It is less expensive.
    c. It can be recycled.

50. What is NOT true about the Java Log currently on the market?
    a. It is not yet widely available in the USA.
    b. It is completely without aroma.
    c. It is made from recycled material.

Grammar – Cloze – Vocabulary – Reading

(75 minutes)

This part of the examination contains 120 problems, numbered **51–170**. There are 40 grammar, 20 cloze, 40 vocabulary and 20 reading comprehension problems. The examiner will not explain any test problems. If you do not understand how to do the problems, raise your hand and a proctor will explain the examples to you.

Do not spend too much time on any one problem. Each problem counts the same. If you do not know the answer to a problem, you may make a reasonable guess. Each problem has only one correct answer. Work fast but carefully. You have 75 minutes to answer all 120 problems.

GRAMMAR

51. Larry and I see each other every ..... , but we're not exactly close friends.
    a. time and again
    b. once a month
    c. now and again
    d. time to time

52. If they asked you to help them move next week, ... ?
    a. didn't they
    b. would you
    c. did you
    d. won't they

53. Sorry ..... at the last minute, but I won't be able to come tomorrow.
    a. to have to cancel
    b. I'm canceled
    c. to canceling
    d. for being canceled

54. Now that the children are grown she has a lot of time ..... her hands.
    a. in
    b. for
    c. at
    d. on

55. I hate to tell you this but, to be honest, it was your directions ..... .
    a. they got us lost
    b. that we got lost
    c. that got us lost
    d. got us lost

56. The supervisor said that no one was to leave ..... the job was completed.
    a. as long as
    b. by the time
    c. until
    d. since

57. The job announcement failed to mention the benefits ..... the successful applicant.
    a. that would be given to
    b. for which they would give
    c. having been given to
    d. of which will be given

58. The instructor explained that the course would be divided ..... three parts.
    a. by
    b. up
    c. into
    d. on

59. It's not that unusual for students ..... an oral presentation.
    a. seeming insecure when they make
    b. who seem insecure to make
    c. to seem insecure when making
    d. seem to be insecure making

60. The researchers were careful ..... variations in temperature and humidity.
    a. controlling
    b. to control for
    c. about taking control of
    d. being in control of

61. The assistant was so upset ..... that she could barely speak.
    a. that what she heard
    b. about what did she hear
    c. to have heard about
    d. by what she had heard

62. Parents who are overly ..... tend to spoil their children.
    a. permitting
    b. permission
    c. permissible
    d. permissive

63. He regrets ..... harder to get better grades when he was in high school.
   a. to not trying
   b. that if only he had tried
   c. not to have tried
   d. not having tried

64. ..... his son's quick thinking, he might not be alive today.
   a. As for
   b. But for
   c. With the exception of
   d. If it hadn't been

65. At this time next week, the couple ..... themselves on a beach in Hawaii.
   a. will sun
   b. will have sunned
   c. will be sunning
   d. are going to sun

66. According to the job announcement on the website, applications ..... by June 30th.
   a. must be submitting
   b. will have submitted
   c. are to be submitted
   d. should submit

67. Mike is regarded ..... the most knowledgeable person in the office.
   a. that he is
   b. as
   c. to being
   d. as though he were

68. She's in such great shape now that it's hard to believe ..... a lot heavier.
   a. her usually being
   b. it was used to being
   c. she used to be
   d. she would have usually been

69. Something in the refrigerator is giving ..... a horrible smell.
   a. away
   b. out
   c. up
   d. off

70. ..... he decides to break up with her or not is no concern of mine.
   a. Should
   b. That
   c. Whether
   d. Although

71. According to the schedule, buses to the capital leave every hour ..... .
   a. on the hour
   b. in an hour
   c. by the hour
   d. hourly

72. ..... he realizes how expensive the trip is, I'm sure he'll change his mind about coming.
   a. Given
   b. Once
   c. The sooner
   d. Only when

73. The beautiful young bride in the photo was ..... her ninety-year-old grandmother.
   a. one and the same as
   b. nothing more and nothing less than
   c. none other than
   d. the one and only

74. She thought to herself, "..... to have helped me with all those heavy packages yesterday."
   a. How kind of him
   b. How kind it is
   c. What kind is he
   d. What kind he is

75. After twenty years ..... abroad, it was only natural that he'd begun to feel homesick.
   a. he had lived
   b. having lived
   c. of living
   d. he was living

76. Out of all the assistants she's ever had, Gene is ..... reliable.
   a. the lesser
   b. less
   c. least of all
   d. the least

77. The director says that they ..... by the end of next week.
 a. must have finished the report
 b. have finished the report
 c. must have the report finished
 d. have the report to be finished

78. He told me he would pick you up at your home around 7 a.m. – provided ..... , of course.
 a. he will remember
 b. he remembers
 c. he would remember
 d. his remembering

79. It was ..... that they were forced to cancel their camping trip.
 a. such bad weather
 b. so bad a weather
 c. too bad weather
 d. so bad weather

80. The doctors tried every means ..... to revive the accident victim.
 a. imaginary
 b. imaginable
 c. imaginative
 d. imagined

81. Should you have any doubts ..... , please feel free to call me.
 a. if ever
 b. whatsoever
 c. whichever
 d. however

82. If you're looking for someone ..... , I'm not the one you should be talking to.
 a. who is blamed
 b. to blame
 c. being blamed
 d. to put on the blame

83. Don't expect a firm answer from him, as it's not in his nature ..... so far in advance.
 a. that he makes plans
 b. making plans
 c. having made plans
 d. to make plans

84. ..... to invest in the stock market should seek advice from a reputable broker.
 a. If anyone wants
 b. Should anyone who wants
 c. Anyone wanting
 d. To want anyone

85. His younger son, Jonathan, is definitely ..... sociable of the two children.
 a. the more
 b. more
 c. the most
 d. most

86. The flight cross-country, from New York to Seattle, is roughly ..... .
 a. five hours of flight
 b. a five-hours flying
 c. five-hours flight
 d. a five-hour flight

87. ..... from working all day, he decided to turn in early.
 a. Tiring
 b. Having tired
 c. Tired
 d. Been tired

88. ..... , she is one of the brightest people I have ever had the pleasure of meeting.
 a. Without a doubt
 b. Not in doubt
 c. Not to doubt it
 d. It's beyond doubt

89. That's the university ..... his father graduated from in the 1980s.
 a. from which
 b. that
 c. when
 d. whom

90. Having studied hard all semester, he's ..... he'll ever be to take the final exam tomorrow.
 a. prepared the best
 b. as well prepared as
 c. the best prepared as
 d. so well prepared that

CLOZE

Passage 1 is about a famous rivalry.

In the second half of the 19th century, scientists as well as society at large were fascinated by the ancient, often enormous fossils that were being discovered in North America. Many of the most exciting finds were ....(91).... largely to the efforts of Edward Drinker Cope and Othniel Charles Marsh, who ....(92).... at the forefront of vertebrate paleontology. Between 1870 and the late 1890s, the two men classified 136 new species of ....(93).... North American dinosaurs. Scientists had previously ....(94).... of only nine.

Today the names Cope and Marsh – like Lewis and Clark or Stanley and Livingstone – remain linked together in history books. ....(95).... these other famous duos, however, Cope and Marsh hated ....(96).... other with a passion. As their competition to ....(97).... dinosaur bones raged across the fossil fields of the American West, Cope and Marsh quarreled continuously in the ....(98).... and within political and scientific circles of the nation's capital. Their race for preeminence sometimes caused them to give different names to the same species and to announce discoveries of new animals ....(99).... having inadequate evidence. Yet, ...(100).... their hatred expressed itself in petty ways, it did spur activity in the field and greatly increased our knowledge of paleontology.

91. a. made c. resulting
    b. discovered d. due

92. a. led c. placed
    b. stood d. located

93. a. distinct c. extinct
    b. instinctive d. distinguished

94. a. knowledge c. thought
    b. aware d. known

95. a. Unlike c. Disliking
    b. Different d. Without

96. a. one c. each
    b. the d. everyone

97. a. unearth c. explore
    b. describe d. conceal

98. a. type c. publication
    b. print d. press

99. a. despite c. by
    b. without d. before

100. a. knowing c. even
     b. while d. as

Passage 2 is about the Milky Way.

If we look up on a clear night, we see that the sky is full of stars. During the summer months in the Northern Hemisphere, a faint band of light ....(101).... from horizon to horizon, a swath of pale white cutting ....(102).... a background of deepest black. ....(103).... the early Egyptians, this was the heavenly Nile, ...(104).... through the land of the dead ruled by Osiris. The ancient Greeks ....(105).... it to a river of milk. Astronomers now know that the band is ....(106).... composed of countless stars in a flattened disk seen edge on. The stars are so close to one another along the line of sight ....(107).... the unaided eye has difficulty discerning the individual members. ....(108).... a large telescope, astronomers find myriads of ....(109).... systems sprinkled throughout the depths of space. They call ....(110).... vast collections of stars "galaxies," after the Greek word for "milk," and they refer to the local galaxy to which the Sun belongs as "the Milky Way."

101. a. distinguishes c. observes
     b. distributes d. stretches

102. a. across c. down
     b. off d. out

103. a. According c. For
     b. From d. By

104. a. flown c. flows
     b. flowed d. flowing

105. a. likened c. resembled
     b. described d. referred

106. a. factually c. truly
     b. actually d. virtually

107. a. and c. because
     b. but d. that

108. a. Through c. Without
     b. Having d. From

109. a. alike c. likely
     b. like d. likable

110. a. very c. such
     b. some d. them

VOCABULARY

111. The shop assistant gave us her ..... that the package would be delivered the next day.
    a. proposition
    b. cooperation
    c. warranty
    d. assurance

112. In the coming elections, the rival politicians will once again ..... for the nation's top post.
    a. ascend
    b. agonize
    c. contend
    d. condescend

113. The couple's ..... relationship inevitably ended in divorce.
    a. turbulent
    b. amiable
    c. inclement
    d. relentless

114. Unable to pay its creditors, the business found itself on the verge of ..... .
    a. depression
    b. recession
    c. bankruptcy
    d. consumption

115. In the final stages of the illness, victims experience ..... pain.
    a. exquisite
    b. excruciating
    c. exuberant
    d. extravagant

116. An only child, he envied his friends who had close relationships with their ..... .
    a. siblings
    b. spouses
    c. rivals
    d. progeny

117. John and his ex-wife have never ..... how their children should be raised.
    a. turned a blind eye toward
    b. feasted their eyes on
    c. seen eye to eye about
    d. set their eyes on

118. The delivery date was clearly ..... in the terms of the contract.
    a. stipulated
    b. speculated
    c. distributed
    d. incited

119. He was so hungry that you could hear his stomach ..... .
    a. fumbling
    b. humbling
    c. mumbling
    d. rumbling

120. The witness was charged with ..... for giving false testimony to the court.
    a. perjury
    b. forgery
    c. evasion
    d. libel

121. The president's party won the election by a(n) ..... large majority.
    a. vastly
    b. superficially
    c. overwhelmingly
    d. proportionately

122. She sells cosmetics in her spare time to ..... her income.
    a. implement
    b. supplant
    c. supplement
    d. proliferate

123. The basketball player's speed and agility ..... his lack of height.
    a. stood in for
    b. made up for
    c. stood up to
    d. did away with

124. Stuck inside on a rainy day, the children soon became restless and ..... .
    a. docile
    b. apprehensive
    c. distorted
    d. fidgety

125. The vehicle is specially designed to travel over ..... terrain.
 a. wobbly
 b. blurry
 c. rugged
 d. jagged

126. If I were you, I'd ..... and insist that he clean up his room immediately.
 a. put my feet up
 b. put my foot down
 c. put my shoe on the other foot
 d. put my foot in my mouth

127. I'd be more than happy to stay for dinner, if it isn't a(n) ..... , of course.
 a. disposition
 b. inhibition
 c. affliction
 d. imposition

128. Hoping to avoid rush-hour traffic, we set out for the airport at the ..... of dawn.
 a. trace
 b. break
 c. crack
 d. opening

129. He's a strict parent with quite ..... ideas about how to discipline his children.
 a. indulgent
 b. accelerated
 c. rigid
 d. lenient

130. He's been feeling tired and ..... for weeks. Why doesn't he consult a doctor?
 a. run down
 b. come down
 c. let down
 d. put down

131. After a few glasses of champagne, she was feeling quite ..... .
 a. muggy
 b. soggy
 c. giddy
 d. grubby

132. He was confident that a degree in business administration would .... his career prospects.
 a. replenish
 b. enhance
 c. inflate
 d. exacerbate

133. The dinner guests were impressed at how ..... the child spoke to them.
 a. respectively
 b. reputedly
 c. irreverently
 d. respectfully

134. The government is committed to ..... environmental research.
 a. submerging
 b. subsidizing
 c. subduing
 d. subverting

135. The rail strike has succeeded in ..... normal train service.
 a. disrupting
 b. resuming
 c. erupting
 d. corrupting

136. But for the prompt intervention of the police, the fight would have turned into a ..... .
 a. brawl
 b. scrawl
 c. crawl
 d. drawl

137. Police have detained a suspect ..... to eye-witness descriptions of a man seen fleeing the crime scene.
 a. equating
 b. adhering
 c. answering
 d. replying

138. Adolescents frequently clash with their parents when they ..... their independence.
 a. invert
 b. convert
 c. divert
 d. assert

139. The newspaper's Sunday entertainment section always contains a listing of ..... events.
  a. becoming
  b. up-and-coming
  c. oncoming
  d. upcoming

140. The burglar ..... disarmed the security system and entered the home unobserved.
  a. adroitly
  b. inadvertently
  c. erroneously
  d. unwillingly

141. The plan was agreed upon by ..... everyone at the meeting.
  a. ultimately
  b. virtually
  c. unanimously
  d. relatively

142. Soldiers receive training in military exercises designed to ..... battle conditions.
  a. incorporate
  b. alleviate
  c. insulate
  d. simulate

143. People who remember facts and figures are said to have ..... memories.
  a. photogenic
  b. short-term
  c. retentive
  d. absorbent

144. Pharmaceutical companies are required to subject their products to ..... testing.
  a. impartial
  b. incessant
  c. unscrupulous
  d. rigorous

145. Tests indicate that the patient's condition is serious and ...... immediate surgery.
  a. requisitions
  b. prescribes
  c. necessitates
  d. implies

146. Her ability to work well with others makes her a great ..... to the company.
  a. contribution
  b. worth
  c. evaluation
  d. asset

147. After careful consideration, she decided not to invest in the risky ..... .
  a. enterprise
  b. preposition
  c. projection
  d. censorship

148. The staff had been given ..... instructions as to how to handle emergencies.
  a. exorbitant
  b. explicit
  c. distinctive
  d. obscure

149. Predictably, the children had ..... a huge appetite on their hike through the forest.
  a. worked in
  b. worked out
  c. worked up
  d. worked off

150. The young man came to the company with excellent ..... from his previous employers.
  a. references
  b. quotations
  c. subscriptions
  d. prescriptions

READING

Passage 1 is about events in Salem Village in the early 1690s.

In 1692 a group of adolescent girls in Salem Village, Massachusetts, became subject to strange fits after hearing tales told by a West Indian slave. When questioned, they accused several women of being witches who were tormenting them. Town officials convened a court to hear the charges of witchcraft, and swiftly convicted and executed a tavern-keeper, Bridget Bishop. Within a month, five other women were convicted and hanged. Despite the convictions, hysteria grew – in large measure because the court permitted witnesses to testify that they had seen the accused as spirits or in visions. By the fall of 1692, more than 20 victims, including several men, had been executed and more than 100 others were in jail, including some of the town's most prominent citizens. As the hysteria threatened to spread beyond Salem, ministers throughout the colony called for an end to the trials. The governor agreed and dismissed the court. Those still in jail were later acquitted or given reprieves.

On a psychological level, most historians agree that Salem was seized by public hysteria, fueled by a genuine belief in witchcraft. They point out that while some of the girls may have been acting, many responsible adults were caught up in the frenzy as well. But even more revealing is an analysis of the identities of the accused and the accusers. Salem, like much of colonial New England at that time, was undergoing an economic and political transition from a largely agrarian, Puritan-dominated community to a more commercial, secular society. Many of the accusers were representatives of a traditional way of life tied to farming and the church, whereas a number of the accused "witches" were members of the rising commercial class of small shopkeepers and tradesmen. Salem's obscure struggle for social and political power between older traditional groups and a newer commercial class was one repeated in communities throughout American history. But it took a bizarre and deadly detour when its citizens were swept up by the conviction that the devil was loose in their homes.

151. How did village leaders react to the girls' accusations?
    a. They immediately arrested the girls and put them on trial.
    b. They rounded up the suspects and hung everyone who was accused.
    c. They executed one woman immediately and put the others on trial.
    d. They treated them seriously and launched judicial proceedings.

152. What prompted the governor to put an end to the trials?
    a. pressure from concerned religious leaders
    b. public outcry at the growing number of citizens executed and jailed
    c. his belief that those still in jail were innocent and should be pardoned
    d. the fact that the townspeople were spreading their hysteria

153. What do many historians believe?
    a. That responsible adults in the village were not really affected by the public hysteria
    b. That the identities of the accusers and the accused should have been analyzed more closely
    c. That the real cause lay in a clash between the town's agrarian and commercial interests
    d. That the accused represented the town's traditional interests

154. What is true of the more than 20 people who were executed?
    a. that they believed in witchcraft.
    b. that they had strong religious convictions.
    c. that they were leading citizens.
    d. that they were women.

155. What does the writer suggest about events in Salem Village?
    a. They set off a string of witch trials throughout America.
    b. They were an extreme example of a common trend in American history.
    c. They are typical of other weird things that have happened throughout American history.
    d. They are an embarrassment to those who have studied them.

Passage 2 is about the discovery of "seeps" in the Gulf of Mexico.

In the 1940s the first offshore oil wells in the Gulf of Mexico began to open some of the world's richest oil fields, but technology limited production to depths of only a few hundred feet. Not until the late 1970s did new engineering techniques enable them to set up drilling platforms in deeper waters to explore "seeps" – cracks or fissures in the ocean floor from which oil, natural gas and related substances slowly leak into the water.

Oil companies have a tremendous economic interest in discovering seeps – proof that rich deposits of oil lie below – and they frequently enlist scientists in their quest. In 1984 some of these researchers made a surprising discovery. Hoping to study how chronic exposure to oil affects marine life – important information for assessing accidental oil spills – they trawled fishing nets above seeps, expecting to find a few sick fish and crabs. Instead, their nets came up so full of mollusks and tube worms that they could hardly hoist them onto the ship.

Scientists had discovered in the 1970s that bacteria, tube worms and more than three hundred other species lived around hydrothermal vents – cracks on the floor of the ocean which spew scalding water and compounds such as hydrogen sulfide. But no one had imagined that the so-called cold seeps on the floor of the Gulf could support such abundant life. Subsequent research revealed that mussels and tube worms feed on bacteria that convert methane and hydrogen sulfide into energy through a process called chemosynthesis. The chemicals from seeps have apparently fueled the development of luxuriant colonies of mussels and tube worms that spread over hundreds of square miles at depths below 1,200 feet. Interestingly, scientists believe that these animals may contribute to the health of the planet. Mussels, for instance, help clear the Gulf of methane, a gas thought to be involved in global warming. How much gas their communities consume is one of the many mysteries that remain about the creatures that inhabit this realm of perpetual darkness.

156. Why are "seeps" so important to oil companies?
- a. They allow oil companies to employ scientists to research the effects of oil spills.
- b. They indicate where offshore drilling efforts should be concentrated.
- c. They offer a chance for the companies to develop deep-water drilling techniques.
- d. They are a rich source of methane and hydrogen sulfide.

157. Why were researchers surprised when they pulled up their nets?
- a. There was no sign of oil coming from the seep.
- b. The mollusks and tube worms revealed no signs of long-term oil exposure.
- c. There were fewer fish and crabs than they had anticipated.
- d. They had expected to find only minimal signs of life on the sea floor.

158. What do hydrothermal vents and seeps have in common?
- a. They were both discovered by scientists working for oil companies.
- b. They both emit gases, oil and cold water.
- c. They both support abundant life under extreme conditions.
- d. They are the only habitats in which tube worms and mussels can survive.

159. How do mussels contribute to the health of the planet?
- a. They absorb gases emitted from seeps.
- b. They spread over hundreds of square miles over the floor of the ocean.
- c. They reverse the effects of global warming.
- d. Scientists have not yet totally unraveled the mystery.

160. According to the passage, what is chemosynthesis?
- a. the process through which bacteria produce methane and hydrogen sulfide
- b. the process that seeps use to produce methane and hydrogen sulfide
- c. the process that bacteria use to produce energy from methane and hydrogen sulfide
- d. the process that tube worms and mussels use to feed on bacteria

Passage 3 is about massage.

Recent research is now confirming that tactile stimulation – or massage – is medicine. At the University of Miami's Touch Research Institute (TRI), more than 50 studies, many still in progress, indicate that massage may have positive effects on conditions from colic to hyperactivity and from migraine to diabetes. It may also help asthmatics breathe more easily, improve autistic children's ability to concentrate, boost immune function – even in HIV-positive patients – and relax burn victims about to undergo débridement, the painful procedure for removing contaminated skin.

For a baby, tactile stimulation can be a matter of life and death. Born eight weeks premature, 11-day-old Brandon must stay in an artificially warmed environment known as an incubator because his own underdeveloped system cannot regulate his body temperature. A TRI researcher reaches through the incubator's portholes and begins to massage the baby. Her hand is larger than the baby's entire back. As her fingers move in firm downward strokes, the baby's translucent skin looks as if it might tear as easily as tissue paper. She is applying gentle pressure – too light and it tickles, too strong and it hurts.

Far from injuring the infant, the massage may be essential to his development. In fact, if Brandon is like most of the premature babies studied at TRI, he will reap astonishing benefits. With three massages a day for ten days, he should be more alert, active and responsive than non-massaged infants of his size and condition. He may have fewer episodes of apnea, a risk factor for sudden infant death syndrome (SIDS). He should also gain weight 47 percent faster and be discharged from the hospital six days sooner on average than non-massaged premature babies – at a current savings of $15,000 each. With 424,000 premature births in America each year and a potential $6 billion in annual savings, one might think that hospitals would rush to establish massage programs, yet they are still not widespread.

161. The writer implies that many of the studies being conducted at the TRI ...
   a. are still in progress and therefore must not raise false hopes.
   b. suggest that massage may have a beneficial effect on many hard-to-treat health problems.
   c. provide conclusive evidence that massage has positive effects on many conditions.
   d. are a clear indication that massage may be more effective than conventional treatment.

162. Why is Brandon in an incubator?
   a. The incubator's portholes make it easier for the nurse to massage him.
   b. His body temperature would otherwise be higher than normal.
   c. It provides him with an artificially warmed environment.
   d. The baby's skin is still very thin.

163. What is true of the University of Miami's Touch Research Institute?
   a. It was set up to study the effects of massage on premature babies.
   b. It has been engaged in massage research for over 50 years.
   c. It treats 424,000 premature babies each year.
   d. It is studying the effects of massage on a wide range of health problems.

164. According to the passage, what happens to premature babies who are **not** massaged?
   a. They gain weight at a slower rate than massaged babies.
   b. They are more susceptible to skin injuries than massaged babies.
   c. They are more alert, active and responsive than massaged babies.
   d. They are less likely to die from sudden infant death syndrome than massaged babies.

165. What does the writer imply?
   a. Hospitals will lose money if they don't introduce massage programs for premature babies.
   b. Hospitals are right not to rush into establishing massage programs for premature babies.
   c. Massage programs for premature babies have been slow to catch on.
   d. Massage programs for premature babies are too expensive to be widely implemented.

Passage 4 is about phytoremediation.

A wide range of pollutants – from uranium to pesticides – have mixed with dirt and water across the United States, rendering water unfit for consumption and land uninhabitable. The methods employed to clean up these pollutants have often seemed as bad as the problems themselves. Contaminated dirt may be excavated, leaving gaping holes that have to be refilled with clean soil while the old dirt is hauled to a landfill where it takes up valuable space. For polluted groundwater, large pumps are often brought out to the contaminated site so that the water can be sucked out of the ground, filtered and pumped back into the earth. The cost of such cleanups is substantial – normally over $100,000 and sometimes more than $1 billion.

But recent scientific advances suggest that there may be solutions to these problems that are not only simpler and much less expensive, but also much more attractive. A patch of golden sunflowers, for example, may be a viable way to remove radioactive wastes from ponds around the Chernobyl nuclear power plant and planting a meadow in Chattanooga, Tennessee, may be the best way to rid the soil of harmful traces of TNT and other explosives. At an increasing number of polluted sites, pumps and bulldozers are being replaced by plants.

The science behind these projects is called phytoremediation. Ever since Europeans first noticed hundreds of years ago that certain plants grow in abundance near natural deposits of zinc and nickel, it has been known that some plants readily absorb toxic materials. Only recently, however, have scientists begun exploring how many pollutants plants can absorb and just how effective they can be. Phytoremediation is still in its infancy, but research suggests that certain plants have the potential to clean up metals like lead and nickel, explosives like TNT, pesticides like DDT, and a host of other wastes.

166. What is **not** true about conventional methods for cleaning up water and soil pollution?
- a. They have been totally unsuccessful.
- b. They may create other ecological problems that are equally as worrying.
- c. They are complicated and costly.
- d. They sometimes result in unsightly scars on the landscape.

167. Which is an example of phytoremediation?
- a. using pumps and filters to purify polluted ground water
- b. removing polluted soil with the aid of bulldozers
- c. observing plants that thrive near zinc and nickel deposits
- d. planting a field with sunflowers to absorb radioactive waste in a nearby pond

168. What does the writer suggest?
- a. Phytoremediation is a well developed science.
- b. Much of the appeal of phytoremediation lies in the fact that it beautifies the environment.
- c. Bulldozers and pumps should no longer be used to remove pollutants.
- d. Scientists have only just begun to explore the possibilities of phytoremediation.

169. Why are landfills mentioned in the first paragraph?
- a. to emphasize that soil excavation is an effective decontamination technique
- b. to illustrate that cleaning up pollutants in one place often creates a problem in another
- c. to show that using bulldozers is preferable to using pumps and filters
- d. to give proof that phytoremediation is being introduced in many places

170. What is probably found in Chatanooga, Tenessee?
- a. a dumping ground for a large pesticide plant
- b. a nuclear power plant
- c. an army munitions factory
- d. large deposits of nickel and zinc

VOCABULARY CONSOLIDATION 3

VEXING VERBS

A Common collocations – Complete each phrase with a word from the box.

agonize	ascend	contend	condescend	distribute	enhance

1. .... that your ideas are correct
2. .... to speak to someone
3. .... your reputation
4. .... a mountain
5. .... over a decision
6. .... leaflets

exacerbate	incite	inflate	replenish	speculate	stipulate

7. .... a tire
8. .... a supply / a guest's drink
9. .... on the future
10. .... an already bad situation
11. .... conditions in a contract
12. .... a riot

B Fine-tuning your knowledge – The numbers below refer to the questions in the Vocabulary section of Practice Test 3. Review the words, then fill each blank with the correct form of the appropriate verb.

122. **implement** / **supplant** / **supplement** / **proliferate**

a. Rabbits have a reputation for .... at an astounding rate.
b. She .... her diet with vitamin pills.
c. The new law will be .... on the 1st of January.
d. Do you think teachers will really be .... by computers one day?

132. **replenish** / **enhance** / **inflate** / **exacerbate**

a. Don't tell him how handsome he is. You'll .... his ego!
b. NASA's photos of distant galaxies have all been .... by computers.
c. Your glass is empty. Can I .... your drink for you?
d. Don't we have enough problems? Lying only .... the situation.

134. **submerge** / **subsidize** / **subdue** / **subvert**

a. After the flood, the fields were .... under several feet of water.
b. Renewed terrorism has succeeded in .... the peace negotiations.
c. The government sent in troops to .... the rebellion.
d. The scientist's research was .... by a grant from the government.

135. **disrupt** / **resume** / **erupt** / **corrupt**

a. If you lose that account, the boss will .... like an active volcano.
b. The devastating earthquake .... the lives of thousands of people.
c. Do you think that violence on television .... the morals of young children?
d. The student plans to work for a year and then .... her studies.

137. **equate** / **adhere** / **answer** / **reply**

a. Have you .... to / .... his letter yet?
b. Don't make the mistake of .... money with happiness.
c. This particular glue will not .... to metal.
d. He knew he'd have to .... to his father if he damaged the car.

145. **requisition** / **prescribe** / **necessitate** / **imply**

a. How dare you .... that I am not telling the truth!
b. Continuing losses .... the downsizing of the company.
c. What did the doctor .... for your cough?
d. Office equipment must be .... through the purchasing department.

NOTORIOUS NOUNS

A Amusing associations – Find the word in the box that is suggested by each prompt.

depression	evasion	forgery	libel	perjury	progeny	rivals	siblings	spouses

1. .... – What Adam and Eve were to each other
2. .... – What Adam and Eve produced after God told them to "Be fruitful and multiply"
3. .... – What refined people euphemistically call their "enemies"
4. .... – What you lack if you're an only child
5. .... – What you commit when you fail to tell the court "the whole truth"
6. .... – What you commit when you sign your mom or dad's name on your report card
7. .... – What you commit when you leak false rumors about someone to a reporter
8. .... – What you're afflicted with when you're "down in the dumps"
9. .... – What liars and tax dodgers have in common

B Fine-tuning your knowledge – The numbers below refer to the questions in the Vocabulary section of Practice Test 3. After reviewing the words, fill in the blanks with the appropriate words.

111. proposition, cooperation, warranty, assurance

a. Nowadays most electrical appliances come with a manufacturer's ....
b. The .... that "all men are created equal" is basic to modern democracy.
c. You have my personal .... that the work will be done on time.
d. Everyone's .... is required if the recycling program is to be a success.

114. depression, recession, bankruptcy, consumption

a. Increased energy .... has had disastrous effects on the environment.
b. People sometimes commit suicide in a fit of ....
c. Unable to pay its debts, the company has had to declare ....
d. Inflation and unemployment are characteristic of an economic .... If the situation is really bad, as in the 1930s, it is known as a ....

127. disposition, inhibition, affliction, imposition

a. He is suffering from a rare tropical ....
b. His boss has a calm .... , which makes it easy to work for her.
c. After a few glasses of wine, she left her ....s behind.
d. Are you sure it's not a(n) .... if we stay the weekend?

128. trace, break, crack, opening

a. The company has several ....s for people with accounting experience.
b. We left the house at the .... of day (ie, at the .... of dawn).
c. No clues were left behind; the burglars disappeared without a ....
d. Winning the lottery the day he lost his job was a really lucky ....
e. After the earthquake, the walls of the house were filled with ....s.

146. contribution, worth, evaluation, asset

a. Her promotion was a direct result of her supervisor's glowing ....
b. Faced with bankruptcy, the company has had to liquidate its ....s.
c. She thanked the entire staff for their valuable ....
d. The company's net .... is estimated at over $3 billion.

150. reference, quotation, subscription, prescription

a. "To be or not to be" is one of the most famous ....s in the world.
b. Don't forget to renew your .... to *National Geographic*.
c. Everyone could see that the .... to his ex-wife upset him.
d. Money is not necessarily a .... for happiness.

ADDLING ADJECTIVES

A Common collocations – Complete each phrase with a word from the appropriate box.

accelerated	blurry	exorbitant	inclement	indulgent	jagged

1. .... courses
2. .... prices
3. .... parents
4. .... weather
5. .... pieces of glass
6. .... photographs

obscure	relentless	rugged	unscrupulous	turbulent	wobbly

7. .... terrain
8. .... rain
9. .... businessmen
10. .... 17th-century poets
11. .... tables
12. .... air

B Fine-tuning your knowledge – The numbers below refer to the questions in the Vocabulary Section of Practice Test 3. After reviewing the words, fill in the blanks with the appropriate words.

115. exquisite / excruciating / exuberant / extravagant

a. She's rarely .... , but she did buy herself an expensive leather jacket last year.
b. What a lovely dress! You've always had .... taste in clothes.
c. Sorry I'm not feeling more .... I must be coming down with something.
d. To be honest, I find Wally an .... bore. It's painful to listen to him.

124. docile / apprehensive / distorted / fidgety

a. Dogs always bark and get excited. Cats are much more ....
b. The article gave a highly .... impression of what had occurred.
c. It's difficult to dress a child who is as .... as Timmy is.
d. If you've studied well, there's no reason to feel .... about the test.

131. muggy / soggy / giddy / grubby

a. I prefer crisp vegetables to ones that are overcooked and ....
b. You'd be .... , too, if you spent all day working on car engines.
c. His new-found fame has gone to his head; he's .... with success.
d. The city air was so hot and .... that she found it hard to breathe.

139. becoming / up-and-coming / oncoming / upcoming

a. They plan their weekends by consulting the paper's list of .... events.
b. I love your new hairstyle; it's so ....
c. The driver lost control of his car and crashed into .... traffic.
d. The .... author is a frequent guest on evening talk shows.

143. photogenic / short-term / retentive / absorbent

a. Cheap paper towels tend to be less .... than more expensive brands.
b. Alzheimer's disease affects a person's .... memory.
c. She hates having her picture taken as she's not at all ....
d. Ed's got an amazingly .... memory; he never forgets anything.

144. impartial / incessant / unscrupulous / rigorous

a. The eminent biographer is noted for his .... attention to detail.
b. The .... drilling outside had given him a splitting headache.
c. His .... business practices will land him in jail someday.
d. When hearing a case, it is a judge's duty to remain ....

AUDACIOUS ADVERBS

Fine-tuning your knowledge – The numbers below refer to the questions in the Vocabulary section of Practice Test 3. After reviewing the words, fill in the blanks with the appropriate words.

121.

vastly
superficially
overwhelmingly
proportionately

a. He glanced through the report .... to get a feel for what it contained.
b. More than 90% of the union members voted to go on strike, a(n) .... large majority.
c. .... more women than ever before are studying engineering.
d. She found his second novel .... more interesting than his first.

133.

respectively
reputedly
irreverently
respectfully

a. The painting was .... sold to the museum for $20 million.
b. The children listened .... as the principal explained the new rules.
c. The Smith boys, Tom and Jerry, finished in first and second place ....
d. The children .... referred to the overweight history teacher as "Old Broadsides," after the famous American warship they had learned about.

140.

adroitly
inadvertently
erroneously
unwillingly

a. The painting had been so .... executed that for years experts had .... attributed it to Botticelli.
b. The mistake was discovered when a restorer .... / .... removed a layer of paint and revealed the signature of one of Botticelli's students.
c. Museum officials admit, rather .... , that the work is now worth far less than what they paid for it.

POETRY IN MOTION

At least one of the words in each group has appeared in the Vocabulary section of Practice Test 3; the others are words that rhyme with it and, as a result, are easily confused. Discuss each group. Then fill in the blanks with the appropriate words.

1.

fumble
mumble
rumble
humble

a. The arrogant politician was .... when his role in the scandal was revealed.
b. He .... a reply, but no one could understand him.
c. She was so hungry that you could hear her stomach ....
d. He .... in his pocket for his keys.

2.

invert
convert
divert
assert
avert
revert

a. The bus driver swerved to the left, barely .... an accident.
b. Despite the evidence, the defendant continues to .... his innocence.
c. Due to an accident on the highway, traffic was .... to a side road.
d. If you .... a glass over a burning candle, the flame will soon go out.
e. After a year of not smoking, he gave in and .... to his old bad habits.
f. The missionaries attempted to .... the natives to Christianity.

3.

brawl
scrawl
crawl
drawl

a. "Hey, y'all," said the Texan with his typical southern ....
b. She types all her essays because none of her teachers can read her ....
c. During rush hour, traffic slows to a ....
d. A Western is not a Western without a typical bar-room ....

4.

simulate
stimulate
stipulate
assimilate

a. It is hoped that generous price discounts will .... sales.
b. The author's contract .... that he would be paid a $1 million advance.
c. Over time, the students finally began to .... the new words.
d. The astronauts train on equipment that .... conditions in space.

PRACTICE TEST 4

Writing

(30 minutes)

Write on one of the topics given below. If you write about something else, your paper will not be graded. If you do not understand the topics, ask the examiner to explain or translate them. You will be graded on the clarity of your writing and the linguistic range and accuracy you show. Write $1\frac{1}{2}$ to 2 pages. You may make any corrections or other changes in the body of the composition.

TOPICS

1. Technology in the 20th century advanced at a greater pace than at any other time in history. In your opinion, what **two** inventions or technological developments of the last century have had the most dramatic impact on modern life? Give reasons for your choices.

2. Advances in reproductive medicine have made it possible for women in their 40s, 50s and even 60s to give birth to healthy children. What special advantages do you think a mature woman and her spouse would have to offer a child? What problems would the family face as the child grows up? On balance, do you agree with the idea of older people bringing children into the world?

For help in writing these compositions, see *Writing Tutorial*, pages 196–197.

Listening Comprehension Test

(35–40 minutes)

This part of the examination is a listening test that will assess your understanding of spoken English. The listening test has three parts. There are 50 questions. Mark all your answers on the separate answer sheet. Do not make any stray marks on the answer sheet. If you change your mind about an answer, erase your first answer completely.

PART 1 – In this part of the test, you will hear a short conversation. From the three answer choices given, choose the answer which means the same thing as you hear, or that is true based on what you hear.

For problems **1–17**, mark your answers on the separate answer sheet. No problem can be repeated. Please listen carefully. Do you have any questions?

1. a. He has to do something before he leaves.
   b. He's moving soon, so he needs a day off.
   c. He already did what she asked.

2. a. He'll leave if she's not back by noon.
   b. He's willing to help her.
   c. He can only help her after one o'clock.

3. a. He's wearing light clothes.
   b. He's just pretending to be cold.
   c. He wants her to turn down the heat.

4. a. They haven't seen the menu yet.
   b. They are just about to eat.
   c. They'll leave if the food is not there soon.

5. a. He agrees that the table is too expensive.
   b. He thinks she's not being practical.
   c. He thinks she needs a larger apartment.

6. a. He thinks Ed will have no objections.
   b. He thinks she should be the one to tell Ed.
   c. He thinks Ed will react negatively.

7. a. She'd like to get to know him better.
   b. She'll go, but she's not keen on the idea.
   c. She would never consider such a thing.

8. a. She thinks only her father should be told.
   b. She sees no reason to tell Al.
   c. She thinks Al should mind his own business.

9. a. She didn't mean to disturb him.
   b. She wants him to do something for her.
   c. She realizes he may be too busy.

10. a. She's too busy to do it.
    b. She thinks Terry has already done it.
    c. She feels Terry would do a better job.

11. a. He was upset about the service he got.
    b. He didn't get his money back.
    c. He liked the first phone better.

12. a. They're both enthusiastic about the novel.
    b. Neither of them has finished the book yet.
    c. She likes the book more than he does.

13. a. Joe's e-mails are not very informative.
    b. Joe may be failing one of his courses.
    c. It's typical of Joe not to keep in touch.

14. a. He can't do anything to change the situation.
    b. He's upset that his wife doesn't believe him.
    c. He's sorry he can't help her.

15. a. Sue always calls if she's going to be late.
    b. Sue doesn't have a cell phone.
    c. Sue's cell phone might be broken.

16. a. He hasn't asked John to help them yet.
    b. He'll be surprised if John doesn't help them.
    c. He's going to call John to remind him.

17. a. He's going to fix something that he broke.
    b. He's upset because she thinks he's lying.
    c. He's intending to do something for her.

PART II – In this part of the test, you will hear a question. From the three answer choices given, choose the one which best answers the question.

For problems **18–35**, mark your answers on the separate answer sheet. No problem can be repeated. Please listen carefully. Do you have any questions?

18. a. He said he'd bring more in the morning.
b. He's not always that generous.
c. He is a bit tiring, isn't he?

19. a. I was just thinking.
b. I'd prefer to do it myself.
c. Would you like to help me?

20. a. Thanks, but it won't be necessary.
b. Sure, I don't see why not.
c. If I were you, I'd go a different way.

21. a. Thanks, I've been looking for it all day.
b. Not that I know of.
c. Haven't you ever seen a baseball before?

22. a. How many times must I tell you?
b. It couldn't be anyone else.
c. I always win. Don't you know that?

23. a. Do I really have to?
b. Not for another hour.
c. I usually take the train.

24. a. To be honest, I'd rather not do it myself.
b The doctors don't hold out much hope.
c. Well, a cup of coffee would be nice.

25. a. Sorry, did I hurt you?
b. I'd like to, but there's just too much traffic.
c. Sorry, I didn't realize I was going so fast.

26. a. They promised to call you when I arrive.
b. I'll ask them to send you some pictures.
c. They've asked me to head up the LA office.

27. a. Do you think these will do?
b. I just can't spare it right now.
c. Sorry, I'm tied up till the end of next week.

28. a. It will only make matters worse.
b. He's much too tall.
c. Because I'm not sure he's right this time.

29. a. I was hoping you'd like it.
b. Just thought I'd call to see how things are.
c. Almost three years old. Can you believe it?

30. a. Do you really think it's that dangerous?
b. I was afraid you'd already gone out.
c. I was just looking for my history notebook.

31. a. Count me in.
b. That sounds just fine.
c. Thanks, I promise to let you know soon.

32. a. I can't stop thinking about it.
b. I still wonder if I made the right decision.
c. Oh, about ten years ago.

33. a. Not until 4 o'clock.
b. It is a bit long, isn't it?
c. About two months ago.

34. a. I'm not convinced.
b. It wouldn't.
c. Sorry, my mind's made up.

35. a. Right after dinner.
b. A few minutes ago.
c. She didn't say.

PART III – In this part, you will hear three short segments from a radio program. The program is called "Learning from the Experts." Each talk lasts about two minutes. As you listen, you may want to take notes to help you remember information given in the talk. After each talk, you will be asked some questions about what was said. From the three answer choices given, you should choose the one which best answers the question according to the information you heard.

Remember, no problems can be repeated. For problems **36–50**, mark your answers on the separate answer sheet. Do you have any questions?

SEGMENT 1

36. Why were Anderson and his colleagues so concerned about the porpoises that were killed in their nets?
- a. They hated to see innocent creatures suffer.
- b. They knew their jobs were at risk if the killing continued.
- c. They did not want to be held responsible for endangering the species.

37. What prompted the fishermen to start experimenting with their nets?
- a. Something they had heard from a federal official
- b. Something they had seen used on school buses
- c. Something they had read by an expert on whales

38. How do "pingers" work?
- a. By emitting a short, low sound every four seconds
- b. By emitting loud, low sounds that last for four seconds each
- c. By emitting continuous sound slightly louder than the noise of the ocean

39. What is true about "pingers"?
- a. They are so successful that they will soon be required in certain waters by federal law.
- b. They have had limited success in reducing dolphin deaths on the West Coast.
- c. They have drastically reduced the rate of dolphin and porpoise deaths on both coasts.

40. How do marine scientists and conservation groups feel about "pingers"?
- a. Despite initial skepticism, they now support pingers without reservation.
- b. They support them, but are worried that the noise may disrupt marine life.
- c. They are against their widespread use until more research can be done.

SEGMENT 2

41. What is the speaker's main point?
- a. More and more workers need psychological counseling.
- b. Coping with job stress is a lot like preparing for major sport competitions.
- c. Employees and companies can benefit from sport psychology techniques.

42. Which is NOT a major goal of sports psychology?
- a. Improved confidence
- b. Improved fitness
- c. Improved performance

43. How could "cognitive restructuring" help an employee whose job performance has fallen?
- a. By concentrating on how well he is doing his job at a given moment
- b. By training him how to make a better impression on his boss
- c. By getting him to identify the areas he needs to improve on

44. How did a sports psychologist help employees at a nuclear energy company pass a licensing exam?
- a. He showed them how to study better.
- b. He told them to focus on their need to pass the exam.
- c. He taught them how to manage their stress as they took the exam.

45. Why does the speaker feel that sports psychology will play an increasing role in the corporate world?
- a. It focuses on long-term results.
- b. It focuses on short-term results and productivity.
- c. It focuses on getting employees to be more relaxed.

SEGMENT 3

46. Why is the museum being hailed as "the best spy museum you'll never see"?
    a. Admission to it is restricted to CIA staff and visitors.
    b. Many of its exhibits involve strictly classified information.
    c. The exhibit includes secret gadgets that are currently in use.

47. What was the jungle transmitter designed to do?
    a. Intercept radio messages broadcast by the enemy
    b. Sense the movement of enemy troops on the ground
    c. Enable soldiers to transmit messages about their location

48. Which statement best describes the current role of pigeons in the CIA's arsenal of weapons?
    a. Live pigeons have been replaced by an ever-improving series of robotic pigeons.
    b. Pigeons have become more useful to the CIA, thanks to lighter technology.
    c. Improved spy technology has resulted in a decrease in the CIA's use of pigeons.

49. Which gadget is described as being the least successful?
    a. The jungle transmitter
    b. Charlie, the robo-catfish
    c. The "insectohopter"

50. Which statement best sums up what the radio guest says about the current status of the CIA's Science and Technology Directorate?
    a. It is currently not as influential as it was during the Cold War.
    b. It is proving even more influential than it was during the Cold War.
    c. Its future depends on its ability to develop harder-to-detect devices.

Grammar – Cloze – Vocabulary – Reading

(75 minutes)

This part of the examination contains 120 problems, numbered **51–170**. There are 40 grammar, 20 cloze, 40 vocabulary and 20 reading comprehension problems. The examiner will not explain any test problems. If you do not understand how to do the problems, raise your hand and a proctor will explain the examples to you.

Do not spend too much time on any one problem. Each problem counts the same. If you do not know the answer to a problem, you may make a reasonable guess. Each problem has only one correct answer. Work fast but carefully. You have 75 minutes to answer all 120 problems.

GRAMMAR

51. For the boss ..... into his office like that, she must have done something really awful.
- a. who he called her
- b. to have called her
- c. had to call her
- d. calling her

52. Plans to build a new airport in the area ..... for two years.
- a. are being discussed
- b. have been discussing
- c. have been under discussion
- d. have been being discussed

53. The beauty of the surroundings ..... for once not a single person had anything bad to say.
- a. were that
- b. were so that
- c. was such that
- d. was too much that

54. I spoke to the twins this morning, and, as it turns out, ... of them can attend the party.
- a. none
- b. neither one
- c. no one
- d. nor one and the other

55. The child wondered what it would be like to grow up in ..... .
- a. a ten-children family
- b. a family from ten children
- c. a ten children's family
- d. a ten-child family

56. It's time someone made it clear to the elderly man that it's dangerous for him ..... at his age.
- a. driving
- b. that he drives
- c. to be driving
- d. to have been driven

57. It's unclear ..... whether or not he has left the office for the day.
- a. as to
- b. if perhaps
- c. that
- d. as if

58. The noise from the upstairs apartment is so unbearable that he really ..... anymore.
- a. hasn't stood for it
- b. doesn't stand it
- c. won't stand still for it
- d. can't stand it

59. In order to prove himself in the new position, he will have to work twice as hard ..... .
- a. as he ever
- b. as ever before
- c. that he did before
- d. than he ever did before

60. She sensed he was the man she would marry ..... she laid eyes on him.
- a. the moment
- b. as soon
- c. from when
- d. since then

61. He loved the car, but ..... was whether or not he could really afford it.
- a. it's of concern to him
- b. it concerned him
- c. he was concerned that it
- d. what concerned him

62. Her project was progressing well, but there was so much that still ..... .
- a. had to do
- b. had to be done
- c. had she to do
- d. she had to do

63. Insurance experts estimated the damage ..... several million dollars.
    a. into
    b. by
    c. at
    d. with

64. I know this is Mark's neighborhood, but which house ..... ?
    a. is he owning
    b. he owns
    c. is owned to him
    d. is he the owner of

65. The journalist felt morally ...... to expose the politician's involvement in the scandal.
    a. compulsive
    b. compelling
    c. compelled
    d. compulsory

66. He spent an hour looking all over the house, but the young kitten was ..... .
    a. nowhere found
    b. not to be anywhere found
    c. not being found anywhere
    d. nowhere to be found

67. She was surprised to hear that Steve ..... to his high school sweetheart since 1995.
    a. had married
    b. was married
    c. is married
    d. had been married

68. ..... out of the window for several minutes when suddenly an idea struck him.
    a. He'd been staring
    b. He'd have stared
    c. He stared
    d. He'd be staring

69. From what I've heard, the couple is doing fine and they have no intention ..... .
    a. to get divorce
    b. that they get divorced
    c. of getting divorced
    d. to having a divorce

70. He says he intends to be home on time – ..... , of course, he gets stuck in traffic.
    a. unless
    b. providing
    c. until
    d. except

71. By the time she arrived, the children ..... their homework.
    a. finished
    b. had finished
    c. have finished
    d. would have finished

72. Gary's promotion is a sure sign that his manager feels he's equal ..... the task.
    a. of
    b. for
    c. to
    d. in

73. If you're asking me to choose between the red one and the blue one, of the two I prefer ..... .
    a. the later
    b. the latter
    c. the last
    d. the latest

74. His memory isn't the greatest anymore, so, just in case, I guess you'd ..... call to remind him.
    a. ought to
    b. rather
    c. might as well
    d. better

75. Ed's an excellent accountant, but ..... his own finances has always been challenging for him.
    a. to have managed
    b. managing to have
    c. having to manage
    d. the managing

76. They were surprised to hear that ..... turned out for the concert.
    a. hardly anybody
    b. almost anybody
    c. almost none
    d. scarcely nobody

77. From what I can see, it's clear we've got ..... everything for the weekend.
   a. plenty of
   b. a lot more
   c. too much
   d. more than enough

78. ..... that the woman he was sitting next to was soon to become his wife.
   a. Little did he know
   b. Little had been known
   c. He knew little
   d. He little knew

79. Mary got engaged last weekend, but she'd ..... anyone till after she tells her parents.
   a. rather we didn't tell
   b. prefers us not to tell
   c. rather not we tell
   d. prefer we not to tell

80. Please inform the boss that my team fully intends ..... the deadline.
   a. to be met
   b. that it meets
   c. of meeting
   d. to meet

81. The children were so fascinated that they hung onto the storyteller's ..... word.
   a. very
   b. every
   c. each
   d. single

82. ..... about Jonathan and Muriel deciding to call off the wedding?
   a. What's this I hear
   b. What I heard
   c. What I'm hearing
   d. What's this heard

83. Under absolutely no circumstances ..... I am about to tell you.
   a. you will reveal that
   b. are you to reveal what
   c. have you revealed that which
   d. you are not to reveal what

84. The police are looking into the robbery, but ..... anyone.
   a. still have they not arrested
   b. they still don't arrest
   c. they have yet to arrest
   d. yet they haven't arrested

85. ..... as tolerant as your parents, the world would be a much better place.
   a. Were everyone
   b. Everyone being
   c. For everyone to be
   d. Everyone should be

86. Your father is furious. ..... take his car without his permission!
   a. How dare you
   b. You needn't
   c. Never do you
   d. May you never

87. From the moment he put glue on the teacher's chair, one never knew what ..... of the boy.
   a. is expected of
   b. to expect
   c. will one expect
   d. has been expected

88. The sad reality is that there is ..... a stress-free job.
   a. nothing like
   b. no such thing as
   c. nothing that compares with
   d. nothing better than

89. As a child he ..... hour after hour playing computer games.
   a. was spending
   b. would spend
   c. used to be spending
   d. was used to spend

90. ..... was while lying on a beach in the Bahamas more than twenty years ago.
   a. Feeling so relaxed, it
   b. When I felt like so relaxed
   c. The last time I felt so relaxed
   d. I haven't felt so relaxed since I

CLOZE

Passage 1 is about octopus tentacles.

Theoretically, there are any number of ways an octopus could use its long, flexible tentacles to move an object, but the method they actually use is surprisingly close to how ....(91).... with rigid skeletons – including humans – do it, scientists say.

When hunting and grabbing food, the octopus uses all the flexibility the tentacle is capable of. But to bring captured prey to its mouth, the octopus ....(92).... the tentacle into a quasi-rigid structure that bends as if it had joints. ....(93).... as a human arm has joints at the shoulder, elbow and ....(94).... that allow it to bend and rotate, the octopus ....(95).... its tentacle to form three segments of roughly equal length. Understanding ....(96).... the octopus controls its eight flexible tentacles all at once could be the ....(97).... for developing the next generation of flexible robotic arms – long a goal among robotics engineers. "If you had something – say, an object – floating in space or water, a straight mechanical arm would be likely to ....(98).... it away," said a project officer at the Office of Naval Research. "But an arm ....(99).... could use to wrap gently around an object and ....(100).... it? Now that would be useful."

91.	a. arms	b. people	c. animals	d. tentacles
92.	a. uses	b. turns	c. breaks	d. molds
93.	a. It's	b. Even	c. Such	d. Just
94.	a. wrist	b. neck	c. ankle	d. knee
95.	a. with	b. bends	c. and	d. used
96.	a. that	b. why	c. how	d. if
97.	a. reason	b. basis	c. method	d. cause
98.	a. pull	b. take	c. reach	d. push
99.	a. you	b. it	c. that	d. whom
100.	a. end	b. bend	c. retrieve	d. inflate

Passage 2 is about the arrival of Europeans in Mesoamerica*.

About 1200 B.C., when the Trojan War was being fought half a world away, an agrarian people raising maize, beans and squash began to build the first city-states in Mesoamerica. From them ....(101).... a calendar to measure time, glyphs to chronicle and commemorate the lives of rulers, tables charting the movement of planets and architecture to ....(102).... that of the Old World.

Europeans arrived in 1519, and in a historical blink of the ....(103).... , Mesoamerica's great cities and ceremonial centers were left in ....(104).... as Spaniards scoured the land for gold. ....(105).... the Spanish conquest, life in Mesoamerica changed almost at ....(106).... . Military clashes, forced labor and Old World ....(107).... – such as smallpox, measles, and typhus – ....(108).... the population. By 1521, the region was subdued, ...(109).... Spanish colonization was ....(110).... effective opposition.

* Mesoamerica – (from Latin, meaning "Middle America") historical term used for the geographical and cultural area extending from central Mexico down through Central America. The area was home to civilizations such as the Mayas and Aztecs.

101.	a. were	b. came	c. having	d. invented
102.	a. defeat	b. antagonize	c. compete	d. rival
103.	a. mind	b. imagination	c. eye	d. head
104.	a. ruins	b. trouble	c. destruction	d. view
105.	a. While	b. Because	c. With	d. For
106.	a. all	b. once	c. times	d. immediately
107.	a. problems	b. symptoms	c. traditions	d. diseases
108.	a. devastated	b. improved	c. cured	d. increased
109.	a. and	b. but	c. until	d. when
110.	a. not	b. under	c. without	d. in

VOCABULARY

111. It's a difficult decision. No wonder he's .... over it.
    a. conspiring
    b. quibbling
    c. assimilating
    d. agonizing

112. Her volunteer work at the hospital is a source of great personal ..... .
    a. appreciation
    b. gratification
    c. initiation
    d. propagation

113. ..... speaking, he feels much better now than before the operation.
    a. Proportionately
    b. Arbitrarily
    c. Relatively
    d. Respectively

114. The excursion had to be postponed due to ..... weather.
    a. inclement
    b. inferior
    c. impertinent
    d. impartial

115. Her headache was so bad that nothing would ..... the pain.
    a. subsidize
    b. alleviate
    c. confiscate
    d. evoke

116. Icy roads and poor visibility made driving on the highway extremely ..... .
    a. apprehensive
    b. relentless
    c. provisional
    d. precarious

117. The faulty toaster was repaired free of charge as it was still under ..... .
    a. interrogation
    b. suspicion
    c. evaluation
    d. warranty

118. The class was canceled as the director was unable to find anyone to ..... the ill teacher.
    a. make up for
    b. stand up to
    c. do away with
    d. stand in for

119. The children were ..... by the magician's wonderful performance.
    a. interrogated
    b. exacerbated
    c. entranced
    d. suppressed

120. The girls laughed at their ..... reflections in the fun-house mirrors.
    a. conspicuous
    b. distorted
    c. jagged
    d. audible

121. He never pays his debts. If you lend him money, you're just ..... .
    a. a fair-weather friend
    b. passing the buck
    c. a glutton for punishment
    d. head over heels

122. During a(n) ..... , unemployment rises as factories are forced to cut back production.
    a. insufficiency
    b. transition
    c. recession
    d. deficit

123. The information in the file is top secret and must not be ..... to anyone.
    a. divulged
    b. repealed
    c. donated
    d. delegated

124. The food critic remarked that the restaurant served mediocre food at ..... prices.
    a. exuberant
    b. exorbitant
    c. exquisite
    d. extraneous

125. The connection between smoking and lung cancer is not at all ..... .
   a. tenuous
   b. compatible
   c. reversible
   d. conceivable

126. Hotels on the island are busily preparing for the summer ..... of tourists.
   a. input
   b. influx
   c. affluence
   d. variation

127. The article went unpublished because it contained several ..... errors.
   a. oblivious
   b. glaring
   c. prestigious
   d. gaping

128. According to the recipe, the stew should be .... for at least an hour.
   a. simmered
   b. ventilated
   c. consumed
   d. preserved

129. The ..... actor has recently been asked to play his first leading film role.
   a. upcoming
   b. oncoming
   c. up-and-coming
   d. forthright

130. Critics were unanimous in their praise of the ..... researched biography.
   a. concisely
   b. meticulously
   c. profoundly
   d. erroneously

131. The wealthy businessman was tried and sent to prison for tax ..... .
   a. alteration
   b. exemption
   c. eviction
   d. evasion

132. In an effort to avoid panic, the government has ..... the seriousness of the incident.
   a. downgraded
   b. downsized
   c. downplayed
   d. downloaded

133. The young man was obviously ..... with great artistic talent.
   a. endowed
   b. consumed
   c. replenished
   d. enhanced

134. She hates having her picture taken as she feels she is not at all ..... .
   a. blurry
   b. discernible
   c. photogenic
   d. obscure

135. She is the ..... of a number of successful clothing boutiques.
   a. proponent
   b. proprietor
   c. entrepreneur
   d. consumer

136. The new tax legislation will be ..... on the first of the year.
   a. implemented
   b. necessitated
   c. requisitioned
   d. incorporated

137. I need some advice about buying a used car. Would you mind if I ..... ?
   a. racked your brains
   b. put my feet up
   c. picked your brains
   d. put my foot in my mouth

138. Simon is one of the most dependable people I know. He has never ..... .
   a. put me down
   b. run me down
   c. let me down
   d. broken me down

139. Effective managers know the importance of ..... responsibility to their subordinates.
   a. attributing
   b. surrendering
   c. delegating
   d. distributing

140. The detective's suspicions were aroused by the ..... in the witnesses' accounts.
   a. discrepancies
   b. controversies
   c. documentaries
   d. differentials

141. Teaching a class of ..... boys is wearing on even the most patient teacher's nerves.
   a. obscure
   b. docile
   c. incessant
   d. raucous

142. The medical journal announced a stunning ..... in cancer research last week.
   a. inclination
   b. breakthrough
   c. exposure
   d. resumption

143. The Nobel Prizes are among the world's most ..... awards.
   a. formidable
   b. imminent
   c. contingent
   d. prestigious

144. The instructions on the can say to stir the paint ..... before applying.
   a. callously
   b. adroitly
   c. vigorously
   d. reputedly

145. Upon entering the apartment, he ..... in the dark for the light switch.
   a. writhed
   b. fumbled
   c. hovered
   d. glimmered

146. At the end of the party the guests thanked the host and hostess for their gracious ..... .
   a. contribution
   b. disposition
   c. expenditure
   d. hospitality

147. Production of electric typewriters is gradually being ..... .
   a. churned out
   b. worked out
   c. phased out
   d. put out

148. Had the police not intervened, the demonstration might have ..... into violence.
   a. inflated
   b. erupted
   c. corrupted
   d. converted

149. The elderly woman preferred to spend the hot, ... day in her air-conditioned apartment.
   a. muggy
   b. soggy
   c. grubby
   d. crispy

150. Photocopying entire textbooks is an ..... of international copyright law.
   a. infliction
   b. obstruction
   c. infringement
   d. indignation

READING

Passage 1 is about a species called *Pfiesteria piscicda*.

Pollution is a threat to many species on earth, but sometimes it can cause species to thrive. Such is the case with *Pfiesteria piscicida*. A one-celled creature called a dinoflagellate, *Pfiesteria* inhabits warm coastal areas and river mouths, especially along the eastern United States. Although scientists have found evidence of *Pfiesteria* in 3,000-year-old sea floor sediments and dinoflagellates are thought to be one of the oldest life forms on earth, few people took notice of *Pfiesteria*.

Lately, however, blooms – or huge, dense populations – of *Pfiesteria* are appearing in coastal waters, and in such large concentrations the dinoflagellates become ruthless killers. The blooms emit powerful toxins that weaken and entrap fish that swim into the area. The toxins eventually cause the fish to develop large bleeding sores through which the tiny creatures attack, feasting on blood and flesh. Often the damage is astounding. During a 1991 fish kill that was blamed on *Pfiesteria* on North Carolina's Neuse River, nearly one billion fish died and bulldozers had to be brought in to clear the remains from the river. Of course, such events can have a devastating effect on commercially important fish, but that is just one way that *Pfiesteria* causes problems. The toxins it emits affect human skin in much the same way as they affect fish skin. Additionally, fishermen and others who have spent time near *Pfiesteria* blooms report that the toxins seem to get into the air, where once inhaled they affect the nervous system, causing severe headaches, blurred vision, nausea, breathing difficulty, short-term memory loss and even cognitive impairment.

For a while, it seemed that deadly *Pfiesteria* blooms were a threat only to North Carolina waters, but the problem seems to be spreading. More and more, conditions along the east coast seem to be favorable for *Pfiesteria*. Researchers suspect that pollutants such as animal waste from livestock operations, fertilizers washed from farmlands and waste water from mining operations have probably all combined to promote the growth of *Pfiesteria* in coastal waters.

151. What is true of *Pfiesteria*?
   a. It has been a menace to fish and humans for over 3,000 years.
   b. It is the oldest life form on earth.
   c. In large concentrations, it poses a threat to fish but not to humans.
   d. It seems to flourish in the presence of certain pollutants.

152. What is the main function of the toxins emitted by the dinoflagellates?
   a. They are quick-acting poisons that kill fish within minutes.
   b. They cause fish to develop wounds on which the creatures feed.
   c. They damage the nervous system of potential predators.
   d. They weaken the fish just long enough for the *Pfiesteria* to attack.

153. What is especially worrying about *Pfiesteria* blooms?
   a. They have devastated the fishing industry in U.S. coastal waters.
   b. They are fatal to humans who come in contact with them.
   c. Conditions are becoming increasingly favorable for their spread.
   d. Researchers have no idea as to exactly what causes them.

154. What were bulldozers used for in the Neuse River?
   a. removing the huge amounts of *Pfiesteria* from the river
   b. excavating holes to bury the dead fish.
   c. cleaning up the sediment at the bottom of the river.
   d. scooping up the vast number of dead fish in the water.

155. In which environment would you **not** expect a *Pfiesteria* bloom to develop?
   a. a cool mountain lake teeming with fish
   b. a river located near a rock quarry
   c. a marsh which absorbs waste water from a nearby pig farm
   d. a river that flows through rich farmland

Passage 2 is about an invention called the GuideCane.

Although a simple cane will suffice for many sight-impaired people, the seeing eye dog has proven to be a perfect navigation tool for the blind. Recently, however, a new aid has surfaced: a simple electronic device called the GuideCane. The idea is the brainchild of a scientist who specializes in creating obstacle avoidance systems that allow robots to move around an environment without bumping into things.

The cane is made up of three parts: the handle, a head and a set of steering wheels beneath the head. Ten ultrasonic sensors are placed in a semicircle around the cane's head. These sensors are like small loudspeakers, each emitting an ultrasound beep, which travels like a sound wave. When the beep hits something ahead of it, the echo is reflected back to the same sensor. By analyzing data from these beeps, the on-board computer inside the head then creates a rudimentary map of its surroundings. If the sensors tell the computer they have detected a chair three feet ahead of it, for example, the computer draws itself a map computing a path around the chair. It then sends this message to the steering wheels, which are propelled by a servo motor, similar to those found in remote-control cars. This is attached to the steering wheels by a small lever underneath the head. As the GuideCane is pushed forward, the wheels change direction on the computer's command.

Unlike other navigational tools, the GuideCane's simplicity makes it easy to use. Just grab the handle, walk ... and, if the cane changes directions, you know something is ahead of you. The cane works reliably with many objects, but not all. When approaching a table, for instance, it might see empty space between the legs, causing the user to bump into the table. Designers are trying to remedy this by putting an upward-pointing sensor on top of the GuideCane's head. The final product is expected to be available within a few years.

156. What is true of the GuideCane?

a. It was invented by someone who designs similar canes for robots.
b. It is a more reliable navigational tool than a seeing eye dog.
c. It is equipped with a set of ten loudspeakers.
d. It is an offshoot of work the designer does with robots.

157. The sensors function by ...

a. emitting audible beeps that are analyzed by an on-board computer
b. emitting and receiving signals that bounce off of objects in their path
c. picking up ultrasound beeps emitted by objects in the environment
d. emitting and picking up reflected light waves

158. How does the user of the GuideCane know that he is approaching an object?

a. The on-board computer prints out a map.
b. An ultrasound message is sent to one of the ten sensors.
c. The steering wheels of the cane change direction.
d. The on-board computer begins to beep.

159. Why is the product not currently available?

a. The on-board computer cannot yet map a path around a table.
b. There are still a few problems that designers must work out.
c. Designers see its simplicity as a drawback.
d. Designers are trying to invent a new sensor that will detect empty space.

160. After analyzing data from the sensors, what does the cane's built-in computer communicate with?

a. the object detected by the sensors
b. the person pushing the cane
c. a servo motor that changes the direction of the wheels
d. an upward-pointing sensor on the top portion of the cane

Passage 3 is about George Washington Carver.

In 1896, George Washington Carver – a former slave who became an agriculturist, inventor and educator – accepted an invitation to head the agricultural department at the all-black Tuskegee Normal and Industrial Institute for Negroes (now Tuskegee University). Upon arrival, Carver found a lack of interest in agriculture, which many students associated with sharecropping and poverty. They tended to be more interested in learning an industrial skill or trade that would allow them to make a living beyond the farm. Carver dignified farming by introducing the disciplines of botany, chemistry and soil study. In a few years, his department, which he renamed "Scientific Agriculture," attracted an increasing number of students.

The second challenge Carver faced at Tuskegee was widespread poverty and malnutrition among local black farmers. For years farmers had planted cotton on the same plots of land, thereby exhausting the topsoil's nutrients. He soon discovered that a lack of nitrogen in the soil accounted for consistently low harvests. Before coming to Tuskegee, Carver had learned that certain plants in the pea family extracted nitrogen from the air and deposited it in the soil. To maintain the topsoil's balance of nutrients, he advised farmers to alternate planting cotton and peanuts and within a few years production increased dramatically. He then created an outreach program in which he traveled to rural parts of Alabama to give hands-on instruction to farmers in this and other innovative techniques.

Widespread peanut cultivation also helped Carver alleviate malnutrition. He stressed that the peanut was a valuable source of protein that could enrich farmers' diets and improve their health. As part of his outreach program, Carver taught farmers' wives how to preserve food and prepare tasty, well-balanced meals. For many black southerners who had never eaten a tomato, which was once widely believed to be poisonous, Carver explained its nutritional value and demonstrated recipes in which it could be used. He was also innovative with the sweet potato and pecan, introducing approximately a hundred uses for each.

161. How did Carver manage to attract students to his department?
   a. by adding a strong scientific element to what was being studied
   b. by insuring that the students were properly disciplined
   c. by adding industrial courses to the curriculum
   d. by promising them an end to sharecropping and poverty

162. What accounted for the desire to learn an industrial skill or trade among Tuskegee students?
   a. They thought agriculture was a boring subject.
   b. They thought factory work would be more interesting than working on a farm.
   c. They wanted to break away from the rural poverty that other blacks had known.
   d. They didn't understand that studying agriculture could be dignified.

163. When Carver first came to Tuskegee, what was true of black farmers in rural Alabama?
   a. They were poor, but relatively well-fed.
   b. Their crop yields were consistently low.
   c. Their soil was rich in nitrogen and therefore not well balanced.
   d. They cultivated peanuts, which were not as profitable as cotton.

164. How did Carver manage to improve conditions for black rural farmers in Alabama?
   a. by enrolling them in his Scientific Agriculture program.
   b. by teaching their wives how to prepare nutritious meals with local ingredients.
   c. by traveling among them and demonstrating how to implement new farming techniques.
   d. by persuading them to grow peanuts instead of cotton.

165. How did Carver help farmers dramatically improve their harvests?
   a. He discovered the soil did not contain enough nitrogen.
   b. He promoted the widespread cultivation of peanuts.
   c. He advised them to improve their diets so they weren't so exhausted.
   d. He suggested that they grow peanuts one year and cotton the next.

Passage 4 is about emperor penguins.

Antarctica in March is like an island panicked by a looming hurricane. Prodded by some innate evacuation order, nearly every creature flees the onslaught of the austral winter. Only emperor penguins make their way south to overwinter in one of the most forbidding environments on the planet. To add to the challenge, they have mating on their minds. After several weeks of courtship during which partners learn to recognize each other's signature song (how else to distinguish one's mate from mobs of look-alike penguins?), each female lays a single softball-size egg. She then strikes out on a two-month oceanic feeding spree, leaving her partner to incubate the egg through the worst of the polar winter with only his body fat to sustain him. Cocooned inside dense plumage – about 80 feathers per square inch – emperors sport a downy undercoat topped by long feathers that overlap like roof tiles. Through shrieking storms and weeks of round-the-clock darkness, the male carefully balances the embryonic emperor on the tops of his feet, where an apron of densely feathered flesh seals out the deadly cold. If all goes well, more than 90 percent of the eggs hatch and the well-fed females trek back into the colony just as the chicks begin whistling for their first meal of regurgitated seafood. When his mate arrives, the male goes berserk trumpeting. He's had the egg on his feet for 65 days, and he's lost between a third and a half of his body weight. It's as if he's telling her that he's good and ready for her to take over.

The method behind the emperor's madness comes to light in December, high summer in the Southern Hemisphere. As the ice on which they've been standing starts to splinter, the fledgling chicks – now just old enough to fend for themselves – take to the sea during the brief period when food is most abundant and the climate is at its kindest.

166. What prompts most animals to leave Antarctica in March?
- a. fear of hurricanes
- b. sheer instinct
- c. knowledge that better conditions exist further south
- d. an inborn desire to live in a less crowded habitat

167. What is true of female emperors?
- a. They play no part in rearing the fledgling chicks.
- b. They lay more than one egg during each breeding cycle.
- c. They visit the males periodically during their two-month feeding spree.
- d. They assume responsibility for rearing the chicks only after they have hatched.

168. What do male emperors nourish themselves on while the eggs are hatching?
- a. food provided by the females
- b. dense plumage
- c. stored body fat
- d. regurgitated seafood

169. What does the writer imply about the emperors' breeding cycle in the final paragraph?
- a. It is timed to allow chicks a better chance of survival.
- b. It appears to serve no evolutionary purpose.
- c. It needlessly endangers the survival of the chicks.
- d. It is a miracle that the species continues to survive.

170. How are emperors uniquely adapted to survive the biting cold?
- a. Each has a distinct mating call.
- b. Their bodies are insulated by specially arranged feathers.
- c. The females are superb hunters.
- d. They can use more than half of their body weight as nourishment.

Vocabulary Consolidation 4

A Preposition and particle power – The following extracts are taken from passages that you have already seen in Practice Tests 1–4. Read each passage quickly, then fill in the gaps with an appropriate preposition or particle.

1. We picture inventors .... heroes .... the genius to recognize and solve a society's problems. .... reality, the greatest inventors have been tinkerers who loved tinkering .... its own sake and who then had to figure .... what their devices might be good .... Our widespread misunderstanding .... inventors as setting .... to solve society's problems causes us to say that necessity is the mother .... invention. Actually, invention is the mother .... necessity, ... creating needs that we never felt before. Far .... welcoming solutions .... its supposed needs, society's entrenched interests commonly resist inventions. .... Gutenberg's time, no one pleaded .... a new way to churn .... books: there were hordes .... copyists whose desire not to be put .... business led .... local bans .... printing.

2. A space suit must provide oxygen and a system .... removing excess CO_2 and water vapor. It must also offer protection .... extreme heat, cold and radiation and facilities .... speech communication and the storage .... body wastes. This is such an imposing list .... requirements that an entire technology has been developed to deal .... them and, indeed, ... the provision of simulated environments and procedures .... testing and evaluating space suits.

3. .... a psychological level, most historians agree that Salem was seized .... public hysteria, fueled .... a genuine belief .... witchcraft. They point .... that while some .... the girls may have been acting, many responsible adults were caught .... the frenzy as well. But even more revealing is an analysis .... the identities .... the accused and the accusers. Salem's obscure struggle .... social and political power .... older traditional groups and a newer commercial class was one repeated .... communities .... American history. But it took a bizarre and deadly detour when its citizens were swept .... the conviction that the devil was loose .... their homes.

4. .... an increasing number .... polluted sites, pumps and bulldozers are being replaced .... plants. Ever since Europeans first noticed hundreds .... years ago that certain plants grow .... abundance near natural deposits .... zinc and nickel, it has been known that some plants readily absorb toxic materials. Phytoremediation is still .... its infancy, but research suggests that certain plants have the potential to clean .... metals .... lead and nickel and a host .... other wastes.

5. Although a simple cane will suffice .... many sight-impaired people, the seeing eye dog has proven to be a perfect navigation tool .... the blind. Recently, however, a new aid has surfaced: a simple electronic device called the GuideCane. The idea is the brainchild .... a scientist who specializes .... creating obstacle avoidance systems that allow robots to move .... an environment .... bumping .... things.

B Phrasal verb crack-down – For each group, match the bold-faced phrases with their definitions.

1.	Bill is so tall you can easily **pick** him **out** in a crowd.	a. treat unfairly and often
2.	Business is bound to **pick up** in December.	b. substitute for, replace
3.	Watch your language! The baby **picks up** everything he hears.	c. criticize unfairly
4.	Why is she always **picking on** me? John was talking, too.	d. notice, spot
5.	Who's going to **stand in for** Jane while she's away?	e. get better, increase
6.	You need to **stand up to** that bully.	f. learn without taking lessons
7.	Why must you **run down** everything I say?	g. resist, defend yourself against

8.	The doctor's schedule is full, but she'll try to **work** you **in**.	a. plan, find a way
9.	I'm still trying to **work out** how I'll tell him.	b. get rid of, reduce (feelings)
10.	He can't seem to **work up** any enthusiasm these days.	c. insult, belittle, humiliate
11.	Taking a long walk will help you **work off** your anger.	d. gradually disappear
12.	I'm tired of the way you always **put** me **down**.	e. include
13.	When the anesthetic **wears off**, expect to be in pain.	f. disappoint
14.	He's 100% reliable. He'll never **let** you **down**.	g. develop

C Idiom round-up – In each group, complete each item with the correct form of a word from the box.

feast	lay	pass	pick	pull	put *(x2)*	rack	twist	wriggle

1. He tried to .... out of mowing the lawn again, but I .... my foot down and he did it.
2. It's about time we .... / .... this rumor to rest, don't you think?
3. I've been .... my brains all day, but I can't remember for the life of me where I met him.
4. The sales report is Ed's responsibility. If he told you it was mine, he's just .... the buck.
5. I really shouldn't go to the movies tonight, but I suppose I will if you .... my arm.
6. .... your eyes on the beautiful BMW convertible that's driving down the road.
7. Seymour has never met the President. He's just .... your leg.
8. I need some advice about buying a new computer. Can I .... your brains for a minute?

blame	business	end	eye *(x2)*	foot	feet	head	heels	mouth	nail

9. They used to be the best of friends, but lately they just don't see .... to ....
10. How dare you accuse me! Joe is the person you ought to be putting the .... on.
11. Mom said we'd better get the room cleaned up or else. I think she means .... this time.
12. Anita's got a new boyfriend. Rumor has it she's .... over .... in love.
13. If you find yourself at a loose .... , perhaps you could help me straighten out the closet.
14. It seems like every time I try to put my .... up, the phone rings.
15. I didn't mean to suggest he was lazy. I guess I really put my .... in my ....
16. I couldn't have said it more perfectly myself. You really hit the .... on the ....

D What's in a name? (adjective review) – Match the people on the right with their descriptions.

Guys

1.	....	He can't see a thing without his glasses.	a.	Turbulent Ted
2.	....	He flies off the handle at the least provocation.	b.	Fidgety Fred
3.	....	He has trouble sitting still.	c.	Wobbly Willy
4.	....	He's the noblest, most charitable of the lot.	d.	Blurry Bob
5.	....	He aspires to be a cowboy some day.	e.	Rugged Randy
6.	....	He's likely to fall down if he's had too much to drink.	f.	Hypothetical Hymie
7.	....	He's always coming down with one thing or another.	g.	Susceptible Saul
8.	....	He's always speculating about what might happen.	h.	Magnanimous Max

Gals

1.	....	She's the loudest person you'll ever meet.	a.	Rigid Rita
2.	....	She hasn't cracked a smile in years.	b.	Eligible Elaine
3.	....	A more qualified person you'd be hard-pressed to find.	c.	Pretentious Priscilla
4.	....	She's always got such a blank expression on her face.	d.	Raucous Rachel
5.	....	She is extremely set in her ways.	e.	Timely Tilly
6.	....	She's always putting on airs.	f.	Docile Dorothy
7.	....	She always shows up just when you need her.	g.	Frowning Frieda
8.	....	She's the quietest, most gentle person I know.	h.	Vacant Vicky

E Verbalizing with adverbs – Match each question with the appropriate answer.

What would you do if . . . ?

1.	....	you were depressed about getting poor grades?	a.	laugh spontaneously
2.	....	you played the stock market without consulting a broker?	b.	collaborate grudgingly
3.	....	your boss forced you to do a project with someone you hate?	c.	object vehemently
4.	....	you had to discuss physics with a Nobel Prize winner?	d.	dress meticulously
5.	....	you wanted to mix white and black paint to make gray?	e.	frown sullenly
6.	....	you were told a joke that was unexpectedly hilarious?	f.	defer respectfully
7.	....	you wanted to impress a manager at a job interview?	g.	invest arbitrarily
8.	....	your parents stopped giving you an allowance?	h.	stir vigorously

What adverb would you use to describe the way in which . . . ?

1.	....	a snail moves after it has just woken up?	a.	distinctly
2.	....	a student studies for a final in under ten minutes?	b.	adroitly
3.	....	you speak to an elderly person who is hard of hearing?	c.	erroneously
4.	....	a man of few words expresses himself?	d.	sluggishly
5.	....	you'd suffer if someone stepped on your favorite CD?	e.	callously
6.	....	a criminal behaves when he doesn't regret what he's done?	f.	concisely
7.	....	a prize-winning ice-skater glides across the ice?	g.	superficially
8.	....	a person you've never seen takes you for his/her best friend?	h.	profoundly

F **Spot check** – Here's another look at some of the groupings tested in the Vocabulary section of Practice Test 4. Circle the choice that best completes each sentence.

1. Winning the final match would be difficult as the other team was a ..... opponent.
   a. formidable
   b. imminent
   c. contingent
   d. prestigious

2. After stealing money from his parents, the child was ..... with guilt.
   a. endowed
   b. consumed
   c. replenished
   d. enhanced

3. They spent the evening ..... computer games from the Internet.
   a. downgrading
   b. downsizing
   c. downplaying
   d. downloading

4. The Congresswoman is a leading ..... of educational reform.
   a. proponent
   b. proprietor
   c. entrepreneur
   d. consumer

5. The newspaper prides itself on its objective and ..... coverage of the news.
   a. inclement
   b. inferior
   c. impertinent
   d. impartial

6. Spain is reputedly a warm country, but there is considerable ..... from one season to the next.
   a. input
   b. influx
   c. affluence
   d. variation

7. The lawyer suspected that the witness was ..... evidence to protect the defendant.
   a. interrogating
   b. exacerbating
   c. entrancing
   d. suppressing

8. The children are looking forward to their ..... holiday with great anticipation.
   a. upcoming
   b. oncoming
   c. up-and-coming
   d. forthright

9. I've never understood why he has such a(n) ..... perception of his limited abilities.
   a. inflated
   b. erupted
   c. corrupted
   d. converted

10. Hiding an escaped convict is considered to be an ..... of justice.
    a. infliction
    b. obstruction
    c. infringement
    d. indignation

11. It's clear he wants to ask her out; his feelings are quite ..... .
    a. conspicuous
    b. distorted
    c. jagged
    d. audible

12. The wealthy businessman ..... a large sum of money to charity each year.
    a. divulges
    b. repeals
    c. donates
    d. delegates

13. It's natural for students to feel nervous when teachers ..... over them during a test.
    a. writhe
    b. fumble
    c. hover
    d. glimmer

14. To curb the budget deficit, the government must cut down on ..... wherever possible.
    a. contribution
    b. disposition
    c. expenditure
    d. hospitality

15. Make sure you put away those potato chips or they'll be ..... by the morning.
    a. muggy
    b. soggy
    c. grubby
    d. crispy

16. Arteriosclerosis is ..... to some degree with medication and proper diet.
    a. tenuous
    b. compatible
    c. reversible
    d. conceivable

PRACTICE TEST 5

Writing

(30 minutes)

Write on one of the topics given below. If you write about something else, your paper will not be graded. If you do not understand the topics, ask the examiner to explain or translate them. You will be graded on the clarity of your writing and the linguistic range and accuracy you show. Write $1\frac{1}{2}$ to 2 pages. You may make any corrections or other changes in the body of the composition.

TOPICS

1. Describe an incident in which someone you trusted really let you down. What did you learn from the experience?

2. Some people feel that education is about learning facts and figures, while others believe it should be more about teaching people how to get along with each other in society. What is your opinion?

For help in writing these compositions, see *Writing Tutorial*, pages 198–199.

Listening Comprehension Test

(35–40 minutes)

This part of the examination is a listening test that will assess your understanding of spoken English. The listening test has three parts. There are 50 questions. Mark all your answers on the separate answer sheet. Do not make any stray marks on the answer sheet. If you change your mind about an answer, erase your first answer completely.

PART I – In this part of the test, you will hear a short conversation. From the three answer choices given, choose the answer which means the same thing as you hear, or that is true based on what you hear.

For problems **1–17**, mark your answers on the separate answer sheet. No problem can be repeated. Please listen carefully. Do you have any questions?

1. a. It's going to take a while.
b. It's already done.
c. It will be done soon.

2. a. She thinks Joe should be embarrassed.
b. She's amazed at how clumsy Joe is.
c. She doesn't see Joe anywhere.

3. a. She is tired because she hates her job.
b. Looking for a new job makes her tired.
c. Being tired doesn't affect her opinion.

4. a. He thinks she's exaggerating.
b. He doesn't want to go with her.
c. He doesn't understand her point.

5. a. He was injured while crossing the street.
b. The back of his car has been damaged.
c. He failed to stop for a red light.

6. a. She didn't want him to know about it.
b. She didn't think it was important.
c. She didn't want to bother him.

7. a. They went to the wrong airport.
b. They boarded the wrong plane.
c. They'll have to change their reservations.

8. a. She's worried that he might be ill.
b. She thinks they're better off without him.
c. She agrees they should start without him.

9. a. They've already missed one meeting.
b. They've argued and still haven't made up.
c. They might have to cancel the meeting.

10. a. He thinks the children are responsible
b. He doubts whether the children will do it.
c. He thinks she's being too strict.

11. a. She's not happy that he's going away.
b. She's willing to help while he's away.
c. She offers to go away with him.

12. a. Jack has just taken over the family company.
b. Jack has just opened his own company.
c. Jack has just received a major promotion.

13. a. They're thinking about moving.
b. Their house was robbed recently.
c. They need to invest in home security.

14. a. They're not sure whether Robert is out of town.
b. Neither of them know why Robert is away.
c. They're concerned about Robert's safety.

15. a. It's been a particularly severe winter.
b. He's been feeling ill for several weeks.
c. Cold weather always depresses him.

16. a. His car had a flat tire at the mall.
b. She thinks he should always take the train.
c. He doesn't have the money for a new car.

17. a. She doesn't think he's being very fair.
b. They both think the instructor is great.
c. She agrees with his negative assessment.

Practice Test 5

PART II – In this part of the test, you will hear a question. From the three answer choices given, choose the one which best answers the question.

For problems **18–35**, mark your answers on the separate answer sheet. No problem can be repeated. Please listen carefully. Do you have any questions?

18. a. Yes, I did.
    b. Strange, I didn't hear anything.
    c. Perhaps, let's see.

19. a. Wasn't it last year?
    b. Pretty soon, I believe.
    c. By 10 p.m. He's really exhausted.

20. a. I suppose I might have.
    b. I'll have to think about it.
    c. Better late than never.

21. a. It looks long enough to me.
    b. I'm very busy right now.
    c. No, could you?

22. a. You will tell her, won't you?
    b. I've got a very soft voice.
    c. I was too embarrassed to ask.

23. a. If it isn't too expensive.
    b. I'm willing to give it a go.
    c. Hardly anyone speaks English.

24. a. I'm used to it. He's that way with everyone.
    b. Actually, I've just been promoted.
    c. To be honest, I could use a raise.

25. a. I can't afford it.
    b. Sorry, guns make me nervous.
    c. OK, let's have a look.

26. a. In the drawer next to the sink.
    b. I usually wear gold.
    c. The fork goes on the left.

27. a. It's almost my turn.
    b. I'll hang up when I'm good and ready.
    c. I had no idea he was a pilot.

28. a. It's several hours yet.
    b. About two hundred miles.
    c. We'll go next week.

29. a. I've never seen such a blaze.
    b. Yes, I put it out just in time.
    c. It was the best I've ever seen.

30. a. I bought mine at the mall.
    b. I found them a bit uncomfortable.
    c. It's hard to say.

31. a. Philip tried, but he dropped it.
    b. Try Philip.
    c. The Yankees, wasn't it?

32. a. Sorry, it's way out of our way.
    b. Unfortunately, there's no other way.
    c. There must be a better way.

33. a. Yes, you may.
    b. I'd take the car.
    c. It's too soon.

34. a. Well, I really appreciate it.
    b. I deserved it.
    c. It was something else.

35. a. Please don't give it another thought.
    b. I hope you can.
    c. I'm glad you did.

PART III – In this part, you will hear three short segments from a radio program. The program is called "Learning from the Experts." Each talk lasts about two minutes. As you listen, you may want to take notes to help you remember information given in the talk. After each talk, you will be asked some questions about what was said. From the three answer choices given, you should choose the one which best answers the question according to the information you heard.

Remember, no problems can be repeated. For problems **36–50**, mark your answers on the separate answer sheet. Do you have any questions?

SEGMENT 1

36. What question concerns the speaker?
   a. Why do so many people in the developing world suffer from malnutrition?
   b. Should genetically engineered foods be used in the developing world?
   c. How can genetic engineering be used to fight malnutrition in the developing world?

37. How do researchers think they can improve the situation?
   a. By genetically engineering large quantities of iron, vitamin A and other nutrients
   b. By genetically engineering rice and other staple crops to be more nutritious
   c. By adding iron and vitamin A to the soil in which rice and other staple crops are grown

38. What have researchers in Switzerland done?
   a. They have developed a strain of rice that is rich in vitamin A but not iron.
   b. They have determined why some rice turns bright yellow.
   c. They have developed a new strain of rice that is rich in both iron and vitamin A.

39. What is true of essential amino acids?
   a. The only way for the human body to obtain them is through protein-rich foods.
   b. Even the presence of small amounts can lead to malnutrition.
   c. The body can only produce them if certain proteins are present.

40. How do genetically modified sweet potatoes differ from ordinary sweet potatoes?
   a. They are not as sweet, but contain three to five times more protein.
   b. They are sweeter and are much richer in protein and essential amino acids.
   c. They are three to five times larger and contain much more vitamin A.

SEGMENT 2

41. What do experts at Mercedes-Daimler say about the car of the future?
   a. It will allow the driver to avoid traffic jams.
   b. It will feed information to drivers and at times take over the controls.
   c. It will be controlled by on-board computers and not the driver.

42. What is the main feature of Daimler's "side-stick" car?
   a. It combines joystick steering with conventional pedals for braking and acceleration.
   b. All controls are on a single joystick to the right or left of the driver.
   c. A pair of joysticks replaces conventional steering and pedal controls.

43. What is true of experienced drivers who have test-driven the "side-stick" car?
   a. They found the car difficult to handle.
   b. They adapted to it much better than 17-year-old novice drivers.
   c. They said they would definitely purchase the car if Daimler were to market it.

44. What might drivers not like about the car of the future?
   a. The fact that the on-board electronics system would sometimes take control
   b. The fact that the car will not perform well despite all the on-board technology
   c. The fact that the car will send out and receive a constant stream of information

45. How do experts at Daimler feel about satisfying customer preferences?
   a. Customer preferences must always be a manufacturer's top priority.
   b. What customers want is important, but safety should always come first.
   c. Nothing must detract from the driver's thrill of being fully in command.

SEGMENT 3

46. What fascinated the researcher most about the explosion of Krakatoa?
    a. The destructive power of the volcanic eruption
    b. The effect of the eruption on Earth's atmosphere
    c. The tidal waves that were caused by the eruption

47. Why did the researcher originally feel that it was probably unrealistic to believe that a connection existed between Krakatoa and the creation of the painting?
    a. The artist would have been too young to remember the Krakatoa eruption.
    b. No volcanic eruptions occurred in the year that Munch finished the painting.
    c. Ten years separated the eruption and the actual creation of the painting.

48. Which was NOT one of the facts that the researcher uncovered on his trip to Norway?
    a. The artist made frequent reference to the eruption in his journals.
    b. Rough sketches of the painting were made in the early-to-mid 1880s.
    c. Norway experienced the 'Krakatoa glow' in the winter of 1883-84.

49. When did the artist experience the emotions that eventually resulted in his painting "The Scream"?
    a. After hearing about the eruption from friends
    b. After reading an article in a local newspaper
    c. While walking at sunset with several friends

50. What is true about the paintings in "The Frieze of Life"?
    a. Most are based on the death of his mother and sister.
    b. Most are based on experiences from the artist's past.
    c. Most feature a haunting blood-red Krakatoa sunset.

Grammar – Cloze – Vocabulary – Reading

(75 minutes)

This part of the examination contains 120 problems, numbered **51–170**. There are 40 grammar, 20 cloze, 40 vocabulary and 20 reading comprehension problems. The examiner will not explain any test problems. If you do not understand how to do the problems, raise your hand and a proctor will explain the examples to you.

Do not spend too much time on any one problem. Each problem counts the same. If you do not know the answer to a problem, you may make a reasonable guess. Each problem has only one correct answer. Work fast but carefully. You have 75 minutes to answer all 120 problems.

GRAMMAR

51. William hates being late for work, but this time he said ..... .
- a. he couldn't help
- b. it couldn't help
- c. he couldn't be helped
- d. it couldn't be helped

52. ..... her advisor, the course turned out to be one of the best she had ever taken.
- a. Recommending
- b. Recommended by
- c. After recommending it by
- d. To be recommended by

53. He couldn't afford any of the cameras he saw, ... they were on sale.
- a. even if
- b. not to mention
- c. despite
- d. let alone

54. The new shopping mall has dozens of stores, many ..... are looking to hire new staff.
- a. that
- b. who
- c. of whom
- d. of which

55. Given that his grades are so poor, ... into a good college.
- a. it's unlikely for him getting
- b. he's unlikely to get
- c. he has little likelihood that he will get
- d. he's unlikely of getting

56. Despite frequent interruptions, she ..... ten pages this morning.
- a. already wrote
- b. has already been writing
- c. has already written
- d. had already written

57. The owners of the company are looking for a sales director ..... to take the company global.
- a. who can be relied
- b. on whom they can rely
- c. who is relied
- d. they can rely

58. Of all the homes we've looked at, ... was within walking distance of a good high school.
- a. not one of them
- b. none of which
- c. only one or two
- d. not even any

59. She suggested we go to a Mexican restaurant as that's what she was in the mood ..... .
- a. of
- b. to
- c. for
- d. in

60. Of the three brothers, Tom is the more artistic, ... Bob and Ralph are more athletic.
- a. even though
- b. nevertheless
- c. otherwise
- d. whereas

61. He was the first to admit that it had been foolish ..... on such icy roads.
- a. of him to drive
- b. for him driving
- c. of having driven
- d. his driving

62. He's suffering from a disease ..... is not yet known.
- a. which cause
- b. the cause of which
- c. which the cause
- d. that is the cause

63. After all that exercise, a nice juicy steak and salad are ..... .
    a. that which you need
    b. what you are needing
    c. just what you need
    d. what do you need

64. Edward is one of the most ..... people I have ever known.
    a. perceptible
    b. perceived
    c. perceiving
    d. perceptive

65. Speaking of Fred, I forgot to mention that I saw his sister just ..... .
    a. the last week
    b. few days ago
    c. the other day
    d. before a week

66. He said he didn't have enough money for his rent, ... a new laptop computer.
    a. not mentioning
    b. apart from
    c. let alone
    d. without speaking of

67. All things ..... , more and more people are enjoying a higher standard of living these days.
    a. into account
    b. considered
    c. told
    d. in general

68. I saw the film again last week and, to my delight, I enjoyed it ..... as I did the first time.
    a. even more
    b. just as much
    c. much more so
    d. so much more

69. John's ..... professor is notorious for giving incredibly difficult tests.
    a. economist
    b. economical
    c. economy
    d. economics

70. ..... such a good bookkeeper is that she seldom makes mistakes.
    a. What makes her
    b. The reason why
    c. Being
    d. Because she is

71. I should have taken her advice when she warned me ..... everything he says.
    a. I didn't believe
    b. not to believe
    c. about believing not
    d. to believe not

72. The rose bushes in my neighbor's garden always look so beautiful ..... trimmed them.
    a. that she's just
    b. right after she's
    c. having her just
    d. whenever they've just been

73. Something strange is going on here, and I wish you would let ..... .
    a. it on me in
    b. it in on me
    c. me in on it
    d. me on in it

74. It is imperative that people ..... aware of the risks involved in taking such medication.
    a. must be
    b. will be
    c. have been
    d. be

75. It's sad to say, but ..... falls in love for the wrong reasons.
    a. many young women
    b. young woman
    c. many a young woman
    d. such young woman

76. He regrets ..... harder to avoid the break-up of his marriage.
    a. not to have worked
    b. not to work
    c. not having worked
    d. him not working

77. He's offered to arrange things while I'm away, but I'd rather ..... till I get back.
   a. him to wait
   b. that he'll wait
   c. his waiting
   d. he wait

78. I probably ..... to call Ed if you didn't just mention his name.
   a. have forgotten
   b. will forget
   c. would have forgotten
   d. forgot

79. The widow's ..... husband was an extremely wealthy man.
   a. lately
   b. later
   c. latest
   d. late

80. On at least two occasions, Myra has shown up at a party wearing a dress ..... .
   a. same exactly with me
   b. the same exact to me
   c. that's the exact same to mine
   d. exactly the same as mine

81. ..... from the long day at work, she decided to go to the party.
   a. However she was tired
   b. Tired though she was
   c. Though tiring
   d. To be tired

82. ..... in Washington, please don't hesitate to pay us a visit.
   a. Are you ever found to be
   b. If you find yourself ever
   c. Should you ever find yourself
   d. If ever you will find yourself

83. I know he didn't mean to insult me, but his comment hurt ..... .
   a. all the same
   b. one and the same
   c. just same
   d. as the same

84. ..... decisions was ultimately the reason for her being dismissed.
   a. She was unable to make
   b. Her inability to make
   c. Incapable of making decisions
   d. Her not being capable to make

85. If she continues to play as well as she's been playing, ... she will the tournament.
   a. chances are
   b. there's a chance of
   c. there are chances
   d. she has a chance that

86. I know I hurt your feelings, but believe me when I say ..... .
   a. it wasn't meant that
   b. my meaning wasn't that
   c. I wasn't meant to
   d. I didn't mean to

87. The class spent the past semester learning how to solve algebraic ..... .
   a. equators
   b. equivalents
   c. equations
   d. equals

88. He said ..... unemployed than go back to his old job.
   a. he should have been
   b. he'd sooner be
   c. he'd better be
   d. he's rather

89. Some people say the accident was George's fault, but that's not ..... I heard it.
   a. what
   b. that
   c. how
   d. the story

90. I'll leave the choice entirely to you; ..... you decide will be fine with me.
   a. whatever
   b. no matter
   c. as long as
   d. provided

CLOZE

Passage 1 is about rescuing sea animals.

A shoreline is the dynamic border between two worlds – the terrestrial and the marine. The ocean's currents, waves and winds sculpt this border, alternately carrying off and depositing sand.

These forces ....(91).... only shape the land, but they also affect the ocean's living populations. Sometimes animals that ....(92).... deeper water are thrown off ....(93)..... . They come close to the shoreline ....(94).... may actually be found on the ....(95)..... . They may be injured, sick or disoriented, and ....(96).... become cold, hungry or dehydrated. Such is the case with various species of dolphin, porpoise, seal, whale and turtle ....(97).... become stranded along the Atlantic coastline. ....(98).... there is help for some animals. In many locations, when beached animals are ....(99).... , professionals and volunteers are on the scene. Sick, cold or injured animals are immediately ....(100).... in a rehabilitation program with the intent of getting them well enough to be returned to their natural habitat. Often the animals are tagged with a transmitter for future tracking.

91. a. might b. not c. that d. if

92. a. live b. drink c. have d. inhabit

93. a. course b. limits c. track d. balance

94. a. where b. so c. or d. but

95. a. water b. run c. beach d. ground

96. a. to b. soon c. had d. should

97. a. have b. and c. can d. that

98. a. Although b. When c. But d. Rarely

99. a. sighted b. seeing c. finding d. examined

100. a. taken b. going c. sent d. placed

Passage 2 is about the scientific method.

So what does a scientist do when he or she uses the scientific method in the exploration of the unknown? First, the scientist tries to learn as much about a subject as time – or funding ....(101)..... . This requires a thorough study of the available literature, the gathering of data from a ....(102).... of sources, discussions with colleagues, and a lot of thinking.

....(103).... data has been gathered and analyzed, the scientist formulates a hypothesis ....(104).... may be a short leap of logic or an intuitive leap of faith. The scientist then designs an experiment to provide evidence in ....(105).... of the hypothesis. ....(106).... form the experiment takes, the scientist must gather substantial ....(107).... of data. Analysis of the gathered data will ....(108).... suggest the validity of the hypothesis or encourage revision and retesting. A hypothesis that has been rigorously tested, analyzed and accepted ....(109).... the scientific community is referred to as a theory. The theory will continue to be an accepted explanation ....(110).... new information is uncovered that disproves the previous explanation.

101. a. gives b. demands c. allows d. has

102. a. variation b. variety c. variance d. variability

103. a. The b. If c. Next d. Once

104. a. that b. or c. which d. and

105. a. support b. addition c. advance d. view

106. a. The b. Whatever c. Which d. However

107. a. range b. numbers c. quantity d. amounts

108. a. not b. neither c. either d. both

109. a. for b. by c. as d. while

110. a. if b. when c. until d. so

VOCABULARY

111. Healthy relationships are based on trust and ..... respect.
    a. casual
    b. eventual
    c. mutual
    d. imperial

112. Some people have no ..... about cheating on their income tax declarations.
    a. queries
    b. inquiries
    c. expectations
    d. qualms

113. Damages from the hurricane have been ..... at millions of dollars.
    a. esteemed
    b. assessed
    c. accessed
    d. apportioned

114. Everyone at the party was taken ..... by his rude behavior.
    a. apart
    b. aback
    c. aside
    d. for granted

115. The mayor's office reports that funds have been ..... for a new hospital.
    a. earmarked
    b. pinpointed
    c. dog-eared
    d. sidetracked

116. She ..... reminded him that he was not the only candidate who was well-qualified for the post.
    a. gratefully
    b. tactfully
    c. resentfully
    d. respectively

117. The director asked his legal experts to ..... a merger agreement.
    a. draw up
    b. write off
    c. run up
    d. bring out

118. As parents they have tried to ..... a strong sense of responsibility in their children.
    a. instill
    b. install
    c. distill
    d. dispel

119. The professor spent hours ..... over his notes for the next day's lecture.
    a. hovering
    b. poring
    c. triumphing
    d. grieving

120. You must be coming down with the flu. It's not like you to feel so ..... .
    a. sluggish
    b. witless
    c. homesick
    d. mediocre

121. The scientist has been at the ..... of genetic research for several decades.
    a. foreground
    b. forehead
    c. forefront
    d. foresight

122. Winning the lottery on the day he was laid off was a ..... of incredibly good luck.
    a. jolt
    b. bolt
    c. stroke
    d. streak

123. The horrible accident had left him with ..... memories that refused to fade.
    a. irresistible
    b. inedible
    c. indelible
    d. illegible

124. When he stayed out till four in the morning, his parents decided it was time for them to ..... .
    a. let bygones be bygones
    b. turn over a new leaf
    c. let sleeping dogs lie
    d. lay down the law

125. He taught his children the importance of ..... the benefits of a good education.
   a. gathering
   b. intercepting
   c. selecting
   d. reaping

126. In the first years of elementary school, children learn the ..... of reading and math.
   a. manifestations
   b. rudiments
   c. ambiguities
   d. supplements

127. Today's job market is characterized by ..... competition for well-paid positions.
   a. ruthless
   b. complacent
   c. vagrant
   d. shrill

128. The eager new employee spent her first few weeks on the job ..... .
   a. letting her hair down
   b. biding her time
   c. learning the ropes
   d. getting a new lease on life

129. Authorities said it would be several days before the flood waters ..... .
   a. alleviated
   b. receded
   c. succumbed
   d. submerged

130. The teacher reprimanded the disrespectful student for ..... her by her first name.
   a. escorting
   b. addressing
   c. classifying
   d. incriminating

131. The director is looking to build up a staff with people who are ..... to new ideas.
   a. resistant
   b. appreciative
   c. tolerant
   d. receptive

132. Frequent exposure to loud noise may result in hearing ..... .
   a. impediment
   b. impeachment
   c. imposition
   d. impairment

133. The older generation has been slow to ..... computer technology.
   a. embellish
   b. embrace
   c. emancipate
   d. emulate

134. Everyone in the room could sense the ..... between the two rival politicians.
   a. amity
   b. unanimity
   c. anonymity
   d. enmity

135. If he continues to spend his money so ..... , his inheritance will be gone in no time.
   a. elegantly
   b. expectantly
   c. extravagantly
   d. equitably

136. Upon hitting the floor, the fine crystal wine glass ..... into a thousand pieces.
   a. shuddered
   b. shimmered
   c. simmered
   d. splintered

137. Government troops were called in to ..... the rebellion.
   a. put down
   b. look down on
   c. cut down on
   d. press down on

138. She wondered what it would be like to be ..... and not have to worry about money.
   a. destitute
   b. abundant
   c. luxuriant
   d. affluent

139. The decorator chose ..... colors to create a more relaxing atmosphere.
   a. substantial
   b. subordinate
   c. subdued
   d. subjective

140. The young executive was shocked at the problems he had inherited from his ..... .
   a. ancestor
   b. successor
   c. forerunner
   d. predecessor

141. Diplomats feel confident that the terms of the peace ..... will soon be agreed upon.
   a. contract
   b. symphony
   c. treaty
   d. truce

142. The Golden Gate in San Francisco is one of the longest ..... bridges in the world.
   a. expenditure
   b. suspension
   c. supposition
   d. expansion

143. The course familiarizes students with word processing and other computer ..... .
   a. promotions
   b. incentives
   c. progressions
   d. applications

144. The boundary between the two properties has been in ..... for many years.
   a. dispute
   b. disrepute
   c. conflict
   d. contrast

145. The population in the southern part of the country is ..... Catholic.
   a. disparagingly
   b. subsequently
   c. predominantly
   d. apparently

146. Is there anything in ..... that you would like me to make for dinner?
   a. brief
   b. principle
   c. succession
   d. particular

147. The graying middle-aged woman envies younger women who are still in ..... .
   a. good standing
   b. their prime
   c. their element
   d. bloom

148. The overweight girl was constantly ..... by her unkind classmates.
   a. lauded
   b. taunted
   c. amused
   d. nurtured

149. Each chapter begins with a(n) ..... of the material that is covered.
   a. oversight
   b. overview
   c. outlook
   d. omission

150. They canceled their weekend sailing plans ..... high winds and rough seas.
   a. on behalf of
   b. in tandem with
   c. on account of
   d. at the expense of

READING

Passage 1 is about an interesting aspect of animal behavior.

Evolution has generated a nearly endless list of behavioral wonders by which animals seem almost perfectly adapted to their world. A prime example is the honey bee's system of communication. A foraging bee returning from a good source of food will perform a "waggle dance" on the vertical sheets of honeycomb. The dance specifies to other bees the distance and direction of the food. The dance takes the form of a flattened figure 8; during the crucial part of the maneuver (the two parts of the figure 8 that cross) the forager vibrates her body. The angle of this part of the run specifies the direction of the food: if this part of the dance points up, the source is in the direction of the sun, whereas if it is aimed, for example, 70° left of vertical, the food is 70° left of the sun. The number of waggling motions specifies the distance to the food.

The complexity of this dance language has paved the way for studies of higher animals. Some species are now known to have a variety of signals to smooth the operations of social living. Vervet monkeys, for example, have the usual set of gestures and sounds to express emotional states and social needs, but they also have a four-word predator vocabulary: a specific call for airborne predators, another for four-legged predators such as leopards, a third for snakes, and a final one for other primates. Each type of alarm elicits a different behavior. Leopard alarms send the vervets into the top branches of trees, whereas the airborne-predator call causes them to drop like stones into the interior of the tree. The calls seem innate, but the young learn by observation which species of each predator class is dangerous. An infant vervet may deliver an aerial alarm at the sight of a vulture, a stork or even a falling leaf, but eventually comes to ignore everything airborne except the martial eagle.

151. What do honeybees and vervets have in common?
   a. They communicate to ensure their survival.
   b. They gradually evolve into highly complex social organisms.
   c. They avoid predators.
   d. They depend on gesture as a means of communication.

152. What point does the writer make about honeybees?
   a. They do not use sound to communicate.
   b. They are the only animals that employ dance language.
   c. They dance when they find food.
   d. They use the sun as a point of reference for flying.

153. When a honeybee finds food, why does it perform a "waggle dance" for its hive mates?
   a. to show how hungry it is
   b. to show how much food is available
   c. to show how far and in what direction they must fly
   d. to show where the sun is in relation to the hive

154. What is remarkable about the language ability of vervet monkeys?
   a. It is limited to a four-word vocabulary for predators.
   b. They can alert each other to dangers from specific predators.
   c. They rely on sounds rather than gestures.
   d. They are the only animals that can express emotions and social needs.

155. According to the passage, what is true about young vervets?
   a. They cannot initially distinguish predators from animals that pose no threat.
   b. They are born with a highly developed sense of who their predators are.
   c. They instinctively know exactly how and when to use the various alarm calls.
   d. They often confuse the different alarm calls.

Passage 2 is about an exciting development in medicine.

Every day thousands of people are admitted to hospitals because of the malfunction of some vital organ. Because of a dearth of transplantable organs, many of these people will die. It's a well-known fact that the waiting list for patients waiting to receive a heart transplant in the United States has been getting longer every year, and lifesaving livers and kidneys are likewise scarce, as is skin for burn victims and others with wounds that fail to heal.

An exciting new strategy, however, is poised to revolutionize the treatment of patients who need new vital structures: the creation of man-made tissues or organs, known as neo-organs. In one scenario, a tissue engineer injects or places a given molecule, such as a growth factor, into a wound or an organ that requires regeneration. These molecules cause the patient's own cells to migrate into the wound site, turn into the right type of cell and regenerate the tissue. In the second, and more ambitious, procedure, the patient receives cells – either his or her own or those of a donor – that have been harvested previously and incorporated into three-dimensional scaffolds of biodegradable polymers, such as those used to make dissolvable sutures used to close surgical incisions. The entire structure of cells and scaffolding is transplanted into the wound site, where the cells replicate, reorganize and form new tissue. At the same time, the artificial polymers break down, leaving only a completely natural final product in the body – a neo-organ.

While tissue engineering has not yet come of age, a glimpse of the future has already arrived. The creation of some tissues for medical use is already a fact, to a limited extent, in hospitals across the U.S. These groundbreaking applications involve fabricated skin, cartilage, bone, ligament and tendon and make musings of "off-the-shelf" whole organs seem less than far-fetched.

156. What overall problem is alluded to in the first paragraph?

a. The number of patients with diseased hearts has increased dramatically.
b. Not enough people are willing to donate their organs.
c. There is a severe shortage of skin for burn victims.
d. The availability of organs for transplant is severely limited.

157. How many different techniques for growing new tissue are described in the second paragraph?

a. one
b. two
c. three
d. four

158. What is true about one technique?

a. A donor's cells generate healthy tissue when injected into a wound or diseased organ.
b. Diseased organs are replaced with structures of biodegradable polymers.
c. Growth factor molecules reproduce themselves and form healthy tissue in a diseased organ.
d. A patient's cells migrate to the problem area, change form and replicate as healthy tissue.

159. What role is envisioned for biodegradable polymers in the growth of a neo-organ?

a. They will serve as a permanent framework for the fully grown organ.
b. They will eventually dissolve, leaving only natural tissue in the fully grown organ.
c. They will be the material from which the neo-organ is grown.
d. They will be the agent which causes the patient's cells to regenerate.

160. According to the passage, what is true about tissue engineering?

a. It is unlikely that the field will come of age in the foreseeable future.
b. Doctors believe that recent developments are still premature.
c. Some promising applications have already begun to be used.
d. Some people feel the concept is strange and unlikely to catch on.

Passage 3 is about an event that occurred at the start of the American Civil War.

On April 20, 1861, just eight days after South Carolina secessionists fired the first shots on Fort Sumter to begin the Civil War, an enormous apparition descended gently upon a sparsely populated village nine miles west of Unionville, South Carolina. A cautious, well-armed group of men carefully ventured out to the open field where the 50-foot-high monstrosity had landed. As they neared it, a young man sporting a tall silk hat and formal Prince Albert coat leapt out of the attached basket, waving frantically. The man, who identified himself as Thaddeus Sobieski Constantine Lowe, told the incredulous crowd that he had just completed an aerial journey from Cincinnati, Ohio – more than 500 miles away – in just nine hours. The purpose of the trip, he explained, was to test the nature of atmospheric wind currents before embarking on a much grander scheme: the crossing of the Atlantic Ocean to Europe by way of passenger balloon. The rural crowd was not concerned with the merits of Lowe's scientific quest. He was quickly branded a Yankee spy, and only through a combination of quick talking and good luck did he escape bodily harm and incarceration. He was allowed to gather up his contraption and transport it in a wagon train to Columbia, the state capital. There, his reputation as an aerialist was well enough known to secure his return to the North.

An unexpected side effect of Lowe's journey was the insight it gave him into conditions in the South on the eve of the Civil War. Military encampments were clustered near rail junctions, with volunteers mustering for the coming conflict. Train cars loaded with Confederate regiments were heading northward, and the tension in the air was palpable to the young aeronaut. Upon returning to Ohio, Lowe turned to one of his financial supporters, an influential newspaper editor who had originally agreed to sponsor the transatlantic balloon flight. Lowe persuaded him to abandon that plan and instead write a letter to U.S. Treasury Secretary Salmon P. Chase, suggesting that the Federal government establish a balloon corps under Lowe's command to provide aerial reconnaissance for Northern armies.

161. Why did Lowe embark on his aerial journey?
   a. as a test run for a future transatlantic flight
   b. to gather military information for the North
   c. to see how far his balloon could fly
   d. in hopes of making it all the way across the Atlantic

162. How did the villagers greet Lowe?
   a. with mild curiosity
   b. with justifiable mistrust
   c. with open aggression
   d. with concerns about his sanity

163. What does the writer imply that the villagers did with Lowell?
   a. They put him on trial for espionage.
   b. They beat him and put him in jail.
   c. They put him on a steam train headed for Columbia.
   d. They allowed higher authorities to decide his fate.

164. What did the experience make Lowe realize?
   a. that crossing the Atlantic in a balloon was a frivolous idea
   b. that his backers would probably abandon the transatlantic project
   c. that it was his civic duty to enlist in the army as soon as he returned to Ohio
   d. that balloons could be utilized to gather vital military information

165. What was clear to Lowe as he passed over the South?
   a. The Southern army was actively mobilizing for the outbreak of war.
   b. The South was better equipped than the North to fight a war.
   c. He had to do something to stop the Southern troops from advancing.
   d. Southern troops were readying themselves for a massive invasion of the North.

Passage 4 is about garbage and waste disposal.

Americans annually dispose of more than 195 billion kilograms of garbage. And that's just the relatively benign municipal solid waste. Each year American industries belch, pump and dump more than 1.1 billion kilos of really nasty stuff like lead compounds, chromium, ammonia and organic solvents into the air, water and ground – about 400 Olympic poolfuls of toxic waste. The really bad news is that most of the planet's 6 billion people are just beginning to follow in America's trash-filled footsteps. "Either we need to control ourselves or nature will," says one expert. "Garbage needs to become a vile thing of the past."

That may seem impossible, but it's not unprecedented. In nature there is no such thing as waste. What dies or is discarded from one part of an ecosystem nourishes another part. Humanity can emulate nature's garbage-free ways but it will require innovative technology and a big change in attitude. In consumer markets, recycling has already spawned an army of alchemists. Jackets are being made from discarded plastic bottles, briefcases from worn-out tires and belts from beer bottle caps. Even though the U.S. has barely begun to get serious about recycling, about 25% of its 195 billion kilograms of municipal garbage is now salvaged, at least temporarily, for some sort of second life.

A less profligate future can already be glimpsed in Kalundborg, Denmark. There, an unusual place called an eco-industrial park shows how much can be gained by recycling and resource sharing. Within the park, a power company, a pharmaceuticals firm, a wall-board producer and an oil refinery share in the production and use of steam, gas and cooling water. Excess heat warms nearby homes and agricultural greenhouses. One company's waste becomes another's resource. The power plant, for example, sells the sulfur dioxide it scrubs from its smokestacks to the wall-board company, which uses the compound as a raw material. Dozens of similar eco-industrial parks are being developed all over the world.

166. What is the writer's major concern in the first paragraph?
- a. American industry produces a disproportionate amount of toxic waste.
- b. Americans produce too much municipal solid waste.
- c. a boom in global garbage production has only just begun.
- d. nothing is being done to control the amount of waste we produce.

167. What is the eco-industrial park in Kalundborg a good example of?
- a. how a properly functioning ecosystem should work
- b. how companies can work together to become more profitable
- c. how recycling municipal waste can benefit several companies simultaneously
- d. how the by-products of one company can be used as the resources of another

168. What is true of the "army of alchemists" mentioned in the second paragraph?
- a. They would benefit from more innovative technology and a better attitude.
- b. They are finding novel uses for discarded plastic, rubber and other materials.
- c. They have created a highly profitable line of unusual consumer products.
- d. Not enough people take their efforts seriously.

169. What is implied about recycling efforts in the United States?
- a. Innovative technology and a change in attitude has vastly improved the situation.
- b. Some progress has been made, but there is great room for improvement.
- c. Progress has been limited and discouraging.
- d. Only a quarter of the population recycles municipal waste.

170. Which statement best sums up the writer's main idea?
- a. Recycling and resource sharing are the keys to a less wasteful future.
- b. Americans produce more garbage than any nation in the world.
- c. We must strive to produce higher quality products from recycled materials.
- d. Nature will take its revenge if we don't take measures to control garbage.

VOCABULARY CONSOLIDATION 5

VEXING VERBS

A Common collocations – Complete each phrase with a word from the box.

dispel	distill	emancipate	embellish	emulate	install	instill	succumb

1. .... confidence in someone
2. .... the truth (ie,exaggerate)
3. .... water / alcohol
4. .... an enslaved people
5. .... an air-conditioner
6. .... to an illness
7. .... a rumor
8. .... someone you admire

dog-ears	earmarks	grieves	hovers	pinpoints	pores	sidetracks	triumphs

9. a helicopter .... in mid-air
10. a child .... his books
11. an accountant .... over his books
12. an interesting question .... a speaker
13. a committee .... funds
14. good .... over evil
15. a widow .... over her dead husband
16. a mechanic .... an engine problem

B Fine-tuning your knowledge – The numbers below refer to the questions in the Vocabulary section of Practice Test 5. Review the words, then fill each blank with the correct form of the appropriate verb.

113. esteem, assess, access, apportion

a. The millionaire's estate was .... between his two children.
b. Damages from the hurricane have been .... at millions of dollars.
c. His integrity is what she .... most about him.
d. Without his password, you won't be able to .... his computer files.

125. gather, intercept, select, reap

a. Police .... the shipment of drugs as it came across the border.
b. She found it difficult to .... just the right gift for him.
c. An angry crowd of protesters .... outside the Police Station.
d. The peasants toiled for days, ... / .... the harvest.
e. Study hard now and you will .... the benefits in the future.

129. alleviate, recede, succumb, submerge

a. She finds reading fiction a perfect way to .... boredom.
b. The flooded village was .... under three feet of water.
c. She's on a strict diet and has so far not .... to temptation.
d. Middle-aged man: "My hairline is not .... My forehead's growing!"

136. shudder, shimmer, simmer, splinter

a. As the earth began to tremble, she .... with fear.
b. The surface of the sea .... softly in the morning sun.
c. The recipe said to .... the sauce for at least an hour.
d. Car windshields are designed to crack rather than ....

148. laud, taunt, amuse, nurture

a. For children to be well-.................................. , they need love as well as food.
b. The students were .... for their excellent exam results.
c. You could tell from their giggles that the joke had ....them.
d. Children have a bad habit of cruelly .... those who seem different.
e. Friendships do not form by themselves; they must be ....

NOTORIOUS NOUNS

A Amusing associations – Find the word in the box that is suggested by each prompt.

anonymity	enmity	expectations	impairment	impeachment		
imposition	incentive	jolt	promotion	qualms	queries	streaks

1. .... – What psychologists call the gift your parents promise you if you pass the ECPE
2. .... – What your hearing suffers when you turn your speakers up too loud
3. .... – What your parents have that they would just love you to meet
4. .... – What you get when you rub your greasy fingers across a clean window
5. .... – What criminals should have more of so there wouldn't be so much crime
6. .... – What happens to naughty presidents who get caught doing things they shouldn't
7. .... – What you get when you stick a wet finger into an electrical outlet
8. .... – What every celebrity secretly dreams of, especially when plagued by paparazzi
9. .... – What students have when teachers don't explain themselves very well
10. .... – What results when you invite a guest for the weekend and he stays a month
11. .... – What a company owner can never hope to get
12. .... – What you'll never find between true friends

B Fine-tuning your knowledge – The numbers below refer to the questions in the Vocabulary section of Practice Test 5. After reviewing the words, fill in the blanks with the appropriate words.

126. manifestations, rudiments, ambiguities, supplements

a. The politician's speech was full of exaggerations and ....
b. Blurred vision and dizziness are the major .... of the condition.
c. Once you learn the .... of the job, you'll feel more at ease.
d. Some doctors do not believe in vitamin ....

140. ancestor, successor, forerunner, predecessor

a. The .... of the laptop computer was a machine the size of a room.
b. He claims that his ....s came to America in the mid-1600s.
c. Her job was made easier as her .... had been very well-organized.
d. If the President dies in office, the Vice-President is his automatic ....

141. contract, symphony, treaty, truce

a. A .... is a long, complex musical composition.
b. A .... is, in effect, a formal written agreement (or ....) between two or more countries. In the case of a peace .... , the warring nations first declare a .... and then spend months negotiating the terms of peace.

142. expenditure, suspension, supposition, expansion

a. The policeman appealed his .... , saying he had done nothing wrong.
b. The plan requires a huge .... of time and money.
c. The energetic new company has plans for rapid ....
d. What you've said is pure .... Come back when you have proof.
e. The car rides much better now that they've had the .... system fixed.

149. oversight, overview, outlook, omission

a. The exhibit was a fascinating .... of the history of feminism.
b. She's fun to be with as she has such a cheerful .... on life.
c. They claimed that the .... of his name from the list was an innocent ....

ADDLING ADJECTIVES

A Automatic associations – Complete each phrase with a word from the box.

abundant	casual	destitute	inedible	resistant	ruthless	shrill	subordinate

1. .... dictators
2. .... meals
3. .... voices
4. .... clauses
5. .... beggars
6. .... resources
7. .... clothes
8. .... bacteria

B Fine-tuning your knowledge – The numbers below refer to the questions in the Vocabulary section of Practice Test 5. After reviewing the words, fill in the blanks with the appropriate words.

111. casual / eventual / mutual / imperial

a. About all they have in common is a strong .... dislike of each other.
b. To the .... observer, they seemed like a happily married couple.
c. Years of hard work led to his .... promotion to the firm's top post.
d. Visitors to the Palace of Versailles are awed by its .... splendor.

120. sluggish / witless / homesick / mediocre

a. It's natural for first-year university students to feel a bit ....
b. If someone says your work is .... , it isn't a compliment.
c. After two years of .... performance, the firm is facing bankruptcy.
d. He regrets having made such a .... remark. He's not usually so foolish.

123. irresistible / inedible / indelible / illegible

a. The earthquake left an .... impression on all who lived through it.
b. Some of the dishes they serve at that restaurant are virtually ....
c. She types her essays as her teachers find her handwriting totally ....
d. The cake proved to be an .... temptation for the poor dieter.

127. ruthless / complacent / vagrant / shrill

a. The ancient marketplace was frequented by .... beggars.
b. The burglars stopped dead when they heard the policeman's .... whistle.
c. The hard-driving director ran the business with .... efficiency.
d. How can you be so .... ? Doesn't it bother you that you're unemployed?

131. resistant / appreciative / tolerant / receptive

a. He's not at all .... of people from different cultural backgrounds.
b. She thanked me profusely and was most .... of my help.
c. He's very open-minded and .... to criticism.
d. Conservative people are, by definition, ... to change.

138. destitute / abundant / luxuriant / affluent

a. Fossil fuels no longer exist in .... quantity.
b. He was homeless and ...., like so many in the .... capital city.
c. The model was famous for her .... waist-long hair.
d. The island is covered in .... / .... vegetation.

139. substantial / subordinate / subdued / subjective

a. The old house was in need of .... remodeling.
b. You're rather .... today. Is anything wrong?
c. Health is the most important thing in life. Everything else is .... to it.
d. Taste in music is a highly .... matter.

AUDACIOUS ADVERBS

Fine-tuning your knowledge – The numbers below refer to the questions in the Vocabulary section of Practice Test 5. After reviewing the words, fill in the blanks with the appropriate words.

116.	**gratefully**	a. Not wanting him to get angry, they .... avoided mentioning his ex-wife's wedding.
	tactfully	b. "How dare you accuse me of lying," she said ....
	resentfully	c. "How can I ever repay your kindness?" she said ....
	respectively	d. Jim and Tim are 10 and 12 years old ....
135.	**elegantly**	a. It's a mystery how he spends so .... on his limited salary.
	expectantly	b. The dispute was settled .... when both sides agreed to compromise.
	extravagantly	c. She's a stunning woman who is always tastefully and .... dressed.
	equitably	d. The dog wagged his tail .... , knowing it was time to be fed.
145.	**disparagingly**	a. I haven't seen them together for months. .... they've separated.
	subsequently	b. The voters in this area have always been .... Republican.
	predominantly	c. She must really dislike him. I've never heard her speak so .... before.
	apparently	d. A loan kept the company afloat for a while, but .... it went bankrupt.

PRICKLY PREPOSITIONAL PHRASES

Fine-tuning your knowledge – The numbers below refer to the questions in the Vocabulary section of Practice Test 5. After reviewing the words, fill in the blanks with the appropriate words.

144.	**in dispute**	a. Which country has rights to the oil on the border is still ....
	into disrepute	b. John is a sensitive boy; .... , Tim, his twin, is very self-centered.
	in conflict	c. Creating a scandal is the quickest way for a politician to fall ....
	in contrast	d. He is in the awkward position of often being .... with his boss.
146.	**in brief**	a. Is there anything .... you'd like to watch tonight?
	in principle	b. He finds long newscasts boring; he'd rather listen to the news ....
	in succession	c. .... I agree with you, but in practice I don't think the plan will work.
	in particular	d. The political party has won three elections ....
147.	**in good standing**	a. To be a club member .... you must pay your annual dues.
	in (one's) prime	b. Always an organizer, she was right .... running the campaign.
	in (one's) element	c. .... she could play five straight sets of tennis, but not anymore!
	in bloom	d. She's always wanted to visit Holland when the tulips are ....
150.	**on behalf of**	a. What good is success if it comes .... your family or your health?
	in tandem with	b. .... all the staff, I'd like to thank you for your dedicated service.
	on account of	c. The scientist wrote the article .... one of his research associates.
	at the expense of	d. They were late for the concert .... a hold-up on the expressway.

Practice Test 6

Writing

(30 minutes)

Write on one of the topics given below. If you write about something else, your paper will not be graded. If you do not understand the topics, ask the examiner to explain or translate them. You will be graded on the clarity of your writing and the linguistic range and accuracy you show. Write $1\frac{1}{2}$ to 2 pages. You may make any corrections or other changes in the body of the composition.

TOPICS

1. Despite stunning medical advances in the past century, the availability of quality treatment for all members of society has yet to be achieved. Public health care exists in many countries, but all too often quality care goes only to those who can pay for it privately. If you could change the public health care system in your country, what **two** aspects would you choose as your top priorities and what changes would you make?

2. Much has been written about parents who push their children to succeed in sports, music or other areas from a very young age. Discuss the positive and negative effects that parents may have on their children when they try to push them in a certain direction.

For help in writing these compositions, see *Writing Tutorial*, pages 200–201.

Listening Comprehension Test

(35–40 minutes)

This part of the examination is a listening test that will assess your understanding of spoken English. The listening test has three parts. There are 50 questions. Mark all your answers on the separate answer sheet. Do not make any stray marks on the answer sheet. If you change your mind about an answer, erase your first answer completely.

Part I – In this part of the test, you will hear a short conversation. From the three answer choices given, choose the answer which means the same thing as you hear, or that is true based on what you hear.

For problems 1–17, mark your answers on the separate answer sheet. No problem can be repeated. Please listen carefully. Do you have any questions?

1. a. He likes Dan, but she doesn't.
   b. Neither of them has seen Dan recently.
   c. Neither of them think very much of Dan.

2. a. She doesn't think there's a problem.
   b. She thinks he's being rude to her.
   c. She's sorry for what she's done.

3. a. He's been dieting a long time.
   b. He's been dieting a short time.
   c. He needs to change his diet.

4. a. She's sorry she made him wash the dishes.
   b. She thinks he should have helped clean up.
   c. She's mad because he didn't cook.

5. a. She wanted him to confirm something.
   b. She didn't want to tell Mary something.
   c. She wanted him to tell Sue something.

6. a. He wishes he weren't so bored.
   b. He's having trouble solving a problem.
   c. He doesn't feel very well.

7. a. He would rather she did it for him.
   b. He can't find the user's manual.
   c. He'd like them to do it together.

8. a. They'll feel better if they take deep breaths.
   b. They both need a break from studying.
   c. They'll continue studying tomorrow.

9. a. They have the same opinion of Larry.
   b. She thinks he should be more like Larry.
   c. She thinks his explanation isn't accurate.

10. a. She suggests they discuss their differences.
    b. She thinks he should help Fran clean up.
    c. She thinks they both need some fresh air.

11. a. She's not sure they have the number.
    b. He's worried about the children being away.
    c. The children will call if there's a problem.

12. a. They forgot to bring the camera.
    b. They didn't bring their camera with them.
    c. They wish they had bought a new camera.

13. a. Her friends are too busy to go out.
    b. None of her friends are married.
    c. She wants to go out this evening.

14. a. He's almost finished with the letter.
    b. He didn't write the letter on time.
    c. He didn't have time to write the letter.

15. a. He wants her to buy him a coat.
    b. His coat needs to be cleaned.
    c. He wants her to dry out his coat.

16. a. Al's job may be in danger.
    b. Al needs to lose weight.
    c. Al's looking for a new job.

17. a. He'll go immediately.
    b. He'll go only if it's important.
    c. The boss is angry with him.

PART II – In this part of the test, you will hear a question. From the three answer choices given, choose the one which best answers the question.

For problems **18–35**, mark your answers on the separate answer sheet. No problem can be repeated. Please listen carefully. Do you have any questions?

18. a. Shall we order some fries, then?
b. I'm just worried about you.
c. I do, too.

19. a. You're right. I'm glad we did.
b. Perhaps, but it's too late now.
c. I agree. We can't really afford it.

20. a. Was anyone hurt?
b. There's no need to be embarrassed.
c. Well, some of us have to work tomorrow.

21. a. I can't remember. It was a while ago.
b. Can I open my eyes now?
c. Yes, it's breathtaking.

22. a. You had a lot to drink last night.
b. She must be jealous.
c. She's always liked clean-shaven men.

23. a. Better than most people, I'd say.
b. We used to be next-door neighbors.
c. It wasn't me. I wonder who told him.

24. a. I did, indeed. It was quite a performance.
b. I've never felt calmer in my life.
c. Actually, it was only drizzling at the time.

25. a. You're right. It's mine.
b. I was afraid you'd be mad at me.
c. Who told you I was the owner?

26. a. Three hundred dollars at least.
b. Less than three weeks.
c. If you're lucky, you'll get $500 for it.

27. a. Mad as a hatter, if you ask me.
b. None whatsoever.
c. Not anymore.

28. a. I'll speed up after I learn the ropes.
b. No, but there was an accident on the bridge.
c. Yes, it was bumper to bumper for miles.

29. a. Sorry, I can't see that far.
b. Ask me again later.
c. I'm not sure. He should've called by now.

30. a. Really? That was fast.
b. I had no idea she was ill.
c. What's bugging her now?

31. a. Sorry, I've got a bad back.
b. Pick you up at 8.
c. Glad I could help out.

32. a. Why do you always get to choose?
b. New Delhi's the capital, isn't it?
c. Exactly what I was thinking.

33. a. No, he worked late and went straight home
b. Yes, but luckily it wasn't serious.
c. I asked him, but he wasn't sure.

34. a. Sorry, I'm going away this weekend.
b. Why wait? Let's do it now.
c. I'd rather not wait that long.

35. a. She didn't invite me.
b. Yes, I'm sure she was there.
c. She's looking forward to it.

PART III – In this part, you will hear three short segments from a radio program. The program is called 'Learning from the Experts.' Each talk lasts about two minutes. As you listen, you may want to take notes to help you remember information given in the talk. After each talk, you will be asked some questions about what was said. From the three answer choices given, you should choose the one which best answers the question according to the information you heard.

Remember, no problems can be repeated. For problems **36–50**, mark your answers on the separate answer sheet. Do you have any questions?

SEGMENT 1

36. Why did the U.S. Air Force establish a chimpanzee colony at Holloman Air Force Base?
  a. To see how long chimps could stay conscious in a decompression chamber
  b. To test the effects of several aspects of space flight
  c. To see if they could be trained to perform tasks while weightless

37. What is true about the experience of the first chimp to be sent into space?
  a. The flight was a brilliant success.
  b. The flight did not go as smoothly as planned.
  c. Shepherd, America's first astronaut, was inspired by the chimp's bravery.

38. What unexpected problem did Enos encounter when he was sent into orbit?
  a. The capsule rolled out of control and stayed in orbit much longer than expected.
  b. The system malfunctioned, causing the chimp to respond incorrectly to avoid being shocked.
  c. The chimp received electrical shocks for performing correct responses.

39. What became of the chimps in the 1960s and '70s?
  a. They continued to be used in research that exposed them to great physical hardship.
  b. They appeared in parades and were celebrated as heroes along with the astronauts.
  c. They were used in research which was not as physically demanding.

40. What is true of the chimps today?
  a. They have been relocated to a special facility to ensure their humane treatment.
  b. After a long legal battle, the US government has had to release them back into the wild.
  c. Despite rising protest, they are still being used in biomedical research.

SEGMENT 2

41. What recent finding has encouraged scientists at the University of California?
  a. Memory loss is an inescapable part of growing old.
  b. Certain brain cells in rhesus monkeys shrink and stop functioning as the monkeys age.
  c. Gene therapy can help restore function to aging brain cells in rhesus monkeys.

42. In what part of the brain did the researchers discover atrophied brain cells?
  a. On the surface of the brain
  b. In communication channels and signal receptors
  c. At the base of the forebrain

43. How did the researchers restore cell activity in the affected area?
  a. They implanted cells that could produce a protein that stimulates nerve growth.
  b. They injected a substance called nerve growth factor into the affected area.
  c. They removed the atrophied cells, fixed the genetic fault and reinserted them.

44. What do researchers hope for the future?
  a. That their findings will soon lead them to a complete cure for Alzheimer's disease
  b. That gene therapy will someday be used to prolong life indefinitely
  c. That similar procedures will someday be applied to human brain cells

45. What opinion do some neurobiologists have about the findings?
  a. They doubt the findings because they feel they are not applicable to humans.
  b. Despite certain reservations, they feel the research is significant.
  c. They claim it is virtually impossible to reverse the natural aging process.

SEGMENT 3

46. What was the surprising finding that the study revealed?
    a. Men actually do more housework than women nowadays.
    b. Considerably less housework is being done than in the 1960s.
    c. Women still do much more housework than men do.

47. What did the study reveal about American men?
    a. They do more housework than both Japanese and Swedish men.
    b. They do less housework than Swedes, but more than Japanese.
    c. They ranked higher than Japanese men, but lower than Swedes.

48. What is responsible for the decrease in housework?
    a. Both men and women are doing more paid work outside the home.
    b. Men who are well paid feel they should not have to do so much housework.
    c. Women who work feel their spouses should do an equal share of the housework.

49. What does the researcher's anecdote about the couple in Chicago show?
    a. That neither males nor females are overly fanatic about doing housework
    b. That women often don't give their men enough credit for the work they do
    c. That many men had their consciousness raised by women friends in the 1970s

50. What shift in society's priorities did another recent study uncover?
    a. People are beginning to rebel against society's putting too many demands on their time.
    b. People are choosing to work harder rather than spend time with their children.
    c. People are opting for more quality time with their children than they did in the 1980s.

Grammar – Cloze – Vocabulary – Reading

(75 minutes)

This part of the examination contains 120 problems, numbered **51–170**. There are 40 grammar, 20 cloze, 40 vocabulary and 20 reading comprehension problems. The examiner will not explain any test problems. If you do not understand how to do the problems, raise your hand and a proctor will explain the examples to you.

Do not spend too much time on any one problem. Each problem counts the same. If you do not know the answer to a problem, you may make a reasonable guess. Each problem has only one correct answer. Work fast but carefully. You have 75 minutes to answer all 120 problems.

GRAMMAR

51. He said he would be able to finish the report by Monday, but only ..... his plans for the weekend.
- a. should he cancel
- b. to cancel
- c. were he to cancel
- d. if he'll cancel

52. He's hoping to qualify for the Olympics, but the competition is ..... his chances are slim.
- a. such that
- b. so
- c. too much of it so
- d. enough that

53. The witness saw two men with guns ..... out of the bank.
- a. to have run
- b. who running
- c. run
- d. to run

54. Is there anyone you would like me to contact ..... an emergency?
- a. in care of
- b. in spite of
- c. in the case of
- d. in the event of

55. He believes ..... whatever he can to protect the environment.
- a. to do
- b. that he do
- c. in doing
- d. to doing

56. ..... told you the mayor is going to run for re-election is dead wrong.
- a. Whomever
- b. Who
- c. The person who
- d. One who

57. She doesn't seem ..... happy working for her new boss.
- a. as she is
- b. that she is
- c. to be
- d. being

58. It's crucial that we arrive on time, so we'd better leave now ..... miss the traffic.
- a. that we
- b. in order that
- c. because we
- d. so as to

59. It is ..... all of us to begin using energy-efficient electrical appliances
- a. above
- b. up to
- c. beyond
- d. over

60. ..... the company not gone bankrupt, she would still be working there today.
- a. Should
- b. If
- c. Were
- d. Had

61. ..... , the boss is not happy about the huge drop in sales last quarter.
- a. Saying it suffices
- b. Being sufficient
- c. Sufficiently said
- d. Suffice it to say

62. I've seen this happen to her before: ..... , the more anxious she becomes.
- a. the more she studies
- b. as much as she studies
- c. while studying more
- d. even though studying more

Practice Test 6

63. Everyone was on time apart from Sarah, who has a habit ..... late.
    a. of being
    b. to be
    c. that is
    d. being

64. From the look of those dark clouds on the horizon, I'd say we're ..... a really bad storm.
    a. up for
    b. in for
    c. down to
    d. about to

65. It's important that we all cultivate friends ..... we can confide in.
    a. so
    b. with whom
    c. that
    d. in whom

66. He's having ..... someone he can trust enough to go into business with.
    a. difficulty to find
    b. difficulty finding
    c. it difficult to find
    d. it difficult finding

67. ..... she was a child, she has been fascinated by historical novels.
    a. Even when
    b. Even though
    c. Ever since
    d. Ever after

68. Jason said they were expecting somewhere ..... 15 and 20 people to attend the party.
    a. from
    b. among
    c. around
    d. between

69. He was not allowed in the restaurant because he was not ..... attired.
    a. in a suit
    b. suitable
    c. suiting
    d. suitably

70. We were hoping he'd go camping with us this weekend, but unfortunately, he's decided ..... .
    a. that he doesn't go
    b. not to go
    c. to not going
    d. he not goes

71. The package ..... this morning, but I'm not sure that it's been done yet.
    a. supposed to send
    b. should have sent
    c. must have been
    d. was to have been sent

72. I know commuting must seem difficult now, but I'm sure you'll ..... it in due time.
    a. become use to
    b. get used to it
    c. accustom to
    d. have use for it

73. She enjoys his company as he's an incredibly ..... human being.
    a. considered
    b. considerate
    c. considerable
    d. considering

74. I have ..... that you will thoroughly enjoy your trip to Hawaii.
    a. no doubts whatsoever
    b. none at all doubts
    c. no doubts not at all
    d. not even single doubt

75. Meteorologists predict that this summer will be the warmest ..... in years.
    a. than we have had
    b. that it has had
    c. that we have had
    d. than it will be

76. I wonder what's ..... her to put her in such an awful mood.
    a. got into
    b. become of
    c. wrong of
    d. troubling about

77. Both children are good students, but everyone says Stan's ..... the two.
    a. more intelligent than
    b. the most intelligent of
    c. the more intelligent than
    d. the more intelligent of

78. ..... too late to take a bus, she called a taxi instead.
    a. It being
    b. Being
    c. As was
    d. It was

79. Never having been to Japan before, ... going in the coming year.
    a. she's planning on
    b. but she's planning to
    c. so her plan is
    d. which is why she plans

80. A recent blog post, ... on a popular science website, said the study had serious flaws.
    a. appeared
    b. which it appeared
    c. it appeared
    d. appearing

81. If you're at a loose end tonight, ... come over to my house and we'll watch a movie?
    a. would maybe you like to
    b. why not
    c. why you don't
    d. how about

82. John ..... next summer on an archeological dig in Egypt.
    a. wishes he had spent
    b. hopes that he could
    c. wishes that he spends
    d. is hoping to spend

83. According to the doctor, the child's diet ..... calcium and iron.
    a. has a serious lack from
    b. lacks seriously of
    c. has serious lack of
    d. is seriously lacking in

84. There's something about him that reminds me ..... my younger brother.
    a. about
    b. for
    c. of
    d. to

85. ..... you say, he's made his decision and has no intention of changing it.
    a. However
    b. No matter what
    c. Nevertheless
    d. Not even if

86. They spent the morning ..... the ruins of the medieval castle.
    a. in order to explore
    b. to explore
    c. exploring
    d. having explored

87. As she wasn't in the mood to cook last night, she decided to ..... .
    a. get something delivered
    b. get something to deliver
    c. have delivered something
    d. have something to deliver

88. I would have visited the Grand Canyon ..... more time at my disposal.
    a. if I have had
    b. if only have I had
    c. had I had
    d. would I have

89. A man who is truly set in his ways, Oliver is probably the most stubborn man that ..... .
    a. I have to meet yet
    b. I have met ever since
    c. I still haven't met
    d. I will ever get to meet

90. The volume on the TV was turned up so loud that ..... think.
    a. I could hardly hear myself
    b. not even I could hear me
    c. I couldn't even hear me
    d. no one could hear myself

CLOZE

Passage 1 is about fear.

Fear is the product of a nervous system evolved to detect danger and produce rapid protective responses automatically. The brain is programmed to respond to routine dangers, ...(91).... it must also learn about new dangers quickly. If people are fortunate enough to ....(92).... a potentially fatal experience, the defense system learns ....(93).... the experience ....(94).... help us avoid similar threats in the future.

Recently, there has been tremendous interest in finding out exactly where the "fear pathways" ....(95).... in the brain, ...(96).... we learn rapidly about fearful events and objects, and how problems with the fear pathways can ....(97).... to common psychological conditions such as anxiety, panic attacks, phobias and obsessive-compulsive disorder. In the past, a region deep inside the brain known as the limbic system ....(98).... suggested to be where emotions and emotional learning were based. More ....(99).... , as more sensitive brain-scanning ....(100).... have been developed, the perception and processing of fear has been localized to a specific area of the limbic system called the amygdala.

91. a. which b. but c. then d. since

92. a. live b. witness c. have d. survive

93. a. about b. if c. from d. that

94. a. to b. and c. can d. which

95. a. locate b. lie c. find d. happen

96. a. that b. when c. how d. and

97. a. cause b. result c. lead d. respond

98. a. was b. has c. they d. and

99. a. recently b. importantly c. over d. often

100. a. technicalities b. technology c. technicians d. techniques

---

Passage 2 is about surviving traumatic events.

Though it may be difficult for the survivors of a plane crash or mass shooting to "look on the bright side," it appears that those who do actually recover best and grow the most as a result of the tragedy. Researchers interviewed the survivors of three traumatic events – a tornado, a plane crash and a mass shooting – a few weeks and then three years after the events ....(101)..... . Those survivors ....(102).... to find something good that came out ....(103).... the experience soon after it happened – for example, those who said, "It made me realize how much I loved my family" or "I decided life was too short not to follow my dreams" – had made a better ....(104).... by the time of the follow-up interview. People who felt they were going to die during the disaster were especially ....(105).... to report personal growth as a result of the experience. Surprisingly, so too ....(106).... survivors who had had prior mental health problems.

According to the lead researcher, the study shows that those ....(107).... lives are in the worst shape may have the ....(108).... to gain from traumatic experience. He also noted that survivors who were inhabitants of small towns ....(109).... to fare better than survivors who lived in big cities, perhaps ....(110).... to the social and material support such towns could offer.

101. a. became b. arrived c. occurred d. placed

102. a. managed b. failing c. able d. tried

103. a. with b. of c. from d. for

104. a. recovery b. growth c. progress d. improvement

105. a. unable b. capable c. bound d. likely

106. a. do b. were c. had d. will

107. a. with b. having c. whose d. that

108. a. least b. best c. more d. most

109. a. tended b. used c. inclined d. prone

110. a. caused b. owing c. because d. leading

VOCABULARY

111. The proposal was so ..... that it was immediately rejected.
   a. prudent
   b. viable
   c. far-fetched
   d. sensible

112. The mother cried out ..... when she realized that her child was lost in the crowd.
   a. voraciously
   b. hectically
   c. frantically
   d. exuberantly

113. She finds it difficult to read magazines printed on ..... paper.
   a. glaring
   b. glowing
   c. glossy
   d. gummy

114. In the aftermath of the crash, charges of negligence were ..... against the airline.
   a. flattered
   b. leveled
   c. hurled
   d. launched

115. She dislikes watching foreign films that have been ..... into English.
   a. transferred
   b. dubbed
   c. conveyed
   d. interacted

116. The gunshot victim was in need of an immediate blood ..... .
   a. transition
   b. transplant
   c. transfusion
   d. transmission

117. I'd have no problem lending you money if I weren't so ..... .
   a. past my prime
   b. wet behind the ears
   c. strapped for cash
   d. in the money

118. He seems to have an ..... talent for getting himself into trouble.
   a. arbitrary
   b. accelerated
   c. incoherent
   d. innate

119. The amateur inventor's garage was full of clever but ultimately useless ..... .
   a. deceptions
   b. contractions
   c. contraptions
   d. apparitions

120. It was a costly mistake which the boss was not willing to ..... over.
   a. fret
   b. gloss
   c. look
   d. lose sleep

121. The museum's latest ..... was a rare series of charcoal sketches by Van Gogh.
   a. requisition
   b. acquisition
   c. imposition
   d. inquisition

122. The doctors said it would take months for him to ..... from the delicate brain operation.
   a. reciprocate
   b. renovate
   c. recapitulate
   d. recuperate

123. The new laundry ..... contains a stain remover as well as a fabric softener.
   a. deterrent
   b. detergent
   c. deference
   d. descendant

124. As he walked down the street, his hat was blown off by a sudden ..... of wind.
   a. gust
   b. gasp
   c. gush
   d. gulp

125. Science and technology made ..... advances in the 20th century.
 a. unobtrusive
 b. unprecedented
 c. unmentionable
 d. unbearable

126. In divorce cases, the judge must decide which parent will be given ..... of the children.
 a. responsibility
 b. possession
 c. adoption
 d. custody

127. The boy felt awed in the ..... of the eminent Nobel Prize laureate.
 a. appearance
 b. name
 c. presence
 d. attendance

128. Mary is ..... employed as a computer programmer for a local manufacturer.
 a. currently
 b. recently
 c. lately
 d. formerly

129. In preparation for her move, she spent the weekend ..... the attic.
 a. phasing out
 b. throwing out
 c. clearing out
 d. putting out

130. The young man bears a(n) ..... resemblance to his maternal grandfather.
 a. oppressive
 b. immaculate
 c. vicious
 d. striking

131. The school lunch program is backed by ..... from the federal government.
 a. subsidiaries
 b. subsistence
 c. funding
 d. fundamentals

132. The executive was dismissed for ..... the terms of his contract.
 a. fracturing
 b. upholding
 c. divulging
 d. breaching

133. The child ..... illness to get out of taking the history test.
 a. forged
 b. feigned
 c. rehearsed
 d. manifested

134. She watches her weight but enjoys ..... a pizza now and then.
 a. indulging in
 b. gnawing on
 c. feeding on
 d. catering to

135. Wise investors prefer ..... their assets to investing all their money in a single stock.
 a. deferring
 b. diverting
 c. differentiating
 d. diversifying

136. Packaged breads contain additives that help ..... the growth of mold.
 a. accelerate
 b. retard
 c. defy
 d. promote

137. If you want to get ahead in life, you must be assertive and ..... .
 a. kill two birds with one stone
 b. beat around the bush
 c. hit the sack
 d. take the bull by the horns

138. If diplomatic efforts fail, the government may be forced to ..... military intervention.
 a. resort to
 b. appeal to
 c. refer to
 d. refrain from

139. The car rides so ...... that you are barely aware of its motion.
- a. firmly
- b. gracefully
- c. smoothly
- d. efficiently

140. The incident ..... a series of angry protests around the country.
- a. triggered
- b. liberated
- c. duplicated
- d. truncated

141. After years of hard use, our living room furniture is not as ..... as it used to be.
- a. flimsy
- b. sturdy
- c. filthy
- d. poised

142. The welfare of her children takes ..... over all of her other concerns.
- a. effect
- b. offense
- c. exception
- d. precedence

143. Those two must have ..... as they've disliked each other from the very start.
- a. got out of bed on the wrong side
- b. got off on the wrong foot
- c. let the cat out of the bag
- d. been slow on the uptake

144. The region is one of the most ..... populated in the world.
- a. spaciously
- b. sparingly
- c. sparsely
- d. spuriously

145. A fire in the baggage compartment caused a ..... in the plane's electrical system.
- a. malfunction
- b. malformation
- c. miscarriage
- d. misconception

146. The reputable gallery ..... paintings by early 20th-century women artists.
- a. settles for
- b. settles on
- c. deals in
- d. deals out

147. She may be over eighty, but there is still a youthful ..... in her eye.
- a. freckle
- b. speckle
- c. sparkle
- d. trickle

148. We found the excess of violence in the film highly ..... .
- a. defensive
- b. repentant
- c. exceptional
- d. objectionable

149. The television station was ..... with complaints after airing the controversial show.
- a. deluged
- b. overcome
- c. innovated
- d. bombed

150. The truth is sometimes cruel and extremely hard to ..... .
- a. grind
- b. chew
- c. swallow
- d. consume

READING

Passage 1 is about autism.

Autism is a brain disorder that prevents individuals from properly understanding what they sense. This leads to problems forming normal social relationships and often leads to inappropriate responses to people or events. The underlying cause of autism is not well understood, but new light has recently been shed by a brain imaging study of a pair of identical twins who differed only in the severity of their autistic symptoms: one suffered from severe autism and the other was mildly autistic, suffering from behavioral and communication problems associated with autism. Using a technique called magnetic resonance imaging (MRI), researchers looked at the sizes of different regions of the brain. When they compared the twins, they found that the severely affected twin had a markedly smaller hippocampus, amygdala and caudate nucleus, regions involved with emotional judgments, learning and memory. Parts of the cerebral cortex involved with attention were also smaller in the severely autistic twin. But both twins also differed from normal children. They had smaller frontal lobes (the area responsible for planning, organization and problem solving) and a smaller superior temporal gyrus, which is involved with language.

The results show two levels of defect. One level separates the twins and seems to underlie the more traditionally defined severe autistic symptoms. The other differentiates the twins from other children, suggesting that the same genetic defects that cause severe autism can cause a milder, broader form of the disease. The fact that genetically identical twins suffer different symptoms shows that autism is more than just a genetic defect. In fact, there were complications at the birth of the twins: the severely autistic twin suffered from cerebral hemorrhaging and respiratory defects which may have caused some of the more severe brain damage.

A larger-scale follow-up study is planned which should show whether the same brain regions are defective in other autistic children, and whether there are genetically related defects in a particular pathway which cause more minor symptoms in non-autistic siblings.

151. According to the passage, what is true about autism?
   a. It always affects identical twins in exactly the way.
   b. It can be detected at birth with the aid of brain imaging studies.
   c. It affects a person's ability to communicate and form normal relationships.
   d. It is a psychological problem that can be cured with extensive psychotherapy.

152. How did researchers determine the differences between the two boys?
   a. They observed the boys' behavior.
   b. They compared images of different regions of the boys' brains.
   c. They measured the strength of the magnet field in different areas of the boys' brains.
   d. They used an imaging technique to study the genetic differences between the two boys.

153. According to the passage, how do normal children differ from autistic children?
   a. They have larger frontal lobes.
   b. They have a much smaller hippocampus.
   c. They have no genetic defects.
   d. They have neither behavioral nor communication problems.

154. What factor accounted for the greater severity of autism in one of the children?
   a. problems that occurred during the child's birth
   b. a difference in the children's genetic make-up
   c. enlargement of certain areas of the child's brain
   d. the child's inability to breathe

155. What does the twin study suggest about autism?
   a. It is now well understood.
   b. It is more prevalent among identical twins than in other children.
   c. It may be the result of both brain damage and genetic abnormalities.
   d. It will usually express itself more severely in one twin.

Passage 2 is about plants in the *Genlisea* family.

Botanical carnivores like the Venus fly-trap restrict their diets to insects, spiders, crustaceans and similar small-fry. These plants are instantly revealed as meat-eaters by the traps they grow to catch their prey. But one group has always puzzled botanists: members of the genus *Genlisea* grow what appear to be traps, but never seem to catch anything. *Genlisea* seem to prefer living in sand or in rocky outcrops – environments poor in nutrients such as nitrogen. This too suggests they are carnivorous. The ability to get nutrients from animals rather than soil gives a plant a competitive advantage in a barren environment, and known insectivores often inhabit such nitrogen-poor habitats.

Genlisea's so-called traps are modified underground leaves. These are hollow, Y-shaped cylinders with a diameter of about 0.2 mm. The openings to the cylinders have inward-pointing hairs, making it easy to enter them but difficult to leave – a common feature of traps in insectivorous plants. Traps this size, though, would not catch many insects. So researchers wondered if perhaps they were being laid for much smaller animals, single-celled protozoa, instead. To find out, they presented some fast-swimming protozoa called ciliates with three species of *Genlisea*, together with a range of other plants that share the habitat of each of the *Genlisea* in question. The ciliates overwhelmingly preferred to swim towards the *Genlisea*, suggesting that the traps were releasing some sort of chemical lure.

But merely being attractive to protozoa does not prove the *Genlisea* is eating them, so researchers designed a follow-up experiment involving ciliates that had been "labeled" with a radioactive isotope of sulfur. Two days after the ciliates had swum into a *Genlisea*'s trap, the sulfur started turning up in the rest of the plant, showing that it and, by inference, other nutrients had been absorbed from the hapless ciliates. Perhaps the most telling evidence of all, however, comes from the researchers' experience in growing the plants. When they started, they found that *Genlisea* are obstinate pot plants. But add ciliates to the soil and there is no stopping them.

156. What has always puzzled botanists about members of the genus *Genlisea* is that the plants ...
- a. are clearly carnivorous.
- b. never seem to catch anything in their leaves.
- c. resemble Venus fly-traps in every detail.
- d. are able to grow in nitrogen-poor soil.

157. How do *Genlisea* differ from other botanical insectivores?
- a. They prefer living in sandy or rocky habitats that are poor in nitrogen.
- b. They prey on insects, spiders and other small animals.
- c. They trap their victims with the aid of modified leaves.
- d. They feed on much smaller, one-celled prey.

158. According to the writer, how does the *Genlisea* attract their prey?
- a. by modifying their leaves
- b. by opening and closing their hollow, Y-shaped cylinders
- c. by emitting a certain substance
- d. by moving the inward-pointing hairs in their traps

159. What did scientists realize when they began to grow the plants?
- a. that ciliates reproduce wildly in the presence of *Genlisea*.
- b. that *Genlisea* cannot be grown under laboratory conditions.
- c. that ciliates grow strong and healthy when they are added to soil.
- d. that *Genlisea* thrive in the presence of ciliates.

160. Why did scientists "label" the ciliates with a radioactive isotope of sulfur?
- a. to see if the *Genlisea* used the ciliates as a food source.
- b. to see how many entered the traps.
- c. to see how long it would take the ciliates to digest the substance.
- d. to see which plants the ciliates preferred.

Passage 3 is about a long-lost settlement in the New World.

Sailing up the coast from Florida in 1562, the French explorer Jean Ribaut landed at Parris Island, South Carolina, pronounced it "one of the greenest and fayrest havens in the world" and built a small fort to defend it. Charlesfort, named after the French king Charles IX, was the first European attempt at settlement in what is now the United States, but until recently no one had found a trace of it.

Ribaut sailed for France after the fort was completed, leaving 27 men behind and promising to return with more supplies and settlers. But France, distracted by religious conflicts between the Catholics and the Huguenots, wasn't interested in another mission and, while pleading his case for a ship in England, Ribaut was imprisoned as a spy. Meanwhile, back at Charlesfort, a fire burned most of the supplies. After the officer in charge hanged one of the men, the crew mutinied, built their own ship and sailed home, abandoning the fort some 11 months after their arrival. In 1566, the Spanish, having established their own foothold at Saint Augustine, Florida, moved into the area and built their own fort, San Felipe, as well as a town called Santa Elena. For a time it served as the capital of Spanish Florida.

Spanish records, though, make no mention of Charlesfort and, before reporting success in 1996, two archeologists had spent 17 years vainly searching for evidence of the lost French settlement. All the while, they were also excavating San Felipe. Not until one of them realized that some pottery from the excavations at San Felipe was actually sixteenth-century French did it hit him: the Spanish had built San Felipe right on top of Charlesfort. Significantly, the French ceramics were concentrated in one area, an unlikely distribution if they had been owned by residents of the larger Spanish settlement. The archeologists suggest that the Spanish never mentioned where Charlesfort was as they didn't want to acknowledge a French claim to their capital.

161. What is true about Charlesfort?
   a. It was the most beautiful fort Ribaut had ever seen.
   b. It was utilized for only a short period of time.
   c. It was built on the remains of a Spanish fort.
   d. When the Spanish arrived, they could find no trace of it.

162. What is true about Ribaut's return to France?
   a. He returned in hopes of convincing the French to fund another expedition.
   b. He returned after the English refused to provide him with a new ship.
   c. He returned to help quell religious problems between the Catholics and Huguenots.
   d. He returned after being accused of spying against the English.

163. What happened to the men that were left in the fort?
   a. Several were hanged for starting a mutiny.
   b. After a fire had burnt down the fort, they fled the island in a small rowboat.
   c. They rebelled and returned to France.
   d. Fearing the Spanish would attack, they abandoned the fort and sailed back to France.

164. Why did archeologists take so long to uncover Charlesfort?
   a. They were not even aware that the French fort had existed.
   b. They were misled by false information in French documents.
   c. They were too busy concentrating their efforts on the excavations at San Felipe.
   d. They hadn't expected that its remains would be under those of the Spanish fort.

165. What is the significance of the pottery found at San Felipe?
   a. Its type and distribution suggest that it belonged to the earlier French settlers.
   b. It shows that Spanish soldiers had defeated the French and taken their fort.
   c. It is evidence that the Spanish settlement was the larger of the two structures.
   d. It proves that the Spanish tried to conceal that the French had been there first.

Passage 4 is about screws.

Inexpensive wood screws are fundamentally modern. Their mass production requires a high degree of precision and standardization. The wood screw also represents an entirely new method of attachment, more durable than nails, which can pop out if the wood dries out or expands. (This makes screws particularly useful in shipbuilding.) The tapered, gimlet-pointed wood screw – like its cousin, the bolt – squeezes the two joined pieces together. The more you tighten the screw – or the nut – the greater the squeeze. In modern steel buildings, for example, high-tension bolts are tightened so hard that it is the friction between the two pieces of steel – not the bolt itself – that gives strength to the joint. On a more mundane level, screws enable a vast array of convenient attachments in the home: door hinges, drawer pulls, shelf hangers, towel bars. Perhaps that is why if you rummage around most people's kitchen drawers you will most likely find at least one screwdriver.

Wood screws are stronger and more durable than nails, pegs or staples. But the aristocrat of screws is the precision screw. This was first made roughly – by hand – and later on screw-cutting lathes, which is a chicken-and-egg story, since it was the screw that made machine lathes possible. The machined screw represented a technological breakthrough of epic proportions. Screws enabled the minute adjustment of a variety of precision instruments like clocks, microscopes, telescopes, sextants, theodolites and marine chronometers.

It is not an exaggeration to say that accurately threaded screws changed the world. Without screws, entire fields of science would have languished, navigation would have remained primitive and naval warfare as well as routine maritime commerce in the 18th and 19th centuries would not have been possible. Without screws there would have been no machine tools, hence no industrial products and no Industrial Revolution. Think of that the next time you pick up a screwdriver to pry open a can of paint.

166. What is true about the wood screw?
- a. It's rarely used in shipbuilding
- b. It's made of wood.
- c. It's used to join two pieces of wood together.
- d. It's just as strong and durable as pegs and staples.

167. Why are nails not as good as wood screws?
- a. They have a more limited range of uses.
- b. They may dry out or expand.
- c. They are not made with as much precision.
- d. They do not hold as tightly or as effectively.

168. What was so significant about the advent of the machined screw?
- a. It made possible a huge range of household conveniences.
- b. It led to the improvement of clocks and sextants.
- c. It facilitated improvements in science, navigation, warfare and industry.
- d. It led to the manufacture of high-tension bolts used in modern steel buildings.

169. Why does the writer call the history of precision-screw manufacturing a "chicken-and-egg story"?
- a. because he is not sure which came first: the screw or the lathe
- b. because lathes produce screws just as chickens produce eggs
- c. because the first hand-made ones were much cruder than machine-made efforts
- d. because precision screws are used in machines that make precision screws

170. What does the writer imply in the final sentence?
- a. High-precision tools should not be used for purposes they were not designed for.
- b. We shouldn't forget that, were it not for screws, there would be no screwdrivers.
- c. It's amazing that something we all take for granted has such historical significance.
- d. People tend to overestimate the historical significance of the screw.

VOCABULARY CONSOLIDATION 6

Vocabulary Consolidation 6

VEXING VERBS

A Common collocations – Complete each phrase with a word from the box.

cater	divulge	dub	fracture	hurl	swallow

1. .... your arm / leg
2. .... a secret
3. .... your pride
4. .... a film into English
5. .... insults at someone
6. .... a wedding reception

convey	grind	indulge	promote	retard	uphold

7. .... yourself with small luxuries
8. .... friendship / a spirit of cooperation
9. .... a message / regrets
10. .... the law
11. .... spoilage
12. .... your teeth

B Fine-tuning your knowledge – The numbers below refer to the questions in the Vocabulary section in Practice Test 6. Review the words, then fill each blank with the correct form of the appropriate verb.

114.

flatter
level
hurl
launch

a. The Navy will .... a new fleet of submarines this summer.
b. In a fit of rage, she .... the vase against the wall.
c. Don't .... yourself. What he said was not meant as a compliment!
d. The publisher will .... the novel with a major publicity campaign.
e. The tiny village was .... by the earthquake.

122.

reciprocate
renovate
recapitulate
recuperate

a. Is it better to .... an old house or buy a new one?
b. It took her longer than expected to .... from the surgery.
c. To .... their kindness, she invited them to spend the weekend with her.
d. The director began by .... what had been decided at the last meeting.
e. The entrepreneur is hopeful that he will .... his investment within a year.

135.

defer
divert
differentiate
diversify

a. The male of the species is easily .... by its bright plumage.
b. If you don't mind, I'd rather .... making my decision until next week.
c. The children .... themselves with coloring books and games.
d. In the 1980s typewriter firms had no choice but to .... or go bankrupt.

138.

resort
appeal
refer
refrain

a. Nowadays many women in business prefer being .... to as Ms.
b. The stewardess .... to the frightened passengers not to panic.
c. Most problems can be solved without having to .... to violence.
d. Knowing the hostess was not a smoker, he .... from lighting his pipe.
e. The idea of taking a year off to travel highly .... to the tired novelist.

140.

trigger
liberate
duplicate
truncate

a. Photocopying machines are used to .... documents.
b. The Greeks .... themselves from Turkish rule in 1821.
c. Space limitations forced the editor to .... the long article.
d. The slightest movement will .... the sensitive burglar alarm.

149.

deluge
overcome
innovate
bomb

a. Companies that fail to .... will not survive the next decade.
b. Several residents were .... by smoke and had to be hospitalized.
c. The area was .... by the sudden rainstorm.
d. Do the police know which terrorist group .... the embassy?

NOTORIOUS NOUNS

A A dozen daffy definitions – Find the word in the box that is suggested by each prompt.

acquisitions	apparitions	contractions	contraptions	exception	freckles
an inquisition	requisition	sparkles	speckles	transfusions	transition

1. .... – What vampires order when they go out for "liquid refreshment"
2. .... – What all of us are in at the start of the new millennium
3. .... – What ostentatious people pretentiously call the expensive things they purchase
4. .... – What grandmothers call computers and microwaves behind your back
5. .... – What poets call "things that go bump in the night"
6. .... – What your mom had the day you came into the world
7. .... – What your parents subject you to when you stay out past your curfew
8. .... – What you see on your clothes when your friend flicks a wet paintbrush at you
9. .... – What a person with a fair complexion gets from sitting in the sun too long
10. .... – What you get in your eyes when you're happy, excited or in love
11. .... – What an employee submits to request a new car to replace the one he's just wrecked
12. .... – What students hopefully won't take when they come across zany exercises like this

B Fine-tuning your knowledge – The numbers below refer to the questions in the Vocabulary section in Practice Test 6. After reviewing the words, fill in the blanks with the appropriate words.

123. deterrent / detergent / deference / descendant

a. The children have good manners and always treat adults with ....
b. She had to put off doing her laundry as she was out of ....
c. A huge watchdog in the yard is a highly effective .... against burglars.
d. She claims to be the .... of a Pilgrim who came to America in the 1600s.

126. responsibility / possession / adoption / custody

a. Unable to have children, the couple is seriously considering ....
b. She was a conscientious student with a well-developed sense of ....
c. Her laptop computer is among her most prized ....s .
d. Police caught the thief red-handed and immediately took him into ....
e. The suspect was arrested for .... of illegal firearms.

131. subsidiary / subsistence / funding / fundamentals

a. The coach enjoys teaching young children the .... of basketball.
b. The local bottling company is a .... of the Coca Cola Corporation.
c. The research project is backed by .... from the federal government.
d. Redeeming cans and begging were the old man's only means of ....

142. effect / offense / exception / precedence

a. Workaholics allow their work to take .... over all aspects of their life.
b. You'll feel better in an hour or so when the pain-killer takes ....
c. I'm sorry you took .... at my joke. I've told it many times and no one has ever taken .... to it before. I didn't mean to give ....

145. malfunction / malformation / miscarriage / misconception

a. Wasn't it Columbus who dispelled the .... that the earth was flat?
b. Convicting an innocent man is a terrible .... of justice.
c. The rocket launch was postponed due to a .... in the fuel system.
d. The baby was born with a serious .... of the heart.
e. The woman was devastated when her pregnancy ended in a ....

ADDLING ADJECTIVES

A Common collocations – Complete each phrase with a word from the box.

far-fetched	flimsy (x2)	glossy	innate	oppressive (x2)	repentant	unbearable	vicious

1. .... dogs
2. .... magazines
3. .... governments
4. .... nightgowns
5. .... sinners
6. .... ability
7. .... / .... heat
8. .... / .... excuses

B Fine-tuning your knowledge – The numbers below refer to the questions in the Vocabulary section in Practice Test 6. After reviewing the words, fill in the blanks with the appropriate words.

111. **prudent** / **viable** / **far-fetched** / **sensible**

a. High heels are not the most .... things to wear on a long hike.
b. A business that continually loses money is obviously not ....
c. Life is so high-tech today that science fiction no longer seems ....
d. He's a .... / .... person who always "looks before he leaps."

113. glaring / glowing / glossy / gummy

a. She loved the look and feel of her cat's .... black fur.
b. She swelled with pride when her son's teacher gave her a .... report.
c. He was momentarily blinded by the .... sunlight.
d. Children who eat lollipops often wind up with .... hands and faces.
e. The hastily written article contained several .... errors of fact.

118. **arbitrary** / **accelerated** / **incoherent** / **innate**

a. After the accident, he was in shock and totally ....
b. Some people have an .... talent for learning languages.
c. I'm tired of your .... rules. What you want is illogical and unreasonable.
d. Hoping to learn some Chinese before the trip, he took an .... course.

125. unobtrusive / unprecedented / unmentionable / unbearable

a. The book's success has been .... in the history of publishing.
b. Her joy was almost .... ; she couldn't wait to tell him the good news.
c. He was a quiet, ... man who kept very much to himself.
d. In the old days many people regarded sex and drugs as .... topics.

130. **oppressive** / **immaculate** / **vicious** / **striking**

a. I've never seen such a(n) .... house. How does she keep it so clean?
b. All heads turned as the .... young woman entered the room.
c. How could anyone have committed such a(n) .... murder?
d. He's a rebellious type who finds all rules and regulations ....

141. flimsy / sturdy / filthy / poised

a. He made a .... attempt to excuse his lateness, but she knew he was lying.
b. The interviewer was highly impressed with the .... young woman.
c. After working on the car all morning, his hands were .... with grease.
d. Houses in earthquake-prone areas need to be as .... as possible.

148. **defensive** / **repentant** / **exceptional** / **objectionable**

a. It was clear that the child had .... artistic ability.
b. She found his rude behavior totally ....
c. The jury was shocked that the murderer showed no signs of being ....
d. He gets very .... when anyone criticizes his work.

AUDACIOUS ADVERBS

Fine-tuning your knowledge – The numbers below refer to the questions in the Vocabulary section in Practice Test 6. After reviewing the words, fill in the blanks with the appropriate words.

112.

voraciously
hectically
frantically
exuberantly

a. The long hike made us .... hungry.
b. The cheerful mailman greeted us .... as he came into the yard.
c. She .... called out for help, but no one could hear her.
d. As closing time drew near, last-minute shoppers rushed .... / .... from shop to shop.

139.

firmly
gracefully
smoothly
efficiently

a. The skaters glided .... / .... across the ice.
b. If you get the suspension system repaired, the car will ride more ....
c. If we work .... and all goes .... , we'll finish by midnight.
d. The children were brought up .... but lovingly.
e. When a car gets excellent gas mileage, we say it runs ....

144.

spaciously
sparingly
sparsely
spuriously

a. If you don't use the pepper flakes .... , the dish will be inedible.
b. He grew up in a tiny village in a .... populated rural area.
c. They loved the big house as it was so .... designed.
d. Although intriguing, the philosopher's argument was .... based on several false assumptions.

TINY BUT DEADLY – A small sampling of one-syllable killers

When you talk about "advanced vocabulary," most of you probably have in mind long, difficult-sounding words like *ostentatious, rehabilitation* and *superciliously*. In fact, there are still many short words in the language that you have probably not yet mastered. Here are a few that appear in Practice Test 6. Discuss the meanings, then fill in each blank with the appropriate form of one of the words.

1.

breach
dub
feign
fret

a. Somehow films that are .... into another language never seem natural.
b. It's no use .... about the test now. What's done is done.
c. The employee was fired for .... his contract.
d. The epidemic was quickly .... "the scourge of the century."
e. He has .... illness so many times that his mother no longer believes him.
f. The tank division had no trouble .... the enemy's defenses.

2.

forge
gloss
gnaw
grind

a. She always .... fresh pepper on her food.
b. Over the years the two men had .... a solid relationship.
c. The loud crunching noise was the dog .... away at a bone.
d. He was sent to jail for .... passports and $100 bills.
e. The ancient sword had been .... with great skill.
f. The politician .... over the fact that he had been implicated in the scandal.
g. Popular science writers usually .... difficult words for their lay readers.

3.

gust
gasp
gush
gulp

a. He drank down the beer in a single ....
b. Strong ....s of wind rattled the window panes.
c. A .... of water sprayed out of the hose.
d. She let out a .... as she saw a figure climb through her bedroom window.

PRACTICE TEST 7

Writing

(30 minutes)

Write on one of the topics given below. If you write about something else, your paper will not be graded. If you do not understand the topics, ask the examiner to explain or translate them. You will be graded on the clarity of your writing and the linguistic range and accuracy you show. Write $1\frac{1}{2}$ to 2 pages. You may make any corrections or other changes in the body of the composition.

TOPICS

1. "Honesty is the best policy," goes the old saying, or is it? We all have moments when we are tempted to stretch the truth – sometimes with a small "white lie" and sometimes with a big "blatant untruth." Describe an incident in which you lied. Would it have been better if you had told the truth or was the lie somehow justified? What did you learn from the experience?

2. With the rising popularity of home computers and the Internet, students are increasingly exploring the possibility of earning university degrees at home through distance-learning programs. But is distance learning right for everyone? Discuss the positive and negative factors that people should take into account before deciding to enroll in such programs.

For help in writing these compositions, see *Writing Tutorial*, pages 202–203.

Listening Comprehension Test

(35–40 minutes)

This part of the examination is a listening test that will assess your understanding of spoken English. The listening test has three parts. There are 50 questions. Mark all your answers on the separate answer sheet. Do not make any stray marks on the answer sheet. If you change your mind about an answer, erase your first answer completely.

PART I – In this part of the test, you will hear a short conversation. From the three answer choices given, choose the answer which means the same thing as you hear, or that is true based on what you hear.

For problems **1–17**, mark your answers on the separate answer sheet. No problem can be repeated. Please listen carefully. Do you have any questions?

1.
a. He would like to go.
b. He thinks they shouldn't go.
c. He's not sure it's a good idea.

2.
a. He thinks he'll have a problem.
b. He'd rather go without her.
c. He'll be fine on his own.

3.
a. She's not speaking to Jenny.
b. She hasn't spoken to Jenny yet.
c. She has no plans to call Jenny.

4.
a. She has bad memories of high school.
b. She thinks he's exaggerating.
c. She's probably older than he is.

5.
a. He thinks she was very impolite to the man.
b. He thinks she should let the man do it again.
c. He'll stop the man if he does it again.

6.
a. He's willing to cooperate with her.
b. He'll be glad to help her make the payment.
c. He'd like to help her, but he can't.

7.
a. He got lost going over the bridge.
b. He doesn't usually take the bridge.
c. He was late because of bridge traffic.

8.
a. She thinks he should be a policeman.
b. She thinks he'll have no problem.
c. She thinks his grades aren't good enough.

9.
a. Neither of them watched the entire game.
b. They both thought the game was bad.
c. She wants him to tell her about the game.

10.
a. Acting in plays always makes Sue nervous.
b. Sue is nervous about making a speech.
c. Sue is afraid she has the wrong address.

11.
a. She wants to check Glen's phone number.
b. She's going to ignore Glen's advice.
c. She wants to find somewhere else to eat.

12.
a. She thinks Al won't do a good job.
b. She thinks Al deserved the promotion.
c. She think the promotion has changed Al.

13.
a. The boss was angry when they told him.
b. The boss doesn't know what happened yet.
c. The boss will be pleased when he finds out.

14.
a. She doubts it will ever happen.
b. She doesn't think it's a good idea.
c. She thinks he should take a deep breath.

15.
a. He's getting dressed to go to a restaurant.
b. He's been invited to a costume party.
c. He's having trouble deciding what to wear.

16.
a. The mall is a few miles out of town.
b. The mall is right in the center of town.
c. The mall is on the main highway.

17.
a. He thinks she should rent the apartment.
b. He thinks she should stay where she is now.
c. He thinks it's much too expensive for her.

PART II – In this part of the test, you will hear a question. From the three answer choices given, choose the one which best answers the question.

For problems **18–35**, mark your answers on the separate answer sheet. No problem can be repeated. Please listen carefully. Do you have any questions?

18. a. Maybe John should do it.
b. It's hard to say.
c. I would have to agree.

19. a. Take your time.
b. I'd take Main Street.
c. It's at the corner of Broadway and 47th.

20. a. Yes, but it's at home.
b. No, I've run out.
c. No, I don't usually wear them.

21. a. It's not a problem.
b. Of course, I know how.
c. I had no idea.

22. a. At the library.
b. They're for my history project.
c. I lent them to my teacher.

23. a. As soon as I'm able.
b. In an hour or two.
c. Whenever I can.

24. a. I believe it was Wendy's.
b. The police are still looking for it.
c. No one will admit it.

25. a. Shall I call to remind him?
b. Well, I give him credit for trying.
c. Don't you remember?

26. a. I wouldn't, if I were you.
b. How about later this afternoon?
c. I'd rather you kept it confidential.

27. a. My husband did it.
b. I flew.
c. It's a long story.

28. a. It would've been nice if you had asked.
b. Sorry, why do you ask?
c. How nice of you to ask!

29. a. Nothing.
b. Don't mention it.
c. You're welcome any time.

30. a. He's always been a workaholic.
b. He got up on the wrong side of the bed.
c. He had the flu last week.

31. a. He's just an optimist, I guess.
b. He can't see very well without glasses.
c. That's just how he is.

32. a. Any time.
b. Sorry, I've got none left.
c. I guess so. How much do you need?

33. a. Not really, it was shorter than I thought.
b. Actually, the flight took off immediately.
c. No, luckily. The train was right on time.

34. a. He asked me to renew it.
b. He'd like me to make a few revisions.
c. He only had time to read the headlines.

35. a. You really should see a doctor.
b. I left early to avoid the traffic.
c. Sorry, I guess I should've called.

PART III – In this part, you will hear three short segments from a radio program. The program is called "Learning from the Experts." Each talk lasts about two minutes. As you listen, you may want to take notes to help you remember information given in the talk. After each talk, you will be asked some questions about what was said. From the three answer choices given, you should choose the one which best answers the question according to the information you heard.

Remember, no problems can be repeated. For problems **36–50**, mark your answers on the separate answer sheet. Do you have any questions?

SEGMENT 1

36. According to the speaker, what is true about burnout?
- a. It starts off innocently enough, with little or no warning of what is to come.
- b. It is easy to predict precisely who will suffer from it and who will not.
- c. It tends to affect employees who are not satisfied with their jobs.

37. What happens during "the awakening" stage?
- a. You become clearly aware that the job is not what you had hoped it would be.
- b. You still believe that the job will satisfy all of your needs.
- c. You work harder to make up for the feeling that something is very wrong.

38. Which of the following are characteristics of "full-scale burnout"?
- a. An overwhelming sense of failure, physical and mental breakdowns, despair
- b. A refusal to give up your high aspirations and impossible goals
- c. Chronic fatigue and irritability, drug and alcohol abuse, depression

39. What does the speaker say about recovering from burnout?
- a. It can't be done if the final stage is reached.
- b. It requires time and the careful readjustment of goals.
- c. If the victim has someone to talk to, he can usually recover in a few months.

40. What advice does the speaker give to someone suffering from burnout?
- a. Invest in businesses owned by family and friends
- b. Work at home as much as possible to avoid stress at the office
- c. Put more energy into family, friends and social activities

SEGMENT 2

41. In the speaker's opinion, what factor has contributed most to the growing success of organ transplants in the United States?
- a. Improved surgical techniques
- b. More efficient transportation techniques
- c. Drugs that suppress organ rejection and infection

42. What problem has this success created?
- a. Tens of thousands of people die because organs cannot be found quickly enough.
- b. The supply of donated organs now falls far short of the demand for them.
- c. It takes several years for patients to get on the waiting list.

43. Under current guidelines, who would be first in line to receive an organ transplant?
- a. The patient who is nearest death and has the financial means to pay the bill
- b. The patient who is nearest death, regardless of his or her ability to pay
- c. The patient who has the best chance of living longer after the transplant

44. What is true about people who sign organ donor cards?
- a. Their families often refuse to allow their organs to be utilized.
- b. Their generous contributions have reduced the shortage of organs.
- c. Their families profit by receiving burial expenses and other financial incentives.

45. How do surgeons intend to cope with the practical and ethical problems that still surround transplantation?
- a. By pressing for laws that will make organ donation mandatory
- b. By pressing for laws that will require family members to receive financial incentives
- c. By developing and utilizing an increasing range of artificial devices

SEGMENT 3

46. How do conventional nursing units differ from Snoezelen rooms?
    a. They expose patients to noise, bright lights and other unnecessary stimulation.
    b. They are designed to stimulate a patient's senses in a much more relaxing way.
    c. They unintentionally cut a patient off from all sources of outside stimulation.

47. In which country did Snoezelen originate?
    a. Switzerland
    b. Great Britain
    c. The Netherlands

48. Why do some people criticize the studies that have been done?
    a. They were done by researchers who were not properly qualified.
    b. They are based on samples that are too small to be conclusive.
    c. They were conducted in Europe and not in the United States.

49. Why are American experts becoming increasingly interested in Snoezelen therapy?
    a. Because they expect a rise in patients who might benefit greatly from it
    b. Because they realize that it may provide a cure for patients with Alzheimer's
    c. Because they don't believe in prescribing medicine for Alzheimer's patients

50. According to the passage, which is not one of the benefits associated with Snoezelen therapy?
    a. Improved brain function
    b. Decreased anxiety levels
    c. Improved sociability

Grammar – Cloze – Vocabulary – Reading

(75 minutes)

This part of the examination contains 120 problems, numbered **51–170**. There are 40 grammar, 20 cloze, 40 vocabulary and 20 reading comprehension problems. The examiner will not explain any test problems. If you do not understand how to do the problems, raise your hand and a proctor will explain the examples to you.

Do not spend too much time on any one problem. Each problem counts the same. If you do not know the answer to a problem, you may make a reasonable guess. Each problem has only one correct answer. Work fast but carefully. You have 75 minutes to answer all 120 problems.

GRAMMAR

51. Remember to put the meat away. It will go bad if it ..... in the refrigerator.
- a. didn't keep
- b. hasn't kept
- c. doesn't keep
- d. isn't kept

52. He said he was interested ..... how to sign up for the introductory computer course.
- a. that he find out
- b. finding out
- c. for finding out
- d. in finding out

53. Dan isn't going to the concert for the simple reason that his parents ..... to.
- a. do not consent
- b. won't allow him
- c. are not letting him
- d. don't want

54. I'd been hoping to go for a walk, but ..... I decided to stay home.
- a. the weather so bad
- b. so bad the weather was
- c. the weather was bad so
- d. it was a such bad weather

55. He didn't say anything about how much weight she had gained ..... .
- a. in case of getting offended
- b. for fear of offending her
- c. to prevent her from offending
- d. because she will be offended

56. Ann Marie said that her grandmother was at the drug store ..... .
- a. having her blood pressure checked
- b. having checked her blood pressure
- c. to have checked her blood pressure
- d. for checking her blood pressure

57. Sorry, we're out of milk again. I used ..... in my coffee this morning.
- a. a little of it
- b. what little there was
- c. the little was there
- d. little left

58. They spent the summer restoring their nineteenth-century ..... cottage.
- a. made-of-stones
- b. stone
- c. stony
- d. stoned

59. As for our going sailing last weekend, we ..... , but the sea was too rough.
- a. had supposed so
- b. supposed to
- c. were supposing so
- d. were supposed to

60. ..... her job, her sons and the housework, she doesn't have a minute for herself.
- a. What with
- b. Because
- c. If it weren't for
- d. Owing

61. The sooner you understand what the boss expects of you, the ..... you'll be.
- a. later
- b. more often
- c. better off
- d. sooner

62. He claims he was motivated to rob the bank ..... his sick child.
- a. for the sake of
- b. thanks to
- c. on behalf of
- d. to account for

63. Apparently, Mary has been good friends with Angela for ..... now.
    a. so long a time
    b. the long time
    c. many a time
    d. quite some time

64. John called a little while ago to say his train ..... at just past noon.
    a. would have arrived
    b. would be arriving
    c. will be arrived
    d. supposed to arrive

65. I appreciate your wanting to help me, but please ..... to all that trouble.
    a. don't go
    b. not go
    c. you shouldn't go
    d. you don't go

66. If ..... , I wouldn't have been able to pay my bills last month.
    a. it wasn't my brother
    b. my brother hadn't been
    c. it hadn't been for my brother
    d. my brother wouldn't be there

67. I hear the Templetons ..... not once, but twice last month.
    a. whose house was broken into
    b. had their house broken into
    c. their house was broken into
    d. were broken into their house

68. ..... hard for the exam, he was sure that he would pass with flying colors.
    a. Having studied
    b. Studied
    c. Because studying
    d. Though he had studied

69. He suggests we leave the house early ..... avoid getting stuck in traffic.
    a. so as to
    b. in order of
    c. so that
    d. due to

70. I'm hoping to meet with the director sometime this afternoon ..... to the office.
    a. the moment I'll get back
    b. no sooner will I get back
    c. as soon as I get back
    d. whenever I'm getting back

71. Everyone says the exam is difficult ..... it lasts all day, with only a few breaks.
    a. since
    b. because of
    c. whereas
    d. which

72. Discipline isn't usually a problem for the faculty as most of our students are ..... .
    a. behaved well
    b. good behaving
    c. of good behavior
    d. well behaved

73. He'd been in the habit of jogging almost every day until a leg injury put him ..... action.
    a. off from
    b. out of
    c. beyond
    d. under

74. Needless to say, the research that went into the thousand-page biography was ..... .
    a. exhausting
    b. exhaustion
    c. exhaustive
    d. exhausted

75. If your car brakes squeal, it's ..... they need adjusting.
    a. surely a sign which
    b. a sure sign that
    c. a sign of surely
    d. a sign to be sure

76. These days it's hard enough to put food on the table, ... saving for a child's education.
    a. to say nothing of
    b. mentioning nothing of
    c. having nothing to do with
    d. to make nothing of

77. I may or may not be able to see the documentary tonight, depending on ..... .
   a. what time it starts
   b. when does it start
   c. it's time it starts
   d. which time is it starting

78. It's company policy: all travel expenses ..... the chief accountant.
   a. are the approval of
   b. have been approved by
   c. are to approve by
   d. must have the approval of

79. I hear the new teacher is popular ..... a great sense of humor.
   a. providing he has
   b. in order to have
   c. due to his having
   d. in the event that he

80. Sorry to interrupt, but the director asked me to tell you he wishes ..... to you immediately.
   a. he had spoken
   b. he would speak
   c. he spoke
   d. to speak

81. My colleague Jeffrey is ..... won a Pulitzer Prize last year for investigative reporting.
   a. one which his wife
   b. one who has a wife
   c. the one whose wife
   d. the one who his wife

82. If it happens again, the boss says he'll put an end to the problem ..... .
   a. once and for all
   b. once upon a time
   c. once in a while
   d. once in a lifetime

83. ..... read her work over again, she wouldn't make so many mistakes.
   a. She'd do well to
   b. If only she would
   c. It's better that she
   d. Not only should she

84. John said he'd drive us to the airport but, ... , we can take a cab.
   a. if need be
   b. if it needs be
   c. if it is needed to be
   d. need that it be

85. To be a book editor, it helps ..... knowledge of a wide range of subjects.
   a. to have a working
   b. working with the
   c. to work with
   d. having worked with

86. On our camping trip, we're taking two tents with us: ours and ..... .
   a. the children
   b. childrens'
   c. children's
   d. the children's

87. ..... the sound of it, I'd say you don't really want to go.
   a. From
   b. Given
   c. Judging
   d. For

88. The problem ..... is whether or not he should accept a job halfway across the country.
   a. that which faces him
   b. of which he is faced
   c. he is faced with
   d. with which he faces

89. ..... that he might have learned from his past mistakes.
   a. To think
   b. You'd think
   c. What you think
   d. You'd thought

90. No matter what people are saying, there's no way ..... blame for this.
   a. for John could
   b. that John is to
   c. of John taking
   d. should John take

CLOZE

Passage 1 is about fire ants.

Known as "the scourge of the South," Amazon-bred fire ants first appeared in Mississippi and Alabama in the late 1940s. With their two-foot-tall, rock-hard mounds able to cause serious damage to the machinery of unsuspecting farmers, the creatures have been ....(91).... for killing chickens, picking crops clean and even blinding infants. Defensive by nature, they will storm ....(92).... threatens their mounds or looks like food. They latch on with barbed jaws and ....(93).... repeatedly with their spiked tails. Their venom ....(94).... humans like a match and causes itchy blisters that ....(95).... for days if left alone or weeks if scratched and infected.

Their spread has been glacial but unstoppable. During the summer, usually after a rain, hundreds of winged ants ....(96).... from their mounds to mate 500 feet in the air. The ....(97).... drop to the ground and die, their ....(98).... in life fulfilled. The females, now queens, drift downward to start new colonies. On a windy day, this may be as ....(99).... as five miles away. They burrow into holes and begin to ....(100).... eggs, as many as 1,500 a day. In a year, a new colony can be 100,000 strong. The process repeats up to eight times each summer, spreading the ants 20 to 30 miles a year.

91. a. charged b. blamed c. accused d. convicted
92. a. whatever b. anything c. and d. when
93. a. wag b. bite c. sting d. pinch
94. a. poisons b. overheats c. burns d. strikes
95. a. consist b. resist c. insist d. persist
96. a. leave b. raise c. uplift d. ascend
97. a. mounds b. males c. insects d. wings
98. a. purpose b. intention c. achievement d. ambition
99. a. long b. closely c. far d. lengthy
100. a. hatch b. lay c. bear d. fertilize

Passage 2 is about George Washington.

George Washington's first great feat was leading the Continental Army to victory over the powerful British forces in the American colonies. To achieve such a stunning success, he had to hold his tiny army of rag-tag volunteers ....(101).... for eight desperate years, always under unbelievably harsh conditions.

....(102).... for his country, Washington was a leader with highly ....(103).... logistical skills. ....(104).... concerned him ....(105).... equipping and sheltering his soldiers and, as far as possible, ...(106).... them out of harm's way. He knew full well that he was outnumbered, outgunned and outgeneraled, and that ....(107).... every effort to supply his troops, his men would have to ....(108).... on empty stomachs and bare feet. So his task was to conserve his meager forces and resources, letting the British ....(109).... themselves out chasing after him. In this way, he managed to ....(110).... the Revolutionary War a guerrilla war, a war of harassment and retreat that was too wearisome and expensive for the British taste.

101. a. together b. back c. alive d. down
102. a. Hopefully b. Sadly c. Fortunately d. Unexpectedly
103. a. paid b. overrated c. qualified d. developed
104. a. It b. What c. This d. Having
105. a. about b. was c. by d. that
106. a. held b. with c. take d. keeping
107. a. however b. despite c. with d. nevertheless
108. a. die b. be c. fight d. eat
109. a. exhaust b. put c. figure d. wear
110. a. make b. turn c. fight d. call

VOCABULARY

111. He was fully aware that it would take years of hard work to ..... his goals.
   a. sustain
   b. contain
   c. retain
   d. attain

112. For someone so young and inexperienced, she is admirably ..... and confident.
   a. poised
   b. possessed
   c. poignant
   d. possessive

113. They were happy to say that they had ..... enjoyed themselves.
   a. extremely
   b. meticulously
   c. thoroughly
   d. authentically

114. To meet the fast-approaching deadline, the staff has no choice but to ..... .
   a. work round the clock
   b. put the clock back
   c. clock their performance
   d. watch the clock

115. He's so egotistical that he thinks the whole universe ..... around him.
   a. revolts
   b. revolves
   c. rotates
   d. evolves

116. With more than 70 novels to her name, Agatha Christie was an extremely ..... writer.
   a. obstinate
   b. extravagant
   c. prolific
   d. reckless

117. The couple needs to ..... out their differences before matters get worse.
   a. wash
   b. dry
   c. rinse
   d. iron

118. The sailors ..... the horizon in hopes of spotting some sign of land.
   a. scorned
   b. scrubbed
   c. scanned
   d. scratched

119. What a coincidence! I bought Gwen that ..... book for her birthday last year.
   a. similar
   b. very
   c. sheer
   d. mere

120. The student was ill for several months and now has many ..... in his knowledge
   a. cavities
   b. blanks
   c. gaps
   d. vacancies

121. The employee got ..... for being late twice in one week.
   a. told off
   b. ticked off
   c. thrown away
   d. put down

122. The towering skyscraper ..... all the other buildings in the area.
   a. overcame
   b. vanquished
   c. belittled
   d. dwarfed

123. The teacher scolded the boy for being disobedient and ..... .
   a. irrelevant
   b. irreparable
   c. impertinent
   d. impeccable

124. Why does he insist on taking German lessons if he has no ..... for languages?
   a. fluency
   b. aptitude
   c. bequest
   d. precision

125. Unless unforeseen ..... develop, the patient's chances of recovery are excellent.
  a. implications
  b. ramifications
  c. consequences
  d. complications

126. When the lock on his suitcase broke, he had no choice but to ..... it open.
  a. shove
  b. rip
  c. pry
  d. crack

127. For as long as I can remember, there has always been ..... between the two brothers.
  a. fraction
  b. traction
  c. friction
  d. suction

128. News of the prime minister's resignation ..... like wildfire.
  a. glimmered
  b. radiated
  c. spread
  d. illuminated

129. The prosecutor was convinced that he had an ..... case against the defendant.
  a. open-ended
  b. open-handed
  c. open-eyed
  d. open-and-shut

130. They came across a bundle of old family photographs while ..... in the attic.
  a. gesturing
  b. ruminating
  c. rummaging
  d. swaying

131. The millionaire's mansion was ..... furnished with the best that money could buy.
  a. rarely
  b. densely
  c. expansively
  d. lavishly

132. The clever swindler ..... on the vulnerability of lonely rich widows.
  a. dwells
  b. leans
  c. preys
  d. dotes

133. You are ..... mistaken if you think you will get away with this without being punished.
  a. vainly
  b. sadly
  c. wrongly
  d. virtually

134. They spent the summer converting the attic into a ..... bedroom.
  a. sparse
  b. scarce
  c. spare
  d. spurious

135. Had the residents paid ..... to the flood warnings, many lives would have been saved.
  a. a compliment
  b. heed
  c. their way
  d. their respects

136. The storm raged for hours, ... battering the tiny fishing boats.
  a. consistently
  b. relentlessly
  c. hardly
  d. inevitably

137. A horde of reporters gathered outside the courtroom to await the jury's ..... .
  a. accusation
  b. objection
  c. claim
  d. verdict

138. John is an extremely ..... character who frequently rubs people the wrong way.
  a. amenable
  b. adjacent
  c. abrasive
  d. adhesive

139. Having had a(n) ..... childhood, she does her best to provide a better life for her children.
   a. deprived
   b. undernourished
   c. diffident
   d. underrated

140. The museum has one of the best collections of Egyptian ..... in the world.
   a. ancestries
   b. antiques
   c. antiquities
   d. antiquarians

141. The army was poorly equipped and unable to ..... off the enemy attack.
   a. fend
   b. repel
   c. defend
   d. propel

142. The odds are ..... against the newcomer's winning the election.
   a. alarmingly
   b. overwhelmingly
   c. barely
   d. extensively

143. It took her a while to figure out the truth, but she finally put ..... .
   a. the cart before the horse
   b. her money where her mouth was
   c. all her eggs in one basket
   d. two and two together

144. When they realized they had won the lottery, the family was ..... with joy.
   a. delirious
   b. deleterious
   c. destitute
   d. devastated

145. Diplomatic efforts to ..... peace between the two nations have thus far been ineffective.
   a. foment
   b. foster
   c. adopt
   d inflict

146. The workers will have to work overtime if the factory is to meet its ..... .
   a. quotation
   b. quota
   c. quote
   d. quotient

147. She always wears gloves when working with ..... plants such as roses and cacti.
   a. gnarled
   b. slippery
   c. prickly
   d. jagged

148. Having been ..... for the past five years, the company finally declared bankruptcy.
   a. undiluted
   b. insolvent
   c. dissolved
   d. liquefied

149. She called all her friends, hoping to ..... the rumors that were circulating about her.
   a. impel
   b. dispel
   c. compel
   d. expel

150. The politician won the election by a ..... of only two percent.
   a. vote
   b. quantity
   c. proportion
   d. margin

READING

Passage 1 is about hearing loss.

Conventional wisdom would have us believe that hearing loss is as inevitable as gray hair and age spots, but research has shown that excessive noise exposure is one of the leading causes of ear damage. Noise damages our ears in two ways. It can strike in an instant, causing what is known as acoustic trauma: one blast from a high-powered hunter's rifle, for example, can rip apart the ear's inner tissues, leaving scars that permanently impair hearing. It can also develop insidiously over a period of decades in what is called noise-induced hearing loss. Dangerous noise levels attack the inner ear's 16,000 hair cells, the tiny workhorses that transport airborne vibrations to our brains, where they are decoded as speech or screech or the wail of a car alarm. Those hair cells do spectacular work, but they are incapable of regeneration. By the time we get the signal that something is wrong – for example, a ringing in the ears or a muffling of sounds – some of the cells may have died.

Though a noise-damaged ear can't be repaired, treatment options for the hearing impaired are improving markedly. Conventional hearing aids have never been all that popular: only about 20 percent of the 28 million Americans with hearing loss wear them. Most people can't put up with the pumped-up volume of background chatter, and no one likes having to adjust the volume when moving from one room to another. But a new generation of fully digital hearing aids, which cost around $3,000, now offers more sophisticated alternatives. Their tiny computer chips filter sound into bands, matching them against a patient's personal hearing-loss profile, softening some pitches and amplifying others. While not all audiologists embrace the expensive new technology, patients using the new devices report 85 to 90 percent satisfaction, compared with only about 60 percent for conventional wearers.

151. What is now known about hearing loss?
  a. It is a natural part of aging.
  b. It is often caused by exposure to excessive noise.
  c. It is usually accompanied by a ringing in the ears.
  d. It usually results from acoustic trauma.

152. What is true about conventional hearing aids?
  a. Only 20 percent of the people who wear them are satisfied.
  b. They are not popular with the younger generation.
  c. Many partially deaf people choose not to wear them.
  d. The volume cannot be controlled, which is a major disadvantage.

153. What is true about noise-induced hearing loss?
  a. It develops gradually over many years.
  b. It almost always results from sudden explosions.
  c. It results from damaged hair cells in the brain.
  d. It can frequently be treated and reversed.

154. What advantage do fully digital hearing aids have over conventional models?
  a. They are more competitively priced.
  b. They amplify background noises more efficiently.
  c. They are smaller and can be adjusted more easily.
  d. They adjust sounds to the wearer's needs.

155. According to the passage, what is the function of the hair cells in the inner ear?
  a. They protect the inner ear from excessive noise damage.
  b. They help transport sound vibrations to the brain.
  c. They discriminate speech from other sounds in the environment.
  d. Without them, our ears would ring constantly.

Passage 2 is about camels.

Camels are divided into two species: the dromedary, or one-humped camel, which once roamed wild in the deserts of North Africa and Arabia but now exists only in a domesticated state; and the two-humped Bactrian camel, native to Central Asia, where domesticated camels abound while a small but shrinking number live in the wild stretches of the Gobi Desert. Bactrians are darker and woollier than dromedaries and have shorter legs.

Bactrian camels are an excellent example of an animal that has adapted well to its environment. They are able to survive on the arid Asian steppes because of the biological strategies that enable them to cope with the severe temperature changes common to Central Asia. Camels can graze on a wide range of plants and thorny vegetation that other mammals avoid. Most striking is their ability to survive long periods without water – a characteristic that humans recognized as useful and used for their own purposes. The camel's body conserves water by producing dry feces and concentrated urine. Body temperature may fluctuate by as much as 57 degrees Fahrenheit during the course of a day, which enables the animal to minimize water loss due to perspiration. Although a camel may look scrawny and emaciated after a long, dry spell and its humps may become flaccid and flop to one side, it fills out quickly as soon as it gets water. In fact, a thirsty camel may drink up to 40 gallons in ten minutes. Its humps serve as storage facilities for body fat, so the camel can survive the grueling journeys across the desert where food is not readily found. Built-in protection against blowing desert sands include the camel's long eyelashes which protect the eyes, and nostrils that can be closed during sand storms. Even the camel's nasal cavities help to reduce water loss by moistening inhaled air. The thick coat of fur and underwool provide warmth during cold desert nights and help insulate against the burning mid-day sun.

156. How does the dromedary compare to the Bactrian camel?
- a. The dromedary is not well suited to life in the desert.
- b. Both have the same geographical range.
- c. The dromedary is lighter in color and not as hairy.
- d. Neither are found in the wild.

157. Which factor helps the Bactrian survive on long desert treks?
- a. It can drink large amounts of water in a short time.
- b. It can utilize energy from body fat in its humps.
- c. It can graze on a variety of plants.
- d. It can sweat profusely.

158. What does the passage suggest would happen to a Bactrian after a long drought?
- a. It would quickly regain its normal appearance.
- b. It would appear thin all over except for its humps.
- c. It would be unaffected and in top physical condition.
- d. It would be weak and on the verge of starvation.

159. Which is **not** related to a Bactrian's ability to protect itself against water loss?
- a. the design of its nasal cavities
- b. the way it produces body waste
- c. its fluctuating body temperature
- d. the length of its eyelashes

160. What is the Bactrian's nose well suited for?
- a. breathing in dry desert air
- b. perspiring
- c. maintaining a steady body temperature
- d. inhaling sand during a desert storm

Passage 3 is about continuing developments in the car industry.

As the new millenium unfolds, cars that don't foul the air are rolling from dream to reality. Boasting zero emissions and featherweight frames, electric cars are regarded as the environmentally sound future of motoring. But while they are relatively quiet and spew no pollution out the tail pipe, so far they suffer from high cost and limited range. Electric cars accelerate swiftly and can drive at highway speeds, but they don't go all that far before they need recharging. Worse yet, fully recharging the battery takes eight hours – easy to do overnight, but not while on a long, continuous trip.

More practical in the short run may be so-called hybrid cars that have both a battery-driven motor and a gasoline engine with the ability to switch back and forth between the two power systems. By alternating automatically between the two motors according to need, the cars can, for example, go into electric mode in the city, thereby not adding to urban smog, and then switch to gasoline mode for longer stretches on the highway. The net result is a spectacular increase in fuel efficiency and far less pollution than from regular cars. There's no hassle either: recharging goes on while the car is in operation, and fuel is as close as the nearest gas station.

A third approach is to power cars with fuel cells, which combine hydrogen with oxygen to form water vapor and electricity. Because hydrogen fuel is not yet widely available, the first fuel-cell cars will probably carry another fuel, possibly methane, to help produce hydrogen.

None of these autos is totally nonpolluting because of the fossil fuels generally used to generate the electricity and hydrogen needed to run the engines. But if the original power source becomes the sun or wind, cars of the future will be much friendlier to the atmosphere than the ones on the road today.

161. According to the passage, what is a main drawback of electric cars currently on the market?
- a. their tail-pipe design
- b. their light frames
- c. their inability to accelerate to highway speeds
- d. the length of time needed to recharge the battery

162. Which car is capable of recharging its battery while in motion?
- a. the electric car
- b. the hybrid car
- c. methane-driven fuel-cell cars
- d. hydrogen-driven fuel-cell cars

163. What does the writer imply about hybrid cars that are driven on the open road?
- a. They employ a nonpolluting battery-driven motor.
- b. They automatically alternate between a battery-driven motor and a gasoline engine.
- c. They are even more efficient and nonpolluting than when driven in city traffic.
- d. They operate in much the same way as conventional cars.

164. According to the passage, what are the major advantages of the hybrid car?
- a. ready availability of fuel and recharging stations
- b. cost and ease of operation
- c. emission reduction and fuel efficiency
- d. reduction of noise and smog on national highways

165. Which type of car may someday present the best solution to current environmental concerns?
- a. electric cars
- b. hybrid cars
- c. fuel-cell cars run on methane
- d. solar- or wind-powered cars

Passage 4 is about factors that influence job performance.

For years psychologists turned to cognitive ability as a predictor of job performance: smarter people were considered more likely to succeed on the job. But intelligence is only part of the story, say current researchers. Although they haven't unraveled the details, most agree that personality traits such as conscientiousness, extroversion, agreeableness, emotional stability and openness to experience also play major roles in a person's job suitability and productivity.

One group of researchers argues that conscientiousness – being responsible, dependable, organized and persistent – is generic to success. Having analyzed 117 studies of personality and job performance, they concluded that conscientiousness consistently predicted performance for all jobs from managerial and sales positions to skilled and semiskilled work. They found that conscientiousness is the only personality trait fundamental to all jobs and job-related criteria. Other traits are valid predictors for only some criteria or occupations.

Another researcher argues that using conscientiousness as a standard of job performance doesn't work for all jobs. For some jobs – particularly creative ones – conscientiousness may be a liability, rather than an asset. In a sample of musicians in Tulsa, Oklahoma, she found that the best musicians, as rated by their peers, had the lowest scores on conscientiousness. She goes on to suggest that researchers should think about matching people to jobs by crossing major personality dimensions with a taxonomy that separates occupations into six themes including realistic jobs (mechanics, fire fighters, construction workers), conventional jobs (bank tellers and statisticians) and artistic jobs (musicians, artists and writers). Her results indicate that while conscientiousness appears to predict performance in realistic and conventional jobs, it appears to impede success in investigative, artistic and social jobs that require innovation, creativity and spontaneity. The conclusion: "There are jobs where you have to have creativity and innovation. If you select employees based on conscientiousness, you won't come close to getting creative or imaginative workers."

166. What did researchers previously believe about job performance?

a. It had little or nothing to do with a person's cognitive ability.
b. It was dependent on how intelligent a person was.
c. It could not be predicted at all.
d. It was determined by a range of personality traits.

167. How is a conscientious worker described in the first study discussed?

a. as someone who is guaranteed to be a financial success
b. as someone who will be successful, no matter what job he does
c. as someone who is trustworthy, reliable and doesn't give up easily
d. as someone who is predictable

168. What conclusion about conscientiousness did researchers in the first study reach?

a. It is a significant indicator of job performance in only a few jobs.
b. It is important, but other factors must be considered in predicting performance.
c. It is the one factor that is basic to all jobs and all aspects of job performance.
d. It is crucial in some jobs, but not that important in others.

169. What do the results of the first study indicate?

a. that conscientiousness may be less desirable than certain other factors in creative jobs
b. that people in realistic and conventional jobs should try to be more conscientious
c. that the first study was seriously flawed and should be ignored
d. that musicians and artists are not as conscientious as mechanics and bank tellers

170. Who would most likely benefit from considering the findings of the two studies?

a. employers and personnel managers
b. students preparing to enter the job market
c. unemployed people in all job categories
d. employees who want to better their prospects for career advancement

VOCABULARY CONSOLIDATION 7

VEXING VERBS

A Common collocations – Complete each phrase with a word from the box.

adopt	foment	foster	inflict	iron	shove

1. .... your way through a crowd
2. .... pain or punishment on someone
3. .... economic growth / a child
4. .... out your differences with someone
5. .... a textbook / a child
6. .... a riot / violence

attain	crack	pry	retain	sustain	rip

7. .... open a nut / an egg
8. .... open a letter
9. .... open a stuck window
10. .... information / water
11. .... your goals / ambitions
12. .... life / an effort / injuries

B Fine-tuning your knowledge – The numbers below refer to the questions in the Vocabulary section in Practice Test 7. Review the words, then fill each blank with the correct form of the appropriate verb.

118. **scorn / scrub / scan / scratch**

a. She hates getting down on her hands and knees to .... the floor.
b. The sailors .... the horizon searching for signs of land.
c. The haughty professor .... the junior members of the college faculty.
d. The cat .... so keep an eye on the baby.
e. It's now possible to .... documents directly into a computer.

122. **overcome / vanquish / belittle / dwarf**

a. The Spanish conquistadors .... / .... the Aztecs.
b. The blind woman has had to .... many obstacles in her life.
c. The referee was literally .... by the towering basketball players.
d. Why are you always .... yourself. You're just as smart as anyone else!
e. Her parents were .... with joy at the birth of their first grandchild.

128. **glimmer / radiate / spread / illuminate**

a. A stove .... warmth; a pregnant woman .... joy and good health.
b. A single bare light bulb .... the room.
c. The lights of the city .... softly in the distance.
d. He .... out the map on the table so everyone could see.

130. **gesture / ruminate / rummage / sway**

a. The trees .... in the tropical breeze.
b. She .... through the closet trying to find her old black sweater.
c. Catching my eye across the crowded room, he .... for me to join him.
d. Since he broke up with her, all she does is sit around the house ....
e. You can try to persuade her, but I doubt that she'll be ....

132. **dwell / lean / prey / dote**

a. Lions .... on zebras and wildebeests.
b. She .... her bicycle against the wall and went into the shop.
c. Prehistoric man .... in forests and caves.
d. Why do you find it necessary to .... on other people's problems?
e. The problem .... on her mind; she could think of nothing else.
f. If his parents hadn't .... on him when he was a child, he wouldn't .... on them so much now.

NOTORIOUS NOUNS

A Amusing associations – Find the word in the box that is suggested by each prompt.

blanks	cavities	fractions	friction	gaps	suction	traction	vacancies

1. .... – What a young math student studies along with percents and decimals
2. .... – What a big hotel and a big company are likely to have in common
3. .... – What you'll have in your knowledge if you play hooky from school
4. .... – What Americans call empty spaces on a form or in a cloze passage
5. .... – What you get in your teeth from chewing too much gum or eating too much candy
6. .... – What is created when liquid is slurped (ie, drunk noisily) through a straw
7. .... – What there is between two people who rub each other the wrong way
8. .... – What your tires no longer have when they lose their grip on the road

B Fine-tuning your knowledge – The numbers below refer to the questions in the Vocabulary section in Practice Test 7. After reviewing the words, fill in the blanks with the appropriate words.

124. **fluency / aptitude / bequest / precision**

a. When the old man died, he left each of his children a .... of $20,000.
b. The delicate brain surgery was performed with painstaking ....
c. Some people have more .... for learning languages than others.
d. Your .... in English will improve if you spend time in the States.

137. **accusation / objection / claim / verdict**

a. If we finish the report, the boss will have no .... to our leaving early.
b. It was a difficult case so the jury took days to return a ....
c. In the wake of the flood, the insurance company was inundated with ....s.
d. What in the world makes you think I did it? I resent your ....

140. **ancestry / antique / antiquity / antiquarian**

a. The historian is a world-renowned expert on Greek and Roman ....
b. If you want to trace your .... or make a family tree, consult a genealogist.
c. The antique-shop owner is one of the most knowledgeable ....s in the area.
d. Octogenarians and nonagenarians are *not* ....s unless they happen to study the ancient past or deal in ....s.

146. **quotation / quote / quota / quotient**

a. Your IQ (or intelligence ....) is a measure of how smart you are.
b. In the USA "inverted commas" are known as .... marks.
c. The government has decided to impose strict ....s on immigration.
d. "To be or not to be" is a famous .... (formal) / .... (informal).
e. When you divide 100 by 2, the .... is 50.

150. **vote / quantity / proportion / margin**

a. The teacher asked them to leave a one-inch .... on both sides of the paper.
b. A large .... of the state is rich farmland.
c. If you want the recipe to serve eight, just double the .... of each ingredient.
d. Caricatures are portraits in which certain features are drawn out of ....
e. An election is a "landslide" when someone gets many more ....s than the others (ie, when someone wins by a large ....).

ADDLING ADJECTIVES

A Common collocations – Complete each phrase with a word from the box.

amenable	delirious	devastated	deprived	gnarled	open-eyed

1. .... of affection
2. .... to change
3. .... with wonder / awe
4. .... with joy
5. .... with age
6. .... with grief

deleterious	destitute	gnarled	jagged	prickly	slippery

7. .... sidewalks / eels
8. .... cactuses (cacti)
9. .... beggars
10. .... hands / trees
11. .... glass / mountains
12. .... substances / effects

B Fine-tuning your knowledge – The numbers below refer to the questions in the Vocabulary section in Practice Test 7. After reviewing the words, fill in the blanks with the appropriate words.

112. poised / possessed / poignant / possessive

a. The film was a .... reminder of the tragedy of war.
b. Upon hearing the good news, he ran around the room like a man ....
c. Some children enjoy sharing their toys; others are more .... by nature.
d. He's always .... and in control, which makes him invaluable in a crisis.

123. irrelevant / irreparable / impertinent / impeccable

a. We were impressed by the local guide's .... command of English.
b. Your comment is .... It has nothing to do with the topic at hand.
c. The .... child was sent to his room for offending the dinner guest.
d. He suffered .... brain damage in the crash and will never walk again.

129. open-ended / open-handed / open-eyed / open-and-shut

a. If parents are too .... , they run the risk of spoiling their children.
b. The ethics of cloning is an .... question that is highly controversial.
c. The prosecutor was sure he had an .... case against the accused.
d. The child looked .... at the mountain of gifts under the Christmas tree.

138. amenable / adjacent / abrasive / adhesive

a. People whose homes are .... to each other are next-door neighbors.
b. She repaired the torn page with a long piece of .... tape.
c. His wife prefers comfort and would not be .... to a camping trip.
d. If you use an .... cleanser on a marble floor, it will dull the surface.

139. deprived / undernourished / diffident / underrated

a. Van Gogh was a(n) .... artist who achieved fame only after he died.
b. The famine victims were severely .... and on the verge of starvation.
c. .... areas are rife with crime and other problems caused by poverty.
d. The writer is a surprisingly .... man who shies away from publicity.

148. undiluted / insolvent / dissolved / liquefied

a. The thermometer contains .... mercury.
b. He downed the .... whisky in a single swallow.
c. A person who is .... cannot pay his debts.
d. She wondered how long the bitter taste of her .... marriage would linger in her memory.

AUDACIOUS ADVERBS

Fine-tuning your knowledge – The numbers below refer to the questions in the Vocabulary section in Practice Test 7. After reviewing the words, fill in the blanks with the appropriate words.

133.

vainly sadly wrongly virtually	a. They were .... disappointed when they failed to win the game. b. "Not one of them is as pretty or as smart as I!" she said .... c. .... everyone I know thinks he was .... accused. d. Not realizing the battery was dead, he .... tried to start the car.

136.

consistently relentlessly hardly inevitably	a. She worked .... , hoping to meet the quickly approaching deadline. b. The disease leads, ... , to paralysis and death. c. It is amazing how .... well the team has played all year. d. .... a day goes by that she doesn't think of him.

142.

alarmingly overwhelmingly barely extensively	a. It is their dream to travel .... when they retire. b. The patient's condition had deteriorated .... in the last few days. c. When the paramedics reached him, he was .... breathing. d. A novel that sells a million copies is .... successful.

SO NEAR AND YET SO FAR

Most of the words below appear in the Vocabulary section of Practice Test 7. Discuss each group, and then fill in each blank with the correct form of the appropriate word.

1.

fend defend offend	a. It was not my intention to .... you. Please accept my apology. b. The well-equipped army easily .... off the attack. c. She believes that children should be taught to .... themselves. d. The elderly couple are having difficulty .... for themselves.

2.

sustain contain retain attain	a. The film .... several scenes which are unsuitable for children. b. Some students are better at .... new vocabulary than others. c. It takes patience and understanding to .... a long-term relationship. d. She would have to work hard to .... the reputation she has worked so hard to ....

3.

revolt revolve rotate evolve	a. The plan slowly .... in his mind. b. It was only a matter of time before the oppressed citizens .... c. As the earth .... around the sun, it also .... on its axis. d. We .... chores at home: eg, I cook one day, my husband cooks the next.

4.

compel dispel expel impel repel propel	a. Cars of the future will be .... by cleaner forms of energy. b. The army failed to .... the enemy invasion. c. The principal was forced to .... the student for serious misconduct. d. She did her best to .... her child's fear of the dark. e. The material is designed to .... water. f. I cannot .... you to respect me if you are not .... to do so of your own accord. [................................ means "force sb to do sth" while .... is more often used to mean "be driven forward by strong desire or emotion."]

PRACTICE TEST 8

Writing

(30 minutes)

Write on one of the topics given below. If you write about something else, your paper will not be graded. If you do not understand the topics, ask the examiner to explain or translate them. You will be graded on the clarity of your writing and the linguistic range and accuracy you show. Write $1\frac{1}{2}$ to 2 pages. You may make any corrections or other changes in the body of the composition.

TOPICS

1. A young person's first role model is often a close relative, a teacher or perhaps a famous public figure. Describe a person that you wanted to be like when you grew up. Include examples of what you admired about this person and how your perception of him/her changed over the years. How do you see this person today?

2. Throughout history, every generation has had to face unique problems and challenges based on the circumstances of the times they live in. What **two** special challenges do you feel young people face today? What steps do you think they can take to prepare themselves to meet these challenges?

For help in writing these compositions, see *Writing Tutorial*, pages 204–205.

Listening Comprehension Test

(35-40 minutes)

This part of the examination is a listening test that will assess your understanding of spoken English. The listening test has three parts. There are 50 questions. Mark all your answers on the separate answer sheet. Do not make any stray marks on the answer sheet. If you change your mind about an answer, erase your first answer completely.

PART I – In this part of the test, you will hear a short conversation. From the three answer choices given, choose the answer which means the same thing as you hear, or that is true based on what you hear.

For problems **1–17**, mark your answers on the separate answer sheet. No problem can be repeated. Please listen carefully. Do you have any questions?

1. a. She's afraid to go herself.
   b. She wants him to answer the door.
   c. She thinks he should bang back.

2. a. He wants her to call Stacey for him.
   b. He's lost Stacey's new address.
   c. He needs Stacey's phone number.

3. a. She'll try to come up with some ideas.
   b. She'll try to get some tickets for him.
   c. She's not sure she can go with him.

4. a. He doesn't have to go to school today.
   b. One of his teachers is in the hospital.
   c. One of his classes was called off.

5. a. He doesn't want to help her.
   b. He told her he'd help, but he forgot.
   c. He intended to help her, but he can't.

6. a. The man is much heavier than Greg.
   b. Greg has put on weight recently.
   c. The man is thinner than Greg.

7. a. They both like the same music.
   b. She'd rather not listen to music.
   c. She wants to think about it.

8. a. She doesn't want him to disturb her.
   b. She didn't realize he was talking to her.
   c. She's been watching the news all day.

9. a. Her sister fell while taking the violin upstairs.
   b. She hates the way her sister plays the violin.
   c. Her sister has just begun learning the violin.

10. a. She thinks they're both working too hard.
    b. She stayed up late to meet a deadline.
    c. She couldn't sleep because she was ill.

11. a. She's thinking about quitting her job.
    b. She's thinking of putting an ad in the paper.
    c. She thinks toys are entertaining.

12. a. She wouldn't think of interfering.
    b. She doesn't approve of the marriage.
    c. She thinks the marriage is a good idea.

13. a. This was Joe's first Mozart concert.
    b. It's Pete who was at the concert with her.
    c. It's Pete who dislikes classical music.

14. a. They're cleaning up the kitchen.
    b. They're working in the garden.
    c. They're clipping coupons from a newspaper.

15. a. Sid got drunk and lost his driver's license.
    b. Sid was put in jail for drunk driving.
    c. Sid's license was taken away as punishment.

16. a. She did little traveling in her last job.
    b. She prefers a job that involves more traveling.
    c. She used to work for a theatrical agency.

17. a. She's enthusiastic about buying a computer.
    b. She's against buying guns.
    c. She suggests they delay the purchase.

Part II – In this part of the test, you will hear a question. From the three answer choices given, choose the one which best answers the question.

For problems **18–35**, mark your answers on the separate answer sheet. No problem can be repeated. Please listen carefully. Do you have any questions?

18. a. How should I know?
b. Have you finished with them?
c. Look over there on the table.

19. a. I'll get it.
b. How much do you need?
c. No, did you?

20. a. I thought you liked going alone.
b. You're always so impatient.
c. Are you saying I did it?

21. a. Maybe later.
b. No, the line's too long.
c. How about some milk?

22. a. The quality's just not what it used to be.
b. I know. They're really affordable now.
c. It's really a shame, isn't it?

23 a. Look, I'm working as hard as I can.
b. I'll accept it if they offer it to me.
c. I'll cross that bridge when I come to it.

24. a. It's still early.
b. I can spare a few hours.
c. As long as you're on time.

25. a. I wish you had asked me first.
b. We have lots of extra forms.
c. You can use my pen, if you like.

26. a. I thought you did it.
b. Maybe next year.
c. I'm a last-minute shopper.

27. a. The police are still working on it.
b. I'm afraid I haven't a clue.
c. The case was dismissed.

28. a. Sorry, we don't accept credit cards.
b. Would you like me to sign it for you?
c. That will be fine.

29. a. No, as long as the report gets done.
b. I was just leaving myself.
c. I wish you hadn't.

30 a. Do you think I should?
b. I decided to buy another one.
c. The sleeves were much too long.

31. a. Nobody's seen it in weeks.
b. As soon as I find the time.
c. I'll look, but I don't think I'll find it.

32. a. She'll have to think about it.
b. I agree. She has been acting strangely.
c. Actually, she's just been offered a part.

33. a. He's got lovely blond curly hair.
b. Most people say me.
c. He's got my personality.

34. a. They're counting on our being there.
b. You can go alone if you prefer.
c. You could've stayed home, you know.

35. a. I said nothing.
b. You never tell me anything.
c. I won't tell a soul.

PART III – In this part, you will hear three short segments from a radio program. The program is called "Learning from the Experts." Each talk lasts about two minutes. As you listen, you may want to take notes to help you remember information given in the talk. After each talk, you will be asked some questions about what was said. From the three answer choices given, you should choose the one which best answers the question according to the information you heard.

Remember, no problems can be repeated. For problems **36–50**, mark your answers on the separate answer sheet. Do you have any questions?

SEGMENT 1

36. According to the speaker, what is resilience?
- a. The ability to live a long, happy and healthy life
- b. The frequency with which bad things happen to good people
- c. The ability to survive and overcome difficult situations

37. Which quality would people with resilience be least likely to have?
- a. A sense that life has treated them unfairly
- b. A sense of feeling connected to others
- c. A tendency to learn from a bad situation

38. What do more and more researchers believe?
- a. Resilience is a matter of genetic inheritance.
- b. Irritable people are more resilient than calm people.
- c. People can develop their resilience through training.

39. How can resilience training help a company's profitability?
- a. By helping employees to recover more quickly from difficult personal situations
- b. By helping workers adapt more quickly to being unemployed
- c. By helping workers improve their relationships with co-workers

40. Why is resilience a must for people in the modern world?
- a. It can save people and companies from being downsized.
- b. It can help people cope with the changing demands and job insecurity.
- c. It can help people prepare to start their own home-based businesses.

SEGMENT 2

41. What makes the village of Batu Putih unique?
- a. The amazingly rich biodiversity of the nearby Supu Forest Reserve
- b. The way its tin-roofed houses are built on unusually high stilts
- c. Its involvement in a WWF-sponsored conservation project

42. What is MESCOT?
- a. A scheme that will enable all villagers to live off the profits of ecotourism
- b. A scheme that encourages ecotourism instead of activities that endanger the forest
- c. A scheme that will totally ban logging and fishing in the area

43. Who was the first to recognize the region's potential for ecotourism?
- a. The villagers themselves
- b. The head of the village
- c. WWF ecotourism planning specialists

44. The WWF advisers are quoted as saying "That gives local communities ownership of the project." What do they mean by this?
- a. Communities will be more committed if they decide by themselves what experiences to offer.
- b. More villagers in the local community will profit if they retain ownership of the village.
- c. It's up to the local community to decide whether or not it will sell its land to the WWF.

45. How will the villagers benefit if their experiment succeeds?
- a. They will have the satisfaction of being a role model for other communities.
- b. They will preserve their natural and cultural diversity as well as revive the local economy.
- c. They will learn how to make their traditional forestry and fishing practices more profitable.

SEGMENT 3

46. Based on early clinical trials, what advantage did coated stents seem to have over uncoated stents?
    a. They would keep arteries open without balloon angioplasty.
    b. They would result in more and healthier new tissue growth
    c. They would keep arteries open longer with less blockage.

47. How many deaths were linked to the Cypher stent in its first six months on the market?
    a Just under 300
    b. More than 60
    c. Just over 30

48. How did the Food and Drug Administration react to the situation?
    a They reaffirmed their faith in the product as long as it were properly used.
    b. They suspended the manufacturer's license and had to recall the product.
    c. They wrote letters to surgeons instructing them how to handle the product.

49. Which of the following has resulted in problems for patients with Cypher stents?
    a. Taking prescribed anti-blood-clotting drugs over a three-month period
    b. Implanting a Cypher stent that fits tightly against the wall of a cleared artery
    c. Using a Cypher stent to support a cleared area of longer than 40 millimeters

50. Which phrase best sums up the manufacturer's response to the situation?
    a. Irresponsible and unprofessional
    b. Concerned and cooperative
    c. Objective and dispassionate

Grammar – Cloze – Vocabulary – Reading

(75 minutes)

This part of the examination contains 120 problems, numbered **51–170**. There are 40 grammar, 20 cloze, 40 vocabulary and 20 reading comprehension problems. The examiner will not explain any test problems. If you do not understand how to do the problems, raise your hand and a proctor will explain the examples to you.

Do not spend too much time on any one problem. Each problem counts the same. If you do not know the answer to a problem, you may make a reasonable guess. Each problem has only one correct answer. Work fast but carefully. You have 75 minutes to answer all 120 problems.

GRAMMAR

51. I've been meaning to invite Sam and his wife to the party, but ..... .
- a. I've not been doing it yet
- b. I still haven't done so
- c. haven't done yet
- d. still don't do it

52. ..... people are buying home computers and shopping online.
- a. Moreover
- b. More of the
- c. More and more
- d. More or less

53. The test ..... four parts: grammar, cloze, vocabulary and reading.
- a. consists of
- b. consists from
- c. is consisted of
- d. is consisting from

54. Frank tends to exaggerate. If I were you, ... what he says with a grain of salt.
- a. I'd taken
- b. I'd take
- c. I'd have taken
- d. I took

55. I can't say when, but ..... the boss will come to his senses and fire her.
- a. some day comes that
- b. there is coming a day that
- c. a day comes when
- d. there'll come a day when

56. ..... are you to reveal this information to the press.
- a. In any event
- b. No matter what happens
- c. Under no circumstances
- d. On any account

57. Reaching into my pocket, I realized that my wallet was gone ..... .
- a. as also was my money
- b. but my money was too
- c. and so was my money
- d. so my money was too

58. Having completely forgotten her birthday, he was forced to send her a ..... birthday card.
- a. belated
- b. lateness
- c. later
- d. latest

59. ..... that William offered you an explanation for his absence, did he?
- a. I don't suppose
- b. Let's suppose
- c. Should I suppose
- d. Supposing

60. Margarita says she likes Gregory better than Dan as he's ..... the two.
- a. funnier from
- b. the funnier of
- c. as much fun of
- d. the funnier than

61. After receiving an emergency text message from his wife, he left the meeting ..... .
- a. not explaining
- b. unexplained
- c. without being explained
- d. without explanation

62. The TV station has received one complaint after ..... about the controversial show.
- a. one another
- b. each other
- c. one other
- d. another

63. Mary said she'd meet us at the theater so we ..... call her now.
    a. haven't to
    b. don't need
    c. not have to
    d. needn't

64. If you want to call her, feel free ..... on my cell phone.
    a. to do so
    b. of doing it
    c. that you do so
    d. for doing it

65. When she heard she had passed the exam, she was ..... herself with joy.
    a. beside
    b. aside
    c. on the side of
    d. at one side of

66. He's up to his neck in financial problems; ..... , he's always cheerful.
    a. otherwise
    b. nevertheless
    c. moreover
    d. in spite

67. ..... the hotel, she was so exhausted that she went straight to sleep.
    a. On reaching
    b. When reached
    c. No sooner did she reach
    d. To have reached

68. Cleaning up will take us no time at all if everyone does ..... share.
    a. the
    b. their
    c. his and her
    d. our

69. If the children look tired, it's because they're not used to ..... .
    a. hardly having to work
    b. having to work so hardly
    c. have worked so hard
    d. having to work so hard

70. As their teacher is ill, the class ..... by a substitute for the rest of the week.
    a. will be teaching
    b. is to be taught
    c. is teaching
    d. has been taught

71. ..... she get home than she greeted her family and sat down with them to eat.
    a. No sooner did
    b. The sooner
    c. As soon as
    d. Only after

72. Everyone in the room was shocked at the child's ..... behavior.
    a. ashamed
    b. shamed
    c. shameless
    d. full of shame

73. Supposing you've run out of gas on a dark country road, what ..... next?
    a. to do
    b. you would do
    c. should you do
    d. would have you to do

74. ..... for such a long time, she was sure she'd recognize him when he got off the plane.
    a. She hadn't seen him
    b. Although she hadn't seen him
    c. As he hadn't been seen
    d. Not having seen him

75. ..... John has been with the company the longest, he trains all the new employees.
    a. While
    b. Since
    c. Therefore
    d. Owing to

76. It's hard to believe, but the twins had a falling out and haven't spoken to ..... in months.
    a. themselves
    b. each of the other
    c. either of them
    d. one another

77. After graduating from college, he ..... an editor in a publishing house.
    a. had become
    b. was become
    c. went on to become
    d. was becoming

78. The changes included in the new tax legislation are ..... all taxpayers.
    a. concerned about
    b. of concern to
    c. concerning
    d. concerned by

79. ..... you learn how to ride a bike, you never forget.
    a. Once
    b. While
    c. As
    d. Since

80. They walked back to where they had parked the car ..... it had been towed away.
    a. having found
    b. found
    c. only to find
    d. only just finding

81. Anyone who is ..... to move a piano up two flights of stairs deserves to hurt his back.
    a. so foolish
    b. foolish enough
    c. too foolish
    d. that foolish

82. According to an article I read, the battle ..... was a turning point in the war.
    a. was fought here
    b. which fought here
    c. to have fought here
    d. fought here

83. When he finally got home, the rest of the family was fast ..... .
    a. sleeping
    b. sleepy
    c. asleep
    d. slept

84. Thankfully, the child was OK, having suffered ..... a few scratches.
    a. little more than
    b. little or nothing but
    c. little by little
    d. for a little

85. The innovative marketing strategy ..... to make a big difference in next year's sales.
    a. is bound
    b. will bound
    c. will probably
    d. is probable

86. The director is certain the contractor can get the job done ..... than we can.
    a. as quick and as accurate
    b. the quicker, the more accurately
    c. quickly and more accurate
    d. more quickly and accurately

87. The embassy reports a marked increase in the number of people ..... political asylum.
    a. to seek
    b. seek
    c. seeking
    d. have sought

88. Reviews of the production were mixed; for every critic who praised it, ... didn't.
    a. someone else
    b. another one who
    c. but others
    d. and another one

89. The resumption of hostilities in the area could result in ..... .
    a. war's declaration
    b. declaring of war
    c. war being declared
    d. war declaration

90. She suffers from a disorder so uncommon ..... her family doctor had never heard of it.
    a. which
    b. even
    c. although
    d. therefore

Practice Test 8

CLOZE

Passage 1 is about scientists.

You have seen them in movies: scientists who are infallible and coldly objective – little more than animated computers in white lab coats. They take measurements and record results as if the collection of data was the ....(91).... object of their lives. The assumption: ....(92).... one gathers enough facts about something, ...(93).... the relationships between those facts will reveal ....(94).... .

But the myth of the infallible scientist evaporates when one thinks of the number of great ideas in science ....(95).... originators were correct in general but ....(96).... in detail. The English physicist John Dalton (1766–1844), for example, still gets ....(97).... for modern atomic theory, although his mathematical formulas for calculating atomic weights have ....(98).... been known to be incorrect. A second ....(99).... in point is the Polish astronomer Copernicus (1473–1543). Credited with correcting Ptolemy's ancient concept of an Earth-centered universe, he was nevertheless ....(100).... in the particulars of the planet's orbits.

91. a. sole b. unique c. lonely d. solitary

92. a. that b. while c. if d. because

93. a. but b. so c. when d. then

94. a. others b. themselves c. them d. those

95. a. that b. because c. whose d. although

96. a. perfect b. wrong c. unsuitable d. full

97. a. known b. attention c. credit d. identified

98. a. long b. hardly c. never d. usually

99. a. situation b. scientist c. example d. case

100. a. mistaken b. blamed c. wronged d. accused

Passage 2 is about settlers in the New World.

The first British immigrants to what is now the United States crossed the Atlantic long after flourishing Spanish colonies had been established in Mexico, the West Indies and South America. ....(101).... all early travelers to the New World, they came in small, overcrowded ships. During their six- to twelve-week voyages, they lived ....(102).... meager rations, and many ....(103).... of disease. Their ships were often battered by storms, and ....(104).... were even lost at sea.

To the weary voyager, the sight of the American shore brought ....(105).... relief. The colonists' first ....(106).... of the new land was a vista of dense woods. True, the woods were ....(107).... by Indians, many of ....(108).... were hostile, and the threat of Indian attack would ....(109).... to the hardships of daily life. ....(110).... the vast, virgin forests, extending nearly 2,100 kilometers along the eastern seaboard from north to south, would prove to be a treasure house, providing abundant food, fuel and raw material for houses, furniture, and ships.

101. a. Almost b. Like c. Not d. Considering

102. a. for b. through c. on d. without

103. a. suffered b. died c. vanished d. afflicted

104. a. some b. those c. others d. few

105. a. the b. up c. little d. immense

106. a. vision b. illusion c. glance d. glimpse

107. a. inhabited b. preoccupied c. popularized d. resided

108. a. which b. who c. whom d. them

109. a. multiply b. intensify c. increase d. add

110. a. But b. Although c. Therefore d. While

VOCABULARY

111. Wanting to do the right thing, she offered to train her ..... before she retired.
   a. descendant
   b. successor
   c. predecessor
   d. forerunner

112. The director of the orphanage ..... accepted the businessman's donation.
   a. authentically
   b. respectively
   c. gratefully
   d. formerly

113. Ellen's birthday party was meant to be a surprise, but someone ..... .
   a. let the cat out of the bag
   b. took the bull by the horns
   c. put the cart before the horse
   d. was slow on the uptake

114. He was so hot that ..... of sweat ran down his face.
   a. freckles
   b. speckles
   c. sparkles
   d. trickles

115. No matter how much she ..... it, the old kitchen floor would never look clean.
   a. simmered
   b. scrubbed
   c. scratched
   d. nurtured

116. The young publishing company has ..... several best-selling novels this year.
   a. written off
   b. drawn up
   c. put down
   d. brought out

117. It's normal for patients coming out of anesthesia to be ..... .
   a. incoherent
   b. irrelevant
   c. illegible
   d. insolvent

118. Modems enable the ..... of computer data through telephone lines.
   a. promotion
   b. omission
   c. transmission
   d. possession

119. I'm sorry to have to tell you that I find your argument totally ..... .
   a. spurious
   b. substantial
   c. vagrant
   d. innate

120. Before it could be published, the poorly written manuscript had to be revised ..... .
   a. sparingly
   b. subsequently
   c. extensively
   d. voraciously

121. The dental examination showed that she had several ..... that needed to be filled.
   a. vacancies
   b. cavities
   c. gaps
   d. blanks

122. It's extremely important that this information not be ..... to anyone.
   a. divulged
   b. radiated
   c. dispelled
   d. expelled

123. The boys were exact opposites: one was outgoing and self-assured; the other, quiet and ..... .
   a. oppressive
   b. scarce
   c. diffident
   d. shrill

124. Convicting the wrong person of a crime is a serious ..... of justice.
   a. malformation
   b. misconception
   c. miscarriage
   d. misquotation

125. The spray smells bad, but it is excellent for ..... insects.
   a. propelling
   b. alleviating
   c. repelling
   d. intercepting

126. Would you mind ..... my report to see if I've omitted anything important?
   a. putting down
   b. looking down on
   c. running up
   d. looking over

127. Wanting to impress the interviewer, she shook his hand ..... .
   a. frantically
   b. firmly
   c. hardly
   d. barely

128. Before having your home renovated, it's wise to get .... from several firms.
   a. quotations
   b. expenditures
   c. inquiries
   d. symphonies

129. The critics agreed that the soloist's performance had been ..... .
   a. subordinate
   b. impertinent
   c. impeccable
   d. inedible

130. She was shattered when she realized that he would never ..... her love.
   a. reciprocate
   b. recapitulate
   c. transfer
   d. duplicate

131. It's no surprise that computer sales have increased ..... typewriter sales.
   a. at the expense of
   b. on account of
   c. on behalf of
   d. in tandem with

132. Experts are still divided as to whether the death penalty acts as a(n) ..... to violent crime.
   a. transition
   b. incentive
   c. deterrent
   d. suspension

133. Unfortunately, the proposal is not ..... as it entails spending too much money.
   a. poignant
   b. exceptional
   c. accelerated
   d. viable

134. "Mom and Dad have always liked you better!" said the child ..... .
   a. lavishly
   b. resentfully
   c. vainly
   d. tactfully

135. The start of the new millennium was a good time for many people to ..... .
   a. let sleeping dogs lie
   b. kill two birds with one stone
   c. clock their performance
   d. turn over a new leaf

136. Be wary when he tells you anything as he has a bad habit of ..... the truth.
   a. embellishing
   b. diversifying
   c. renovating
   d. adopting

137. It is impossible to predict what ..... the new tax law will have.
   a. expectations
   b. impositions
   c. ramifications
   d. malfunctions

138. She enjoyed the music at the restaurant as it was soft and ..... .
   a. unobtrusive
   b. glaring
   c. undernourished
   d. shimmering

139. Whenever he sees his ex-wife, they end up quarrelling and ..... insults at each other.
   a. cracking
   b. lauding
   c. bombing
   d. hurling

140. Stuttering is a speech ..... that can often be corrected with therapy.
   a. deference
   b. impediment
   c. aptitude
   d. manifestation

141. She slammed her foot on the brake pedal and the car stopped with a ..... .
   a. gasp
   b. jolt
   c. gush
   d. bolt

142. What she hates about big cities is that everyone rushes around so ..... .
   a. inevitably
   b. alarmingly
   c. hectically
   d. gracefully

143. She's an optimistic person who never ..... on the negative aspects of a situation.
   a. dwells
   b. preys
   c. feeds
   d. leans

144. The little girl was .... when she heard that her puppy had been run over.
   a. destitute
   b. irreparable
   c. unmentionable
   d. devastated

145. He's a private person who dislikes it when others ..... into his personal affairs.
   a. rip
   b. pry
   c. recede
   d. launch

146. At seventy years old, it's natural for a woman to ..... .
   a. beat around the bush
   b. be wet behind the ears
   c. feel past her prime
   d. lay down the law

147. Everyone says he's a(n) ..... actor with very little talent.
   a. underrated
   b. prolific
   c. flimsy
   d. mediocre

148. She finds it difficult to lose weight because she always ..... temptation.
   a. succumbs to
   b. refrains from
   c. hovers over
   d. caters to

149. I'm glad to see you two are speaking again. What made you call a ..... ?
   a. vote
   b. truce
   c. treaty
   d. name

150. The mischievous students did their best to ..... the teacher with irrelevant questions.
   a. sway
   b. sidetrack
   c. emulate
   d. vanquish

READING

Passage 1 is about avalanches.

In the high mountain regions where cross-country skiing is popular, the most common type of avalanche happens when a weak layer in the snow gives way, precipitating the snow on top down the hill – the so-called "dry-slab avalanche." For years skiers have used standard tests such as the Rutschblock test or the shovel shear test to gauge the stability of slopes. The tests involve digging a hole in the snow and, crudely, jumping up and down, or pushing the snow sideways with a shovel to judge its strength. These tests allow the skier to identify weak layers in the snow-pack, estimate their strength and so assess the risk of an avalanche. A recent study of the mechanics of dry-slab avalanches appearing in the *Journal of Glaciology* suggests that these tests may not tell the whole story.

The authors of the study show that the standard tests do not measure important factors affecting the likelihood of an avalanche. Although the presence of a weak layer is a prerequisite for an avalanche, the trigger for an avalanche depends on the strength of the overlying layers of snow and on the growth of cracks in the snow. The analysis shows that the risk of an avalanche is affected by factors such as the temperature of the snow's surface layer, its hardness and its thickness – even the size of the skis has an effect. In many cases, these influences increase the probability of an avalanche, so that an area may not be safe even if the standard tests indicate that it is. Unfortunately, the temperature, strength and thickness of layers of snow change rapidly from place to place on a slope and so cannot easily be taken into account by the recreational skier.

The conclusion is that the commonly used tests for avalanche safety may be unable to reveal vital information. As in many action sports, the element of risk cannot be eliminated, only reduced to a level that the participant finds acceptable.

151. What do the authors of a recent article suggest about avalanches?
    a. They are remarkably accurate, despite their crudity.
    b. They should be performed by recreational skiers on a more frequent basis.
    c. They are only reliable if they are performed by trained experts.
    d. They cannot be relied upon to reveal the full risk that skiers face.

152. What condition **must** be present for an avalanche to occur?
    a. appropriate temperature
    b. cracks in the surface of the snow
    c. the existence of a weak layer under the snow's surface
    d. a thick surface layer of snow

153. According to the passage, what is true about layers of snow on a mountain?
    a. Underlying layers are always weaker than top layers.
    b. Top wet layers pose no danger to the skier.
    c. Their qualities vary greatly on different parts of a slope.
    d. Their stability cannot be estimated, even by experts.

154. What does the study conclude?
    a. Skiing involves an unacceptable level of risk.
    b. Fewer people should take up skiing because of the risks involved.
    c. Skiers should be discouraged from performing the standard tests.
    d. No matter what skiers do, an element of risk will always exist.

155. Which is **not** mentioned as a factor that affects the probability of an avalanche occurring?
    a. ski size
    b. air temperature
    c. the thickness of the snow's surface layer
    d. the strength of underlying layers of snow

Passage 2 is about a device called the CyberTracker.

Interpreting nature's vocabulary of footprints and foliage, Stone Age hunters not only tracked their prey but also acquired a practical understanding of recurring patterns in animal behavior. But the tracker's knowledge was never written down. Even today, among the few remaining hunter-gatherer communities in Africa, Asia and Australia, the best trackers can neither read nor write. And as their dwindling, isolated communities face social marginalization, their tribal cultures and means of survival are under threat. Now, a scientist is using computer technology to revive the dying art of tracking.

After spending 11 years on periodic field trips with tribal communities in the Kalahari Desert, physicist Louis Liebenberg decided that their ancient tracking skills could not just be documented but could indeed be saved by the use of modern technology. Working with computer experts, he came up with the CyberTracker, a handheld computer that enables native trackers to record animal behavior. The CyberTracker has a user interface that employs a keyboard with symbols rather than letters: animals are listed by clear silhouettes while functions such as drinking, running and eating are identified by easily understood symbols. By simply touching the appropriate icons on the screen, the user can record detailed information on everything from feeding patterns to the exact location of habitual hunting grounds. Linked to a Global Positioning System satellite network, the CyberTracker feeds data into statistical and graphics software that can compile maps and chart the migrations of various animal populations.

In addition to helping indigenous people preserve their traditions, the invention makes the tribesmen's knowledge available to others, opening up potential applications for managing wildlife populations and combating poachers. Kruger National Park is already planning to use 100 CyberTrackers for wildlife tracking and research on animal behavior and movements. And Liebenberg himself is training a team to help distribute the technology in southern Africa and beyond. If he succeeds, the CyberTracker could symbolize the fusion of Stone Age and Space Age.

156. What concerns the writer about the art of tracking?
- a. Modern trackers are uneducated and not as skillful as their Stone Age ancestors.
- b. Tribesmen are unwilling to reveal their secrets to the next generation.
- c. Ancient hunter-gatherers did not pass their skills on to their descendants.
- d. Like other tribal practices, it may die out unless it is documented.

157. Why does the writer consider the CyberTracker to be an important innovation?
- a. It will force trackers to acquire basic literacy and computer skills.
- b. It could facilitate the work of wildlife managers and animal researchers.
- c. It marks the first time that Space Age technology has been aided by ancient customs.
- d. It will help indigenous people become better hunters.

158. What makes the CyberTracker so easy for native trackers to use?
- a. its size and portability
- b. its specially designed keyboard
- c. its simplified Global Positioning System
- d. its statistical and graphics software

159. What happens to the information that is recorded by a CyberTracker?
- a. It is processed by software that can generate maps and chart animal movements.
- b. It is distributed internationally by a specially trained team.
- c. It is sent to a satellite network that informs the user of his exact location.
- d. It is checked for accuracy by wildlife management specialists.

160. The CyberTracker would be an aid in understanding all of the following, except ...
- a. animal migration patterns.
- b. animal feeding patterns.
- c. the time of projected poaching raids.
- d. the exact location of hunting grounds.

Passage 3 is about modern medicine.

On July 2, 1881, less than six months into his first term, President James A. Garfield was shot by a ne'er-do-well named Charles Julius Guiteau. In a futile search for the bullet, his doctors performed two operations, never bothering to wash their hands, let alone sterilize their equipment. Garfield died later that summer, apparently from the infections contracted during the surgery. Guiteau was convicted and hanged, but he always denied that he had killed the president. "The doctors did that," he said. "I simply shot at him."

Garfield had the misfortune of being shot a few years too soon, but his fate is a vivid reminder of just how recently medicine has emerged from the dark ages. Even as he lay dying, epochal changes were coming to medical science. The French scientist Louis Pasteur had begun to perceive the links between microbes and disease, and other researchers would soon unveil the causes of such perennial killers as cholera and tuberculosis. By 1900, such staples as aspirin and the X-ray had entered medical practice and physicians were engaged in an unprecedented riot of discovery. Five decades later, antibiotics had essentially cured many bacterial diseases – and by 1960, modern vaccines had miraculously given millions of children protective immunity against measles and polio. Today, armed with a new understanding of genetics and immunology, researchers are inching toward similar triumphs over a range of chronic and hereditary ailments.

Yet, as the 21st century progresses, modern medicine's limitations and failings are as striking as its successes. The rise of AIDS reminds us that new plagues are still possible. The recent emergence of new, drug-resistant strains of tuberculosis and malaria makes clear that the microbial world is no less inventive than we are. And the persistence of pre-modern suffering across large stretches of the world – including the developed world – serves as a strong antidote to complacency.

161. Which statement best summarizes the main idea of the passage?
   a. Garfield would not have died if he had been shot in the early 20th century.
   b. The 20th century witnessed remarkable advances in medicine.
   c. Despite advances in medical science, there is still much work to be done.
   d. Modern medicine has not been as successful as many people claim.

162. According to the passage, which area saw major advances in the first half of the 20th century?
   a. immunology
   b. the fight against infectious diseases
   c. inherited illnesses
   d. the eradication of childhood diseases

163. What does the writer imply about progress in the treatment of chronic and hereditary ailments?
   a. It has been slow but promising.
   b. It has not yet been made.
   c. It will not be a major priority in the 21st century.
   d. It could not have been possible without the discoveries of Louis Pasteur.

164. Why does the writer include the anecdote about President Garfield?
   a. to show how his death led to the introduction of new surgical procedures
   b. to persuade us that Guiteau should not have been hanged for what he did
   c. to imply that Garfield's doctors should have been sued for malpractice
   d. to illustrate how primitive medicine was in the late 19th century

165. What is true of tuberculosis and malaria?
   a. Both diseases were successfully eradicated in the 20th century.
   b. They continue to be a major cause of suffering in industrialized countries.
   c. New forms have appeared that do not respond to 20th-century drugs.
   d. Scientists have been slow to find a cure for both diseases.

Passage 4 is about successful thrillers.

Best-selling novelist Robert Ludlum (1927–2001) knew what makes a successful thriller. And that, above all, is velocity. Reviewing Ludlum, a famous reviewer once said, "I sprained my wrist turning his pages."

Narrative velocity is a trick. Looks easy. Isn't. The thriller writer works hard to make speed. Short sentences help. So do bodies. That are dead. And discovered in certain places. Often the dead people were carrying secret papers. Often there's a blonde in the hotel lobby. The man who finds the body often finds the blonde. Or the blonde finds the man. Because she's looking for the papers, too.

But short sentences and dead bodies are not enough. A writer of page-turners needs a good plot. People worry about things (the spouse, the kids, the job, the waistline), and they are tired of these worries. They want to worry about something else. They want distractions – systemic, hair-pulling distraction. They want plot. And plot means Good battling Evil. Good by itself is not interesting. Evil, on the other hand, is. The Evil has to be strong enough to threaten the hero of the story. But Good has to win in the end. Or Hollywood won't buy the book.

It often helps to throw in topics the public wants to worry about. In the 1960s and 1970s, people worried about the Cold War. In the 1980s and 1990s, they worried about business, rogue viruses and cloning. A few worried whether Hitler could be cloned. Creepy serial killers are always popular. Terrorists will continue to be big for the next few years. Especially terrorists who end up dead.

And then, if all these elements are present and the writer is lucky, the thriller lives many lives. First, it's a glossy hardcover with a nice advertising budget. Then a best-seller. Then a paperback. Then a movie. Years later, it achieves a sort of afterlife, usually in its paperback form and most often on a shelf in a summer house, somewhere where books linger. The book waits until someone picks it up. The reader flips through it. The references are a little dated. But the book looks interesting. Good is threatened by Evil, and the sentences move along. The blonde is smoking a cigarette in a hotel lobby. There's trouble.

166. What is the tone of the famous reviewer's comment in the first paragraph?
- a. factual and objective
- b. sarcastic and critical
- c. humorous and admiring
- d. cautionary and negative

167. Which of the following best describes "narrative velocity"?
- a. how often a reader is made to turn the page
- b. how fast the writer moves the story forward
- c. how many pages the writer takes to tell the story
- d. how long the reader takes to finish the novel

168. Which of the following is most important in the creation of a page-turner?
- a. the amount of speed
- b. the number of dead bodies
- c. the reader's wrist strength
- d. the right story line

169. What ingredient must be present if the novel is eventually to be made into a film?
- a. Evil that is eventually defeated by Good
- b. a blonde in a hotel lobby looking for secret papers
- c. spouses who worry about their kids, jobs and waistlines
- d. one or more dead bodies with secret papers in hotels

170. What does the writer imply about the thriller that lives many lives?
- a. It loses something once it becomes a paperback.
- b. It somehow manages to retain its original appeal.
- c. Their authors are very rich people.
- d. The movie is never *as good as the book.*

VOCABULARY CONSOLIDATION 8

A Preposition and particle power – The following extracts are taken from passages that you have already seen in Practice Tests 5–8. Read each passage quickly, then fill in the gaps with an appropriate preposition or particle.

1. The ocean's currents, waves and winds not only shape the land, but they also affect the living populations. Sometimes animals that inhabit deeper water are thrown .... course. They come close .... the shoreline or may actually be found .... the beach. They may be injured, sick or disoriented and soon become cold, hungry or dehydrated. Such is the case .... various species .... dolphin, porpoise, seal, whale and turtle that become stranded .... the Atlantic coastline. But there is help .... some animals. .... many locations, when beached animals are sighted, professionals and volunteers are .... the scene. Sick, cold or injured animals are immediately placed .... a rehabilitation program .... the intent .... getting them well enough to be returned .... their natural habitat. Often the animals are tagged .... a transmitter .... future tracking.

2. Bactrian camels are an excellent example .... an animal that has adapted well .... its environment. They are able to survive .... the arid Asian steppes because .... the biological strategies that enable them to cope .... the severe temperature changes common .... Central Asia. Camels can graze .... a wide range .... plants and thorny vegetation that other mammals avoid. Most striking is their ability to survive long periods .... water – a characteristic that humans recognized .... useful and used .... their own purposes. Body temperature may fluctuate .... much .... 57 degrees Fahrenheit .... the course .... a day, which enables the animal to minimize water loss due .... perspiration. Although a camel may look scrawny and emaciated .... a long, dry spell and its humps may become flaccid and flop .... one side, it fills .... quickly .... soon .... it gets water. .... fact, a thirsty camel may drink .... 40 gallons .... ten minutes.

3. More practical .... the short run may be so-called hybrid cars that have both a battery-driven motor and a gasoline engine .... the ability to switch back and forth .... the two power systems. .... alternating automatically .... the two motors according .... need, the cars can, ... example, go .... electric mode .... the city, thereby not adding .... urban smog, and then switch .... gasoline mode .... longer stretches .... the highway. The net result is a spectacular increase .... fuel efficiency and far less pollution than .... regular cars. There's no hassle either: recharging goes .... while the car is .... operation, and fuel is .... close .... the nearest gas station.

4. .... 1900, such staples .... aspirin and the X-ray had entered medical practice and physicians were engaged .... an unprecedented riot .... discovery. Five decades later, antibiotics had essentially cured many bacterial diseases – and .... 1960, modern vaccines had miraculously given millions .... children protective immunity .... measles and polio. Today, armed .... a new understanding .... genetics and immunology, researchers are inching .... similar triumphs .... a range .... chronic and hereditary ailments.

B Phrasal verb crack-down – For each group, match the bold-faced phrases with their definitions.

1.	....	Will somebody please tell me what I did to **tick** him **off**?	a. cause to appear
2.	....	You can be sure the boss will **tell** him **off** for being late.	b. insult, belittle
3.	....	All he's done is **run up** the phone bill since he was laid off.	c. plan out and write
4.	....	We asked the lawyer to **draw up** an agreement.	d. make angry
5.	....	You always **put** my cooking **down**. Am I that bad a cook?	e. increase, accumulate
6.	....	The doctors **put** his heart attack **down to** his obesity.	f. criticize angrily
7.	....	Falling in love tends to **bring out** the best in most people.	g. say sth is caused by

8.	....	If he doesn't **come up with** a plan soon, we're finished.	a. say spontaneously
9.	....	Children **come out with** the strangest things sometimes.	b. reduce, lessen
10.	....	I always **come down with** a cold when I have time off.	c. regard as inferior
11.	....	The doctor told him to **cut down on** his salt intake.	d. try to avoid
12.	....	They **look down on** people who aren't as rich as they are.	e. stand, tolerate
13.	....	**Look out for** pickpockets when you travel abroad.	f. become sick with
14.	....	Strict teachers refuse to **put up with** noise in their classes.	g. find or produce

C Idiom round-up – In each group, complete each blank with the correct form of a word from the box.

bag	basket	cat	eggs	foot	hair	lease	life	prime	ropes	sack	uptake

1. The boss's new secretary is lovely, but she's a bit slow on the .... I'm afraid she got off on the wrong .... with him, but perhaps things will improve once she's learned the ....
2. Catherine found out about her surprise party. I wonder who let the .... out of the ....
3. A good stock broker will tell you it's financial suicide to invest all your money in one stock. Don't you know you should never put all your .... in one .... ?
4. My four-week vacation in Hawaii has given me a whole new .... on .... !
5. I thought Denise was past her .... but she went dancing and really let her .... down last night. She'd better hit the .... early tonight or she'll be useless at work.

VERBS:	beat	bide	kill	lay	turn	watch	work
NOUNS:	birds	bush	clock (*x2*)	law	leaf	stone	time

6. I hear his parents have finally .... down the .... He's grounded until his grades improve
7. The class is so boring that all the students do is .... the .... from the moment they come in.
8. We need gifts for Mom and Dad. If we go to the mall, we can .... two .... with one ....
9. To meet its quota, the factory will have to .... round the .... for the next few months.
10. I hate the way you always .... around the .... Why don't you just say what you mean?
11. Lazy students tend to .... their .... and not get serious until right before a big test. You'd think some of them would learn after a while and .... over a new ....

D Elusive epithets (adjective review) – Match the people on the right with their descriptions.

GUYS AND GALS

1.	....	He works like a snail, but in the end he gets things done.	a.	Prudent Prudence
2	....	She's a ruthless competitor.	b.	Sturdy Stanley
3.	....	He's a bit short on brain power.	c.	Vagrant Valerie
4.	....	She's the most cautious of the lot.	d.	Vicious Victoria
5.	....	He's as strong as an ox and built like one, too	e.	Reckless Rex
6.	....	She's as stubborn as a mule.	f.	Obstinate Olivia
7.	....	Don't lend him your car as he may not return it in one piece.	g.	Witless Wally
8.	....	She's a wanderer at heart and currently in need of a home.	h.	Eventual Evan

...AND ANIMALS

1.	....	They're big and furry and no one can stand them.	a.	insolvent insects
2.	....	They're undistinguished members of the rodent family.	b.	diffident ducks
3.	....	They're tiny winged creatures that can't make ends meet.	c.	gnarled gnus
4	....	They're round, spiky and bad-tempered as well.	d	prickly porcupines
5.	....	They're reptiles that are poor and extinct.	e.	mediocre mice
6.	....	They're small and furry and have high, unpleasant voices.	f.	destitute dinosaurs
7.	....	They're antelopes that are afflicted with arthritis.	g.	unbearable bears
8.	....	They're water fowl that lack self-confidence.	h.	shrill shrews

E Verbalizing with adverbs – Match each question with the appropriate answer.

What would you do if you ...

1.	....	felt something brush against your neck in a dark forest?	a.	laugh exuberantly
2.	....	had just enough money to get you through the month?	b.	exit gracefully
3.	....	had to tell someone that the seat of his pants was ripped?	c.	scream frantically
4.	....	had just been told an uproarious joke?	d.	work more efficiently
5.	....	were introduced to a king or queen?	e	dress elegantly
6.	....	were invited to a formal dinner party?	f.	spend sparingly
7.	....	were told that your deadline has just been moved up?	g.	whisper tactfully
8.	....	wanted to leave a party without offending the host?	h.	bow / curtsy graciously

What adverb would you use to describe the way in which ...

1.	....	an ice-skater glides across ice?	a.	relentlessly
2.	....	a ravenously hungry teenager consumes a pizza?	b.	thoroughly
3.	....	an award-winning historian researches a topic?	c.	lavishly
4.	....	a cook should use red-hot chili peppers?	d.	voraciously
5.	....	a physiotherapist massages a tense muscle?	e.	resentfully
6.	....	rain falls when it comes down heavily for hours on end?	f.	smoothly
7.	....	a selfish child reacts to having to share his toys?	g.	sparingly
8.	....	a multi-millionaire would decorate his new mansion?	h.	firmly

F Spot check – Here's another look at some of the groupings tested in the Vocabulary section of Practice Test 8. Circle the choice that best completes each sentence.

1. She has had an easy time adjusting to the new job as her ..... was well organized.
   a. descendant
   b. successor
   c. predecessor
   d. forerunner

2. She ..... the stew for over two hours so the meat would be nice and tender.
   a. simmered
   b. scrubbed
   c. scratched
   d. nurtured

3. His handwriting was so ..... that not even he could read what he had written.
   a. incoherent
   b. irrelevant
   c. illegible
   d. insolvent

4. The bright young woman ..... an air of charm and confidence.
   a. divulged
   b. radiated
   c. dispelled
   d. expelled

5. An illegal shipment of weapons was ..... by alert customs officials last week.
   a. propelled
   b. alleviated
   c. repelled
   d. intercepted

6. We all agreed that the steak was so well done that it was virtually ..... .
   a. subordinate
   b. impertinent
   c. impeccable
   d. inedible

7. Adolescence is a difficult period of ..... for both teenagers and their parents.
   a. transition
   b. incentive
   c. deterrent
   d. suspension

8. ..... the house will entail the installation of new wiring and plumbing.
   a. Embellishing
   b. Diversifying
   c. Renovating
   d. Adopting

9. The teenager found it impossible to live up to his parents' high ..... .
   a. expectations
   b. impositions
   c. ramifications
   d. malfunctions

10. One look at her ..... eyes told him that she was still furious about what had happened.
   a. unobtrusive
   b. glaring
   c. undernourished
   d. shimmering

11. His failure to meet deadlines is yet another ..... of his unsuitability for the job.
   a. deference
   b. impediment
   c. aptitude
   d. manifestation

12. The child let out a ..... of delight when she saw the tiny kitten.
   a. gasp
   b. jolt
   c. gush
   d. bolt

13. The thought that he had been responsible for the tragic accident ..... on his mind.
   a. dwelled
   b. preyed
   c. fed
   d. leaned

14. The ..... writer has written more than a dozen highly acclaimed novels in the past two decades.
   a. underrated
   b. prolific
   c. flimsy
   d. mediocre

15. The helicopter ..... overhead as the rescuer attempted to reach the victim.
   a. succumbed
   b. refrained
   c. hovered
   d. catered

16. The fans linked arms and ..... from side to side as they chanted their slogans.
   a. swayed
   b. sidetracked
   c. emulated
   d. vanquished

Extra Cloze Practice

Passage 1 is about ways to attract birds.
Observers use two main ways to attract birds to come closer to them: encouraging them to nest in nest-boxes and providing them with food. For example, when winter arrives, a bird table suitably positioned ....(91).... view of the windows of a house will provide invaluable opportunities to ....(92).... glimpses of the birds feeding. Getting the creatures to ....(93).... is surprisingly easy, with success being achieved with offerings ....(94).... simple as nuts or scraps of fat. An old bone or coconut shell ....(95).... from a string will tempt the ....(96).... of common garden birds, while carefully ....(97).... the food on offer will attract less common species such as the Great Spotted Woodpecker. In years when winters are especially harsh, it's ....(98).... to know that these humble strategies might just be responsible for saving the lives of a vast number of birds.

Observers in the ....(99).... tend to recommend two basic types of nest-box: ....(100).... that have an open front for ledge-builders like the robin, and those with smaller entrances for flycatchers and similarly small species. Bird tables and other similar equipment are readily obtainable from local nurseries.

91. a. beneath b. beyond c. within d. amid
92. a. take b. catch c. perceive d. watch
93. a. approach b. fly c. enter d. withdraw
94. a. quite b. that c. whose d. as
95. a. dangling b. holding c. attaching d. waving
96. a. number b. most c. majority d. mass
97. a. variation b. varying c. variety d. variance
98. a. comforting b. disturbing c. fortunate d. troubling
99. a. know b. making c. offing d. running
100. a. these b. them c. they d. those

Passage 2 is about getting a good night's sleep.
Many people suffer from an inability to sleep through the night, prompting them to seek help to alleviate the problem. Wishing to ....(101).... medication, they may ....(102).... with alternative bedtime remedies such as drinking something hot or ....(103).... in a relaxing bath. But, while going to bed in a tranquil ....(104).... of mind must surely be beneficial to ....(105).... sleep, it does not necessarily guard against waking up again in the ....(106).... of the night.

So what's to be done? A simple, but ....(107).... overlooked strategy might just be the answer. Nowadays it's fairly ....(108).... for people to leave on either a television or radio while they sleep. They might also have an alarm clock, a computer or even a cell phone just inches from their head. Insomniacs would do well to ....(109).... all flashing, buzzing and otherwise ....(110).... electronic devices from their bedrooms. Doing so would go a long way toward increasing their chances of achieving a satisfying and restorative night's sleep.

101. a. prevent b. avoid c. prescribe d. abstain
102. a. deal b. struggle c. attempt d. experiment
103. a. making b. having c. taking d. soaking
104. a. place b. state c. peace d. mood
105. a. promoting b. dropping c. falling d. staying
106. a. midst b. midpoint c. middle d. midway
107. a. frequent b. usual c. typical d. often
108. a. commonplace b. mundane c. conservative d. monotonous
109. a. retreat b. reduce c. expel d. eliminate
110. a. irritated b. disturbing c. annoyingly d. alarming

Passage 3 is about a well-known painter.
Bruegel the Elder was a Flemish painter who lived from approximately 1525 until 1569. He is also known as "Peasant Bruegel," not to signal his origins but ....(91).... to call attention to his favorite subject matter and to ....(92).... him from his sons, Pieter and Jan, who were also artists. His paintings combine an intense ....(93).... with the everyday lives of ordinary people with a ....(94).... observation of landscape. His ....(95).... of the world around him was unflinching in its depiction of human frailty, cruelty and suffering, ...(96).... he also painted some gentler ....(97).... of people at work and play. Sometimes there are even ....(98).... of bawdy humor that might not seem ....(99).... today, ...(100).... his landscapes that depict seasons of the year provide historians with a rich source of information about farming in the 16th century.

Produced at a time when Bruegel's world was under foreign rule, his paintings above all interest art historians who are fond of debating whether or not they had hidden meaning.

91. a. rather b. also c. only d. than
92. a. compare b. vary c. isolate d. distinguish
93. a. fascination b. appreciation c. passion d. interest
94. a. superficial b. sketchy c. keen d. blunt
95. a. belief b. view c. knowledge d. sight
96. a. since b. so c. because d. but
97. a. scenes b. skits c. episodes d. objects
98. a. emotions b. actions c. touches d. clues
99. a. offended b. appropriate c. unsuitable d. convenient
100. a. therefore b. hence c. whereas d. nonetheless

Passage 4 is about a change in America's diet.
America's love affair with meat is changing. Although the hamburger has long been a ....(101).... of American culture and the United States still consumes more meat than anyone other country in the world, observers have noted that the ....(102).... of both organic vegetables and whole-grain products is definitely on the ....(103).... . Vegetarianism is no ....(104).... seen as an oddity, and there is evidence of a distinct cultural shift away from meat consumption. ....(105).... these facts is a study that showed a six percent decline in meat consumption between 2006 and 2010. According to researchers, this can, in part, be ....(106).... to difficult economic times, but ....(107).... factors also seem to be at work: nowadays young people are simply moving away from the "meat and potatoes" orientation of their parents and grandparents. ....(108).... all, it seems that a greater awareness of health issues is playing a role. The fact that ....(109).... consumption of red meat has been .....(110).... to increased risk of heart attack, stroke and cancer is undeniably a major contributing factor in the growth of the meatless diet.

101. a. mark b. symptom c. symbol d. logo
102. a. development b. popularity c. triumph d. growth
103. a. wane b. run c. loose d. rise
104. a. longer b. farther c. sooner d. less
105. a. Supporting b. Researching c. Claiming d. Approving
106. a. inscribed b. caused c. explained d. attributed
107. a. aging b. generational c. parental d. ancestral
108. a. Above b. Beyond c. For d. At
109. a. exceptional b. exhaustive c. excessive d. exaggerated
110. a. associated b. identified c. linked d. shown

Passage 5 is about two kinds of toadstool.*

Amanita Phalloides, more commonly known as the Death Cap, can grow as tall as five inches in height. As its name ....(91).... , it is deadly poisonous when ingested; consuming just one of these toadstools can ....(92).... in death. Whitish-green in color, its cap averages about three inches in diameter and is darker toward the center, ...(93).... underneath it has radiating green or yellow rib-like fibers known as gills. Commonplace in European forests, the Death Cap often ....(94).... up in the fall under oaks and other broad-leaved trees. ....(95).... the toadstool's legendary toxicity, experts strongly advise that mushroom hunters keep their ....(96).... .

At first glance, *Amanita citrina* or the False Death Cap bears a close ....(97).... to the Death Cap. ....(98).... not poisonous, the fungus is, however, inedible, with all of its parts ....(99).... a strong, unpleasant smell, particularly when it is broken open. The cap is lemon-colored with white patches, while the gills underneath are white, as ....(100).... the flesh. Common throughout Europe, the fungus appears in woodlands between August and November.

* **toadstool** – an alternate term for *mushroom* (a fungus consisting of a stem with a domed cap), particularly one that is inedible or poisonous.

91. a. suggests b. recommends c. proposes d. infers

92. a. lead b. cause c. occur d. result

93. a. whereby b. as c. while d. since

94. a. appears b. sprouts c. jumps d. grows

95. a. Because b. Given c. Due d. Considered

96. a. shirts b. heads c. distance d. word

97. a. comparison b. look c. examination d. resemblance

98. a. Though b. However c. Despite d. Being

99. a. letting b. communicating c. giving d. emitting

100. a. is b. if c. for d. though

Passage 6 is about trees.

The largest living organism on earth is the giant sequoia tree. This ....(101).... species can survive for 3,000 years or even longer. It is the widest of all trees, ...(102).... a base diameter that can reach up to 35 feet across. It is ....(103).... among the tallest of all living ....(104).... and can rise up to a height of more than 300 feet. The bark of its trunk and branches can be as ....(105).... as four feet thick, and it is ....(106).... of the fastest growing trees in the world. Its initial growth ....(107).... is one to two feet a year ....(108).... it reaches 200 to 300 feet high, at ....(109).... point it begins to level out.

While the giant sequoia is the most massive tree overall, the record for greatest height is ....(110).... by California's coast redwood. This amazing tree can grow taller than a 30-story skyscraper, with the tallest on record found to be just under 380 feet high.

101. a. mighty b. ferocious c. flimsy d. scrawny

102. a. has b. with c. and d. by

103. a. still b. just c. too d. also

104. a. things b. objects c. beasts d. creatures

105. a. good b. strong c. much d. loud

106. a. some b. one c. most d. much

107. a. rate b. pace c. ratio d. time

108. a. when b. so c. since d. until

109. a. some b. no c. which d. that

110. a. held b. given c. awarded d. broken

Passage 7 is about a famous monument in Ireland.

The Spire of Dublin was completed in January of 2003 by Ian Ritchie Architects. Built as part of a plan to ....(91).... the city after years of neglect, it now ....(92).... tall in the middle of O'Connell Street, which is ....(93).... far the most popular and well-known of Dublin's thoroughfares. Although the structure's completion was originally ....(94).... to coincide with the ....(95).... of the new millennium, difficulties in obtaining planning permission and meeting environmental regulations resulted in a three-year ....(96).... .

Over time, the towering 390-foot, needle-shaped, stainless-steel structure has been ....(97).... to by a variety of names: the Millennium Spire, the Spike and the Stiletto in the Ghetto, to name ....(98).... a few. ....(99).... , its official name is the Monument of Lights, ...(100).... in Irish is *An Túr Solais*. The spire is clearly visible throughout the city and has become a popular meeting point.

91. a. revitalize b. remunerate c. replenish d. reinforce

92. a. raises b. stands c. walks d. sits

93. a. thus b. as c. by d. the

94. a. meaning b. having c. planning d. intended

95. a. daybreak b. dawn c. dusk d. twilight

96. a. delay b. hesitation c. cancellation d. intermission

97. a. called b. given c. spoken d. referred

98. a. and b. but c. yet d. them

99. a. Concurrently b. Inevitably c. However d. Fortunately

100. a. as b. that c. which d. it

Passage 8 is about the color indigo.

There is an interesting history behind indigo. ....(101).... on context, the word can variously mean a tropical plant (*Indigo tinctoria*), the dark-blue dye that comes ....(102).... this plant, or the dark-blue color which, in 1672, in his famous ....(103).... on light, English physicist Sir Isaac Newton identified as the color of the spectrum ....(104).... between blue and violet.

The origins of indigo (the plant) are shrouded in mystery, ...(105).... are those of woad (*Isatis tinctoria*), ...(106).... plant which yields a dye that also produces indigo (the color). ....(107).... the European discovery of the seaway to India in 1498, great amounts of indigo began being imported from Bengal, eventually resulting ....(108).... trade restrictions in some parts of Europe to protect the woad industry. By 1859, strained relations between profit-hungry indigo plantation owners and exploited indigo farmers ....(109).... in a peasant uprising. In more recent times, indigo has achieved fame as the original color of denim blue jeans. In ....(110).... , woad's reputation has not fared as well. The plant is considered an invasive species in parts of the United States, and attempts have been made to eradicate it.

101. a. Basing b. Depending c. Judging d. Relying

102. a. of b. by c. from d. with

103. a. treatise b. treatment c. treat d. treaty

104. a. fallen b. falls c. fell d. falling

105. a. which b. as c. so d. and

106. a. the b. also c. another d. similar

107. a. After b. When c. During d. Because

108. a. from b. in c. to d. by

109. a. burst b. caused c. erupted d. triggered

110. a. short b. contrast c. consideration d. part

Passage 9 is about watermills.

Water is first thought to have been utilized as a means of powering mills by the ancient Greeks. Among the many who ....(91).... on the existence and usefulness of these mills over 2,000 years ago was Antipater of Thessalonica. Not only did he ....(92).... the water-powered, wheel-driven mill ....(93).... an effective means of grinding grain, but he also saw ....(94).... it an admirable way to ....(95).... the load of human labor. ....(96).... , the Romans constructed some of the earliest watermills outside of Greece, improving on Greek technology and thereby ....(97).... the requisite knowledge and skills throughout the Mediterranean. In addition to grinding flour, these more complex mills ....(98).... used for such industrial purposes as marble cutting and textile manufacture.

A watermill functions by diverting a source of moving water (such as from a river or stream) to a water wheel, usually via a channel or pipe. It is the ....(99).... of the water that pushes the wheel, which in ....(100).... drives an axle shaft that powers the machinery or tool that is attached to it. Occasionally, multiple mills are constructed in a stack formation so that water passes through numerous mills turning many wheels.

91. a. commented b. observed c. mentioned d. referred

92. a. praise b. approve c. believe d. ascribe

93. a. being b. was c. to d. as

94. a. to b. by c. in d. through

95. a. illuminate b. lighten c. enhance d. intensify

96. a. Previously b. Subsequently c. Formally d. Consequently

97. a. sprinkling b. stretching c. scattering d. spreading

98. a. which b. had c. were d. to

99. a. temperature b. force c. waviness d. dripping

100. a. motion b. theory c. progress d. turn

Passage 10 is about flying.

People have always dreamed of being able to fly. The myths of the classical world are full of wondrous ....(101).... creatures; the ancient Chinese are ....(102).... to have attempted to use kites to lift themselves into the air; and in the late fifteenth century Leonardo da Vinci sketched designs for several complex flying machines ....(103).... on his studies of how birds flew. In subsequent years, many ....(104).... their hand at designing ornithopters, or flapping-wing machines, yet more often than ....(105).... the machines ....(106).... with disaster, crashing to the ground with often fatal consequences for their pilots. Airships and hot air balloons had a greater measure of success, as ....(107).... Lilienthal's hang glider in the 1890s, but ....(108).... than fly through the air, these floated on it.

The Wright brothers won the race to get a heavier-than-air machine ....(109).... the ground in 1903. After that, though, France began to lead the way in aviation technology and soon built planes that broke records for distance, altitude and speed. It is ....(110).... to these early triumphs that words of French origin such as *fuselage* and *aileron* are now part of the language of aviation.

101. a. winged b. flighty c. unflappable d. airy

102. a. meant b. sure c. believing d. known

103. a. relied b. based c. counted d. dependent

104. a. used b. had c. tried d. attempted

105. a. not b. never c. ever d. usually

106. a. coincided b. met c. experienced d. encountered

107. a. was b. though c. did d. had

108. a. sooner b. instead c. other d. rather

109. a. off b. up c. over d. beyond

110. a. owed b. equivalent c. thanks d. said

Passage 11 is about an animal known as the numbat.

The numbat (*Myrmecobious fasciatus*) is one of Australia's most interesting-looking marsupials. It's a small, colorful creature with a long, bushy tail at one ....(91).... and a finely pointed snout (or muzzle) at the other. The overall color of its fur ....(92).... from back to front, with its long-haired tail ....(93).... to be gray flecked with white, its snout a light brown, and the fur on its upper back often a bright brick red. But ....(94).... really sets it ....(95).... are its distinctive markings, including from four to eleven vertical white bands on its dark brownish-black hindquarters and a dark horizontal stripe bordered by white on ....(96).... side of its snout running from ear to mouth.

The numbat – or banded anteater, as it is sometimes misleadingly called – is unique ....(97).... that it is the only marsupial in the world to ....(98).... solely on termites. ....(99).... discovering a termite mound, the numbat will dig down to reveal the corridors and then lick up the swarming insects with its sticky tube-like ....(100).... . An adult requires up to 20,000 termites a day. Once common in semi-arid and arid regions of southern Australia, numbats in the wild now numbers fewer than 2,000.

91. a. side b. tip c. point d. end
92. a. extends b. varies c. shifts d. transfers
93. a. accustomed b. meaning c. usually d. tending
94. a. what b. something c. that d. which
95. a. back b. up c. apart d. free
96. a. either b. both c. one d. every
97. a. in b. that c. as d. owing
98. a. consume b. diet c. nourish d. feed
99. a. While b. Upon c. By d. In
100. a. lips b. nose c. tongue d. teeth

Passage 12 is about a well-known psychologist.

Jean Piaget (1896–1980) was a Swiss developmental psychologist and philosopher. His ....(101).... to educational psychology was tremendous. In ....(102).... , he believed that the child is an active and intelligent learner who is ....(103).... hard-wired to adapt to his or her environment. A child's understanding is, in the ....(104).... , determined by perception, ...(105).... fosters intellectual development in a series of four stages: first by forming simple and concrete knowledge and ....(106).... by engaging in higher ....(107).... higher levels of logical abstraction. At these higher levels, the child can ....(108).... judgments about how the world might be rather than how it is now.

....(109).... of Piaget often argue that his stages are too rigidly defined and that his ideas ignore the crucial social aspects of learning: in particular, the roles ....(110).... by human interdependence and language. But despite these and other criticisms, most professionals are quick to acknowledge the impact that his ideas have had on educators.

101. a. impact b. contribution c. donation d. influence
102. a. nutshell b. fact c. essence d. retrospect
103. a. genetically b. electronically c. digitally d. inefficiently
104. a. much b. most c. part d. main
105. a. it b. but c. which d. so
106. a. than b. recently c. later d. consequently
107. a. and b. always c. the d. ever
108. a. have b. do c. say d. make
109. a. Detractors b. Supporters c. Enemies d. Believers
110. a. acted b. played c. developed d. served

Passage 13 is about technological change.

For those embracing change, technological innovation can't come fast enough. For others, it has ....(91).... so a little too quickly. In the last decade, Internet use has ....(92).... , and the vast majority of people have become cell-phone users. Smartphones, now the ....(93).... for young people, have opened up ....(94).... to online content, social networks and instant messaging as never before. Born into a technologically ....(95).... world, the so-called "digital native" spends an average of 8.5 hours each day ....(96).... up to digital technology. This is having a serious ....(97).... on our brain circuitry, which is slowly being rewired.

On the positive side, technology is ....(98).... our brains to multitask and become better ....(99).... to engage in complex reasoning and decision making. On the ....(100).... , our love affair with technology is influencing our social behavior, causing us to use – or rather overuse – our electronic devices in every imaginable situation. Research suggests that we are now less able to stay focused and our ability to empathize with others has seriously been diminished.

91. a. done b. come c. made d. been

92. a. burst b. revolutionized c. mushroomed d. erupted

93. a. requirement b. norm c. prototype d. mold

94. a. doorways b. possibilities c. eyes d. access

95. a. soaked b. soggy c. saturated d. flooded

96. a. hooked b. plugged c. logged d. connected

97. a. problem b. harm c. damage d. effect

98. a. making b. training c. ordering d. begging

99. a. at b. able c. off d. suitable

100. a. negativity b. drawback c. downside d. contrary

Passage 14 is about a family of insects called fairyflies.

Fairyflies (*Mymaridae*) are the tiniest of insects. Due to their incredibly minute size, they often go ....(101).... by humans. Their apparent invisibility, ...(102).... with their hair-fringed wings and fragile bodies, give ....(103).... to their common name. However, fairyflies are not ....(104).... flies at all, but rather small wasps the size of a pinhead, typically measuring a ....(105).... 0.020 to 0.039 inches long.

Parasitic by nature, fairyflies live ....(106).... the eggs and larvae of other insects. ....(107).... their ability to find and consume the eggs of their hosts, a number of species are especially prized by farmers for use as a kind of organic pesticide.

As ....(108).... as their coloration goes, fairyflies are usually non-metallic hues of black, brown or yellow. They live in temperate and tropical regions, with the highest concentration of species being found in tropical forests in the southern hemisphere. Fairyflies have been in ....(109).... for roughly 66 million years, and ....(110).... have been found in fossilized amber from the Cretaceous period (between 146 and 65 million years ago).

A new species of fairyfly was recently discovered in the rainforests of Costa Rica and was aptly named *Tinkerbella nana* after the beloved fairy Tinker Bell in *Peter Pan*.

101. a. unwelcome b. unwarranted c. uncovered d. unnoticed

102. a. together b. compared c. mixed d. united

103. a. way b. emphasis c. rise d. credit

104. a. actually b. only c. virtually d. factually

105. a. just b. mere c. little d. scarcely

106. a. with b. from c. by d. off

107. a. Owing b. Judging c. Given d. Provided

108. a. long b. far c. much d. soon

109. a. existence b. danger c. operation d. extinction

110. a. survivors b. prototypes c. specimens d. models

Passage 15 is about driving an enormous truck across the Australian outback.

An arduous five-day, 2,500-mile journey through central Australia separates the driver and rig from their final destination: a supply depot outside the northern city of Darwin. Along the way, the four-tanker rig (or road train) will ....(91).... at least three tires, which is ....(92).... much a typical occurrence, considering the length of the ....(93).... over searing hot roads.

In the Australian outback, distances are huge, and there are ....(94).... few railways. This vast open space is ....(95).... by single-lane highways that are straight and empty, ...(96).... it is along these ....(97).... the massive rigs must travel. It is the best way to ....(98).... freight from city to city and from one side of the ....(99).... to the other.

A common hazard along the way is wandering cattle from ranches near the road. But, of course, the highways are also ....(100).... for kangaroos. Though a rig goes no faster than 60 miles per hour, with an average weight of 100 tons, it's just too massive to maneuver out of the way, let alone stop in an attempt to avoid hitting the creatures.

91. a. flatten b. deflate c. break d. blow

92. a. fairly b. as c. pretty d. so

93. a. haul b. vehicle c. transportation d. cargo

94. a. but b. merely c. yet d. barely

95. a. scarred b. traversed c. etched d. dissected

96. a. but b. for c. though d. and

97. a. ones b. they c. that d. are

98. a. transact b. transpose c. transfer d. transcend

99. a. world b. continent c. peninsula d. ocean

100. a. perilous b. endangered c. jeopardized d. treachery

Passage 16 is about multitasking.

Multitasking has now become the norm. Working mothers do it at home, ...(101).... monitoring emails and making business calls while making dinner, tidying the kitchen and helping with the children's homework ....(102).... at the same time. While this is ....(103).... on, their kids are media multitasking – surfing the Internet, ...(104).... their Facebook status, texting their friends – and also doing their schoolwork. We all do it, but research ....(105).... that multitasking using digital media is ....(106).... that effective or actually very good for our health.

The problem is that the brain can't really ....(107).... attention to more than one thing at a time. By switching between two or more tasks, we become slower and that much ....(108).... accurate at each. ....(109).... , multitasking also excites the brain by releasing an addictive hormone. Unfortunately, in the ....(110).... of such stimulation, we are left feeling flat and find it difficult to concentrate solely on one task. In short, multitasking with digital media can seriously diminish our ability to focus and to filter relevant information. It may also result in loss of sleep.

101. a. virtually b. coincidentally c. simultaneously d. instantly

102. a. together b. both c. all d. just

103. a. holding b. turning c. coming d. going

104. a. updating b. uplifting c. uploading d. upholding

105. a. denies b. suggests c. recommends d. proclaims

106. a. either b. neither c. just d. not

107. a. draw b. pay c. focus d. concentrate

108. a. more b. as c. less d. not

109. a. Moreover b. Nonetheless c. Consequently d. Happily

110. a. lack b. absence c. desire d. event

WRITING TUTORIAL

Writing Tutorial

This section is meant to be a crash course on surviving the 30-minute Composition portion of the Final ECPE. It consists of 16 guided tasks that correspond to the 16 topics in Final Tests 1–8. Each task contains discussion and brainstorming activities as well as step-by-step instructions for developing each topic.

The purpose of these tasks is to give you practice in planning, organizing and developing your ideas into an effective composition. As you work through the section, you will become familiar with the main composition types that appear on the exam (see chart on next page). You will also be shown how to structure your compositions so they have a clear Introduction, Main Body and Conclusion. Finally, you will be given ample practice in the "art" of developing your paragraphs by starting with a clear topic sentence which you then build on by linking together a series of reasons, examples and other supporting statements.

For more tips on how to handle the Composition section, see page 10.

"Tell them..." on the mountain – *A parable to remember on the day of the exam*

Once upon a time at the top of a high, high mountain, there lived a wise old retired English teacher who had an incredibly pragmatic approach not only to life but to composition writing. Students would come from far and wide to learn the secrets of his craft. Most listened, scratched their heads and muttered, "Nonsense!" but as Michigan Mama made the long trek up the mountain, she sensed that her journey had not been in vain. Reaching the top, she greeted him as he gestured for her to sit.

"Have you the answer, old sage?" she said, after catching her breath. "Have you got the key to help my students write competent, articulate, well-organized, exam-passing compositions?"

"I might," he said humbly. "Only **you** *can decide."*

"Tell me, old sage. I'm all ears."

"It is simple, my child. We all know that a composition needs an Introduction, a Main Body and a Conclusion, but what confuses everyone is what to do when they come to writing each of these parts."

" Yes...?" said Michigan Mama expectantly, sensing she was about to hear The Truth.

"Well, it's simple," he said, as he wrote in her notebook.

- Tell them what you're going to tell them.
- Tell them.
- Tell them what you told them.

Michigan Mama read the shaky scrawl and gazed up at him in awe. "It **is** *that simple, isn't it?" she said. "No more long, wandering introductions which don't prepare the readers for what's ahead. No more messy conclusions that introduce all kinds of new ideas that the readers aren't prepared for in the last paragraph..."*

"You **are** *a genius," she said, radiant with gratitude. "I must go and, well, ... tell them!"*

SUMMARY OF MAIN COMPOSITION TYPES

PROTOTYPE

Introduction	→	Tell them what you're going to tell them
Main body	→	Tell them
Conclusion	→	Tell them what you told them

TYPE 1 — Narrative

Introduction
Restate the topic in your own words and briefly introduce the person or incident you will be writing about.

Main body
- Establish background to what you are about to describe (eg, how you met someone, where you were going, what you were doing).
- Narrate what happened. Break into 2–3 paragraphs: the lead-up to the key moment and the key moment itself in 1–2 paragraphs and the aftermath in a separate paragraph. Use time links where possible.

Conclusion
Discuss the influence the person / incident has had on you and what you learned.

TYPE 2 — Problem / Solution

Introduction
Restate the situation in the topic in your own words. State simply that the situation involves problems (name them, if appropriate), but solutions do exist.

Main body
Devote a separate paragraph to each problem.
- Start with a clear topic sentence announcing the problem. Then analyze the problem with a series of reasons, examples and results.
- Using a clear transition statement (eg, "One way to remedy this would be to ..." or "If I were in charge, I would ..."), present one or more solutions. Use links and elaborate with reasons, examples, results.

Conclusion
Summarize by restating message in introduction. Close, if possible, with a thought-provoking statement about putting solutions into effect.

TYPE 3 — For and Against

Introduction
Briefly restate the issue in the topic. State simply that the issue has advantages and disadvantages or reasons to be "for" or "against" it. (Save your opinion for end.)

Main body
Devote a separate paragraph to each side of the argument.
- Start with a clear topic sentence announcing one side of the argument.
- Develop with 2–4 aspects. Use linking words and elaborate, where needed, with reasons and/or examples.

Conclusion
End by weighing up both sides and expressing your opinion.

TYPE 4 — Opinion

This type may ask your opinion about what you would choose in a certain case or about what the key aspects of an issue are. You might also be asked if you agree or disagree with something.

Introduction
Briefly restate the topic and your opinion (eg, your choices or whether you agree).

Main body
Devote a separate paragraph to each choice, key aspect or side of the argument.
- Start with topic sentence announcing the choice, aspect or side of the argument.
- Develop with several reasons and/or examples to justify your choice/opinion, using linking words to signal each elaboration.

Conclusion
End by restating your opinion and leaving readers with a thought-provoking idea.

FINAL TEST 1

TOPIC 1 – A Personal Time Capsule

Opinion (Type 4)

A Before you begin

1. Consider what criteria to use to make your selections. To do this, think about what aspects of your life and times you want to show future generations or what overall impression you want to create.

....

....

2. Either alone or in groups, list five items that you might include in your time capsule. For each, list one or more reasons why you would include this item.
   a) ....
   b) ....
   c) ....
   d) ....
   e) ....

3. Compare results with the class. Discuss which items have the best potential for inclusion: ie, which can be developed in an interesting way - perhaps with a **description** and one or more **reasons**.

B Suggestions for development

INTRODUCTION – Tell them what you're going to tell them

- Restate topic or capture reader's attention by starting with image of someone finding the capsule.

- If you like, lead in to your ideas by posing rhetorical questions. For example:
  What picture would I want to give future generations?
  What objects would I use to create that picture?

- Mention your two choices without elaborating.

MAIN BODY (Paragraphs 2 and 3) – Tell them

- Start each paragraph with a clear topic sentence announcing each choice plus reason. For example:
  Paragraph 2: *To begin with, I would include ... to show ...*
  Paragraph 3: *The second item I would include would be ... as a reminder of ...*

- Develop each paragraph with a brief description of the object (what it looks like, what it contains).

- Elaborate in more detail the message you hope the object will send to future generations.
  In this way whoever found the capsule would see / would understand ...

CONCLUSION – Tell them what you told them

- Begin with a clear topic sentence that restates objects and summarizes why you chose them.

- You can stop here ... or you can continue, if you wish, with thought-provoking questions:
  Will these items seem strange to those who find them?
  Will ... still exist as we know it today?

- End with thought-provoking wish for the future:
  I can only hope that future generations will ...

TOPIC 2 – Implications of People Living Longer

For and Against (Type 3)

A Before you begin

1. List the positive aspects of elderly people living longer

....

....

....

....

2. List the negative aspects of living in a society with increasing numbers of elderly people.

....

....

....

....

B Suggestions for development

INTRODUCTION – Tell them what you're going to tell them

- Restate the topic in your own words in one or two sentences.
- State simply that the situation has both negative and positive implications. For example:
  This can have both positive and negative consequences / implications.

MAIN BODY (Paragraphs 2 and 3) – Tell them

Paragraph 2 – Positive implications

- Start with a clear topic sentence citing main or first positive aspect. For example:
  On the positive side, the longer people live, the more time they have to ...
- Develop with a series of examples, using linkers such as:
  Some people ... Others ... Still others ... / First of all, ... Secondly, ... Moreover, ...
- Finish, if you like, with a summary statement, about overall benefits to families and society.
  In all cases ... In short, ...

Paragraph 3 – Negative implications

- Shift to negative side of the issue with a clear topic sentence. For example:
  On the other hand, there are many negative implications.
  or *But despite the advantages, there are also a number of negative aspects.*
- Develop your argument by citing each disadvantage and elaborating it with 1–2 reasons or examples.
  Firstly, the fact that more people are living longer can result in ...
  Furthermore, ... This means that ... Last but not least, ...
- Finish, if you like, with a summary statement about overall negative effects (see Paragraph 2 above).

CONCLUSION – Tell them what you told them

- End by weighing both sides and expressing your opinion about what can be done to maximize the positive aspects and minimize the negative ones. For example.
  All things considered, ... It is my firm belief that with proper planning ...

FINAL TEST 2

TOPIC 1 – Keys to a Healthy "Proactive" Lifestyle

Opinion (Type 4)

A Before you begin

1. Either alone or in groups, list all the "keys" you can think of. Compare lists with your classmates and jot down all the ideas below.

   a) ....

   ....

   b) ....

   ....

   c) ....

   ....

   d) ....

   ....

   e) ....

2. To determine which areas have the best potential for development, make notes next to each item (ie, reasons, examples, advice). See where you have the most / best ideas, then decide on two.

B Suggestions for development

INTRODUCTION – Tell them what you're going to tell them

- Restate the topic in your own words, **or**
- State how everyone wants to be healthy and follow with a rhetorical question, such as:
  But what actually is involved in maintaining a healthy lifestyle?
- State your opinion about the two main areas by combining link and clear statement of keys:
  Link: *To my mind, ... / In my opinion, ... / From where I stand, ...*
  Choices: *... there are two main ingredients: [choice A] and [choice B].*
  ... [choice A] and [choice B] are the two major keys.

MAIN BODY (Paragraphs 2 and 3) – Tell them

- Start each paragraph with a clear topic sentence announcing each choice. For example:
  Paragraph 2: *For me, the most important factor for a healthy future is ...*
  Paragraph 3: *The second most vital ingredient for a healthy lifestyle in my opinion is ...*
- Develop each paragraph with reasons, examples and advice. Use links such as:
  Without .... , we are asking for problems. / Take couch potatoes, for example. ...
  As a result, ... / No matter how busy we are, we can still ... . / It also wouldn't hurt us to ...
  Finally, we could also try ... After all, ...

CONCLUSION – Tell them what you told them

- End with clear topic sentence that restates the two keys and what you can gain. Use a phrase like:
  To sum up, / In short, / In brief, we have everything to gain by ... and ...
- Round off, if you like, with a sentence or two, leaving readers with the clear idea that a few changes in their habits will put them on the road to a healthier lifestyle.

TOPIC 2 – Life in the Future

Opinion (Type 4)

A Before you begin

1. Jot down ideas for each category then compare your notes with the rest of the class. You can take a technological approach to the topic or use your imagination and have some fun.

Transport: ....
Education: ....
Energy: ....
Leisure: ....
Houses: ....
Medicine: ....

2. Look at your notes and decide which two areas you could develop most effectively with reasons, elaboration and/or imaginative examples.

B Suggestions for development

INTRODUCTION – Tell them what you're going to tell them

- Restate topic by referring generally to changes in the first five decades of the 21st century. You might want to contrast the last 50 years of the 20th with the first 50 years of the 21st. For example:
  There is no doubt that life in the second half of the 21st century will be ...
  or *If changes in the last half of the 20th century are anything to go by, the first half of the 21st century will ...*

- Announce the two areas that you have chosen to discuss with a clear statement of opinion, such as:
  In my opinion, the transformation will be particularly striking in ... and ... .

- Finish, if you like, with clever general reference to looking into a crystal ball. For example:
  If I were asked to peer into my crystal ball, here's what I think I'd see.

MAIN BODY (Paragraphs 2 and 3) – Tell them

- Start each paragraph with a clear topic sentence that announces each choice. For example:
  Paragraph 2: *First of all, I'd see a world where ... of the future will be ...*
  Paragraph 3: *The other field where major transformations will occur will be in ...*

- Develop each paragraph with a sequence of 2–4 predictions with occasional elaboration and examples. Use a series of links such as:
  (a) *For starters, ...* *What's more, ...* *And, finally, ...*
  or (b) *In the future ...* *It's even conceivable that ...* *Finally, it's not unlikely that...*

CONCLUSION – Tell them what you told them

- Summarize by restating choices and making thought-provoking statements about your predictions:
  Of course, nobody can say for sure what the future will bring, but at least in the areas of [choice 1] and [choice 2] ...

Writing Tutorial

FINAL TEST 3

TOPIC 1 – Giving Gifts

Opinion/Narrative (Types 4/1)

A Before you begin

1. Exchange stories with your classmates about the best and the worst gifts you're ever received.
   - Say what the gift was and who gave it to you.
   - Establish the background: eg, What was the occasion? Why was the gift chosen?
   - Why was the gift appropriate / inappropriate?
   - How did the gift make you feel? Did it change your relationship with the giver?

   As you listen to your classmates speak, see if you can suggest ways to strengthen their stories by getting them to include more descriptive detail or reasons.

2. Discuss the meaning of the following gift-related sayings. Could any be used to illustrate your stories or those of your classmates?

   It's the thought that counts.
   Never look a gift-horse in the mouth.
   Beware of Greeks bearing gifts.
   It's better to give than to receive.

B Suggestions for development

INTRODUCTION – Tell them what you're going to tell them

- Restate the topic in your own words in one or two sentences.
- If you like, pose one or two rhetorical questions to lead into your two experiences. For example:
  But does it have to be that way? Has gift-giving really lost its meaning?
- Make a simple statement about what your experience on two occasions has shown you, such as:
  My experience on two different occasion tells me that ...

MAIN BODY (Paragraphs 2 and 3) – Tell them

- Start each paragraph with a clear topic sentence that introduces each gift. Try to make a clear contrast between the two gifts in the way you word the two sentences. For example:
  Paragraph 2: *One of the best gifts I've ever received was ...*
  Paragraph 3: *But not all gifts are chosen with such care. I'll never forget...*
- Develop each paragraph by using elements from one or both of these progressions:

  (1) Establish background.
  Narrate what happened as you got the gift.
  Summarize your reaction.

  (2) Establish background.
  Analyze why gift was good / bad.
  Discuss the result.
- Consider using one of the sayings in A2 as a clever way to round off one or both paragraphs.

CONCLUSION – Tell them what you told them

- Summarize what you learned from the two experiences by starting with a clear lead-in statement followed by thought-provoking analysis and/or advice. Use phrases such as:
  To sum up, we can see that ...
  To my mind, a gift is most meaningful when ...
  So next time you're out hunting for a gift ...
  As the old saying goes, " ... "

TOPIC 2 – Single-parent Families **Problem/Solution (Type 2)**

A Before you begin

1. Divorce is not the only reason for single-parent families. What other situations can arise?

....

....

2. After discussing the topic with your classmates, make notes about specific problems and solutions in your notebook or on the blackboard under the following areas:

- Problems related to living with parent of one sex
- Problems related to parent working
- Psychological problems
- Other problems

After you have finished, decide which two areas have the best potential for logical development.

3. What special qualities do single parents need to help children solve these problems?

....

B Suggestions for development

INTRODUCTION – Tell them what you're going to tell them

- Restate the topic in your own words, using a standard lead-in phrase such as:
  It's undeniable that ... *It's a sad fact of modern life that ...* *It is widely recognized that ...*
- Say simply that the situation has created many problems, but solutions do exist. For example:
  This has created many problems, but with ... [qualities from A3], solutions can be found.

MAIN BODY (Paragraphs 2 and 3) – Tell them

- Start each paragraph with a clear topic sentence that announces the problem. Use phrases such as:
  One major problem is ... / The second major problem is ... / Perhaps the greatest problem is ...
- Develop the first half of each paragraph by either elaborating on the problem or citing other problems that may follow:
  In other words, ... *That is to say, ...* *This means that ...*
  This may lead to... *This can also result in ...* *A final consequence is that ...*
- Shift to second part of paragraph with a clear transition statement. Then go on to offer one or more solutions, elaborating where needed with reasons, examples and results. Use links such as:
  There are various ways to remedy this. *In the case of ... , for example, ...*
  or *For these reasons, the single parent must ... .* *It is also vital that the parent ...* *This can be done by ... .*

CONCLUSION – Tell them what you told them

- Conclude by briefly restating the main message in the introduction. For example:
  In short, with [qualities from A3] , many problems can be solved.
- If you like, add dramatic restatement comparing single-parent families and traditional families:
  If everyone is [qualities from A3], the children of single parents will be just as ... as the children of traditional families.

FINAL TEST 4

TOPIC 1 – 20th-century Technology

Opinion (Type 4)

A Before you begin

1. Brainstorm with the entire class and list as many major technological achievements of the 20th century as you can. Don't stop until you've reached at least 20. Here's a few to get you started:

jets	television	nuclear power	computers

2. Working alone or in groups, narrow the list to four and jot down as many dramatic impacts as you can. (Some may have good *and* bad impacts.) Share ideas with the class and jot down anything you hadn't considered.

Tip

*The key phrase in the question is "**dramatic** impact." Anything that is not dramatic – eg, the fact that computers can be used to play games or make birthday cards – should be deleted.*

3. Now review your notes and decide which two achievements have the best potential for development.

B Suggestions for development

INTRODUCTION – Tell them what you're going to tell them

- Restate the topic by referring to the vast range of developments and the enormous impact they have had on modern life. Then narrow your focus to the two of your choice. For example:
  Restate *The 20th century spawned a vast number of new inventions, many of which ... .*
  Narrow *The two that have had the most dramatic effect, in my opinion, are ... .*

MAIN BODY (Paragraphs 2 and 3) – Tell them

- Start each paragraph with a clear topic sentence stating your choice and, if you like, a general reason or some hint of whether the choice has had an overall positive or negative impact on society. For example:
  Paragraph 2: *I choose the ... because it has dramatically ...*
  Paragraph 3: *Another invention which has had an enormous impact is ...* **or**
  ... has had an even greater impact on our lives – though not necessarily for the better.

- Develop each paragraph by presenting a sequence of specific impacts (with elaboration or examples as needed) or by contrasting the past with the present. For example:
  To begin with, ... / As a result, ... / In addition, ... I say this because ... / Last but not least, ...
  Before the invention of ... , ... / Nowadays, however, ... / It has also been said that ...

- If you have presented good and bad aspects, finish with a balanced summary, such as:
  Although ... has been criticized for ... , there is no question that it has had a major positive / negative impact on our lives.
  or *To be fair, though, the disadvantages must be balanced against the fact that ...*

CONCLUSION – Tell them what you told them

- Summarize by referring to both choices and making a dramatic restatement of their impact:
  In conclusion, despite the fact that neither ... nor ... have had a totally positive effect on our lives, they are still in my opinion the inventions that ...

TOPIC 2 – Should older adults become parents? **For and Against (Type 3)**

A Before you begin

1. Imagine you are walking by a primary school. A silver-haired gentleman in his early 60s – obviously somebody's grandfather – is waiting at the entrance. Suddenly a six-year-old rushes up to him, shouting, "Daddy! Daddy!" How would you react?

2. List the special advantages that mature parents could offer their child.

....

....

....

....

....

3. List the disadvantages that need to be considered.

....

....

....

....

4. Reconsider your answer to (1) above. Does a loving and financially secure mature parent have something to offer a child that a younger, inexperienced and financially insecure parent may not?

B Suggestions for development

INTRODUCTION – Tell them what you're going to tell them

- Restate the topic in your own words, giving brief social background if you can.
  In today's society, more and more women are choosing to ...

- If you wish, lead in to the end of the introduction with a rhetorical question, such as:
  Is this a positive direction for society to be moving in?

- State that the issue has both positive and negative aspects.
  A closer look shows there are both positive and negative aspects to consider.

MAIN BODY (Paragraphs 2 and 3) – Tell them

- Begin each paragraph with a clear topic sentence. For example:
  Paragraph 2: *On one hand, few would dispute that mature parents can offer a child special advantages.*
  Paragraph 3: *There are also significant disadvantages, however.*

- Develop each with 2–4 aspects, using links and elaborating where needed with reasons / examples.
  \+ *The first is that older parents ... / They will also ... / In other words, ... / Finally, ...*
  – *To begin with, as parents grow older ... / Problems may also stem from ...*
  Perhaps the most pressing problem of all is ... / This puts pressure on the parents to ...

CONCLUSION – Tell them what you told them

- End by weighing up both sides and expressing your opinion, using linking phrases such as:
  In the final analysis, the potential ... to the child far outweigh the ... .
  On balance, I see nothing wrong with ... / I strongly disagree with ...

FINAL TEST 5

TOPIC 1 – A Big Let-down

Narrative (Type 1)

A Before you begin

1. Exchange stories about people who have disappointed you. Use these hints to organize your ideas:
   - Say who the person was and briefly describe the background of your relationship.
   - Tell what happened to disappoint you so much.
   - Discuss what happened afterwards: eg, Did you try to re-establish the relationship?
   - What lessons did you learn from the experience?

   As you listen, think of ways to improve each story. Could more detail or elaboration be added?

2. Discuss the meaning of the following sayings and expressions. Could any be used in your story?

   A friend in need is a friend indeed.
   Learn to take the bitter with the sweet.
   It's a dog-eat-dog world.
   Every cloud has a silver lining.
   to chalk something up to experience
   to show one's true colors
   a bitter pill to swallow
   a "true-blue" friend / a "fair-weather" friend

B Suggestions for development

INTRODUCTION – Tell them what you're going to tell them

- Introduce the topic by commenting on the importance of trust and friendship. For example:
  I used to think that friends were "true-blue" and would never let you down.
- Lead in with a brief statement that your experience with "Friend X" taught you differently.
  I found out differently, however, when my good friend X let me down last year.

MAIN BODY (Paragraphs 2 and 3) – Tell them

Paragraph 2:

- Establish the background of your friendship.
- Round off by introducing the incident that changed everything. Use an attention-grabbing link such as:
  Little did I know that ... / One day, however, ... / How was I to know that ...

Paragraph 3 and subsequent paragraphs, if needed:

- Go on to narrate what happened. To show the passage of time, use narrative time links such as:
  At first, ... / Then ... / Suddenly, ... / Not until ... did I realize ... / After a while ... /
  In a day or two ... / But the worst was still to come ... / In the end ...
- If the story naturally breaks up into different parts, place each in a separate paragraph.
- Consider using direct speech to break up the narrative or to emphasize key moments:
  "Out! Both of you!" she screamed. *"This is all your fault!" he said.*

CONCLUSION – Tell them what you told them

- Conclude by looking back at the experience and saying what you learnt. Start with a link such as:
  In retrospect, ... / With hindsight, ... / When all is said and done, ...
- If you wish, incorporate a saying from A2 above as an impressive finishing touch.

TOPIC 2 – **What is education**? **Opinion (Type 4)**

A Before you begin

1. Read the question carefully, then take a vote:
   - How many think education is about learning facts and figures? ....
   - How many think it's about teaching people to get along with each other in society? ....
   - How many think it's about both? ....

2. Reasons why people believe education is about learning facts and figures:

   ....

   ....

   ....

   ....

3. Reasons why education should be about teaching people to get along in society:

   ....

   ....

   ....

   ....

4. No matter how you voted, you should consider both points of view. You can elaborate your opinion at the end of each paragraph or you can wait till the conclusion.

B Suggestions for development

INTRODUCTION – Tell them what you're going to tell them

- Restate topic or, if you wish, open with a rhetorical question. For example:
  Is it just about book learning, or is it (also) about preparing children to be part of society?

- Clearly state your opinion. Use links such as:
  I am of the opinion that ... / I firmly believe that ... / There is no question that ...

MAIN BODY (Paragraphs 2 and 3) – Tell them

- Start each paragraph with a clear topic sentence introducing each point of view. For example:
  Paragraph 2: *Few people would deny that a solid basic education is needed to ...*
  Paragraph 3: *There is, however, another side to consider: that is, education's role in ...*

- Develop with reasons and/or examples by using links such as:
  For starters, ... / It is also vital that ... because ... / Furthermore, ...
  By this I mean that ... / For example, ... / Children should also be taught ... / Finally, ...

CONCLUSION – Tell them what you told them

- Conclude by weighing what both sides have to offer and firmly restating your opinion.

- If you believe that education should perform *both* roles, you may want to comment on the fact that many school systems place too much emphasis on one type of education and that something should be done to restore the balance. For example:
  To my mind, much too much emphasis is placed on ... and not enough on ... / I strongly believe that ... / The world would be a much better place to live in if ... / For me, ...

FINAL TEST 6

TOPIC 1 – Public Health Care — Problem/Solution (Type 2)

A Before you begin

1. Discuss the changes in public health care that have occurred in your country over the past century. Then, either alone or in groups, jot down three problem areas that exist and make notes as to how you would elaborate each in a composition. Compare results with the class and add to your notes.
   a) ....
   b) ....
   c) ....
2. For each problem above, jot down one or more solutions.
   a) ....
   b) ....
   c) ....
3. Review your notes and determine which two areas have the best potential for logical development.

B Suggestions for development

INTRODUCTION – Tell them what you're going to tell them

- Restate the topic generally, then mention the overall problem in your country.
  It is one of the sad realities of modern life that ... . In my country, for example,...
- State simply which two areas you would focus on if you were in a position of power:
  If I were in charge, ... / If I were the Secretary (Minister) of Health, I would focus on ...

MAIN BODY (Paragraphs 2 and 3) – Tell them

- Begin each paragraph with a clear topic sentence announcing the problem. For example:
  Paragraph 2: *The question of ... is probably the greatest problem facing public health in .. today.*
  Paragraph 3: *The second problem I would address is the fact that ...*
- Develop the first half with an analysis of the problem. Use a series of links such as:
  It is well-known that ... . I find this totally unfair because ... . It also implies that ... .
  or *This is especially true ... . All too frequently ...*
- Shift to second part of paragraph using a clear transition link. Then go on to offer one or more solutions supported with reasons, examples and results. Use a series of links such as:
  If I were in charge, I would make it my highest priority to ... . I would also ... .
  or *If it were up to me, I would strive to ... . This would lead to ... . I would also look into ... .*

CONCLUSION – Tell them what you told them

- Summarize by restating the main problem areas and end, if you wish, by dramatically asserting your opinion that solutions exist, but the government must work harder to put them into effect:
  All things considered, ... / To sum up, ... / In short, ...
  It is my firm belief that with a little extra effort the government could ... .

TOPIC 2 – Parents Who Push Their Children to Succeed **For and Against (Type 3)**

A Before you begin

1. Discuss the good and bad effects of parental pressure on children who:
   - have athletic, artistic or musical ability
   - don't like attending language lessons
   - are intelligent but don't like to study
   - get excellent grades at school

2. List negative aspects of parents pushing their children to succeed, plus notes on how to elaborate.
   a) ....
   ....
   b) ....
   ....
   c) ....
   ....

3. List positive aspects of parents pushing their children to succeed, plus notes on how to elaborate.
   a) ....
   ....
   b) ....
   ....
   c) ....
   ....

B Suggestions for development

INTRODUCTION – Tell them what you're going to tell them

- Begin by stating the fact that is mentioned in the question.
  There is no doubt that ... / It is an undeniable fact that many parents ...

- If you wish, pose a rhetorical question and say that there are no easy answers. For example:
  Is it right for parents to do this? As with many things in life, there is no easy answer.

- State simply that the situation has both negative and positive implications:
  Parental pressure can certainly have ... effects on children, but it may also ...

MAIN BODY (Paragraphs 2 and 3) – Tell them

- Begin each paragraph with a clear topic sentence. For example:
  Paragraph 2: *On the negative side, when children are pressured to succeed, they ...*
  Paragraph 3: *On the other hand, parental pressure also has a positive side.*

- Develop with a series of 2-4 aspects, using links and elaboration where necessary:
  Firstly, ... This is because ... Secondly, ... For example, ... In some cases, this causes...

CONCLUSION – Tell them what you told them

- End by weighing up both sides and expressing your opinion. For example:
  To sum up, it is clear that ... In many respects, it's a question of degree: too much pushing can ... , but a gentle push in the right direction can ...

FINAL TEST 7

TOPIC 1 – Lying

Narrative (Type 1)

A Before you begin

1. Discuss the difference between little "white lies" and big "blatant untruths."

2. Exchange stories about lies you have told. Use these hints to organize your thoughts:
   - Establish the background: ie, explain the circumstances that led up to the telling of the lie.
   - Narrate the events that led up to the telling of the lie and how you felt when you told it.
   - Tell what happened after: eg, Did you get caught? Did you regret telling the lie?
   - Say what you learned from the experience.

   As you listen, think of ways to improve each story. Does it contain enough detail and elaboration?

3. Discuss the meaning of the following expressions. Could any be incorporated into your story?

   the moment of truth
   be caught in a lie
   lie through one's teeth
   live a lie
   honesty is the best policy
   the truth will out
   fall for something hook, line and sinker
   be caught red-handed

B Suggestions for development

INTRODUCTION – Tell them what you're going to tell them

- Restate the topic in your own words.
- If you wish, use rhetorical questions to lead in to your story. For example:
  But what about a big "blatant untruth"? Are we ever justified in telling one of those?
- Suggest answer to rhetorical questions by referring to story and the lessons to be learned:
  If "yes" is your answer, you might want to think again when you read ....

MAIN BODY (Paragraphs 2 and 3) – Tell them

Paragraph 2:
- Establish the background and narrate events leading to the lie, using time links where possible.
- Close with the telling of the lie and a statement of how you felt after telling it.

Paragraph 3 and subsequent paragraphs, if needed:
- Tell the second part of the story, using time links where appropriate.
- Summarize what happened at the end and relate back to the theme of lying.

CONCLUSION – Tell them what you told them

- Conclude by looking back at the experience and saying what you learned. Use links such as:
  In retrospect, ... / With hindsight, ... / In the final analysis, ... / At the end of the day, ...
- If you wish, finish up by referring to quote in topic or another expression in A3 above:
  In the end, I learned the hard way that "Honesty really ***is*** *the best policy."*

TOPIC 2 – **Distance Learning** **For and Against** (Type 3)

A Before you begin

1. If you had your choice (and money was not a problem), would you get a degree via distance learning or by attending classes at a regular college or university? Why?

2. Discuss whether or not you would recommend distance learning to these interested individuals:
   a young mother with two pre-school children *a full-time teacher, married, wanting Masters*
   a bright 20-year-old confined to a wheelchair *a full-time bank clerk, single, wanting a BA*

3. List the major advantages offered by distance learning, plus notes on how to elaborate.
   a) ....
   ....
   b) ....
   ....
   c) ....
   ....

4. List the drawbacks of distance learning, plus notes on how to elaborate.
   a) ....
   ....
   b) ....
   ....
   c) ....
   ....

B Suggestions for development

INTRODUCTION – Tell them what you're going to tell them

- Restate the topic in a sentence or two, using a standard introductory phrase. For example:
  There is no doubt that ... / It's an undeniable fact that ... / Nowadays more and more ...

- Pose problem in the question and follow with clear reference to advantages and disadvantages:
  But for all the publicity distance learning has received, it's safe to say that ... .
  Before enrolling, one should consider the advantages and disadvantages.

MAIN BODY (Paragraphs 2 and 3) – Tell them

- Begin each paragraph with a clear topic sentence announcing advantages or disadvantages.

- Develop with a series of 2–3 points, elaborating where possible and using links such as:
  Firstly, ... This means that ... . It is also beneficial for... . The second advantage is ...
  To begin with, no one should underestimate ... . There is also the fact that ... .
  This could become a major problem if ... . Finally, distance learners would miss out on ...

CONCLUSION – Tell them what you told them

- Summarize by weighing both sides and expressing your opinion.

- Consider closing with a thought-provoking comparison between distance learning and the traditional university experience ... or with one or two pieces of advice for potential enrollees.

FINAL TEST 8

TOPIC 1 – Role Models

Narrative (Type 1)

A Before you begin

1. Using the categories below, list people who have been role models for you over the years.
   Close relative: ....
   Teacher / coach: ....
   Public figure (athlete, singer, actor, etc): ....

   Has your admiration for these people decreased or increased as you have become more mature?

2. Exchange stories about one of your role models. Use these hints to organize your thoughts:
   - Say who the person is/was and briefly describe how your fascination/admiration began.
   - Give examples of what you admired about the person.
   - Say how your relationship and/or your perception of the person developed over time by briefly describing one or more incidents.
   - Say how you view the person now and what lasting influence he/she has had on you.

   As you listen, think of ways to improve each story. Could more detail and elaboration be added?

B Suggestions for development

INTRODUCTION – Tell them what you're going to tell them

- Introduce the topic by saying that you, like many of us, have had role models. For example:
  Like all children, I went through passing phases of wanting to be like ... .

- List a few examples from A1 above. Then announce the person, explaining briefly who he/she is.
  First there was ... . / Then ... . / Others ... , but no one inspired my admiration / captured my imagination like [name of role model + brief explanation].

MAIN BODY (Paragraphs 2 and 3) – Tell them

Paragraph 2:
- Establish background (eg, how you met / how you first became aware of the person). For example:
  I was roughly 10 years old when "X" ...
  "X" has played a major role in my life since ...
  For as long as I can remember, "X" ...
  "X" was born in ...

- Say what first fascinated you about the person and give examples of what you admired:
  Something immediately attracted me ... . He / she had a kind of .... He / she also had ...

- Briefly describe the key incident or event that resulted in the person's becoming your role model.

Paragraph 3:
- Narrate what happened over the course of time, using time links where appropriate.

- Discuss whether the person's influence faded or became stronger as the years have gone by.

CONCLUSION – Tell them what you told them

- Sum up by looking back on the relationship and discussing the person's long-term influence on you.
  In retrospect, ... / With hindsight, ... / Looking back, I now realize that ...
  There's no doubt in my mind that "X" will continue to inspire me because ...

TOPIC 2 – 21st-century Challenges **Problem/Solution (Type 2)**

A Before you begin

1. The topic asks you to discuss two problems that face young people today. Brainstorm with the class and list as many as you can think of. Here's some to get you started:

automation	*depersonalization of society*
dwindling natural resources	*crime*

2. Working alone or in groups, narrow the list to four problems and make notes as to how you would develop each challenge with reasons, examples and possible solutions. Exchange ideas with the rest of the class and jot down any interesting suggestions.

3. Now review your notes and decide which two areas have the best potential for development.

B Suggestions for development

INTRODUCTION – Tell them what you're going to tell them

- Restate topic in your own words.
- If you wish, pose a rhetorical question that leads into your opinion statement. For example:
  What are the most important challenges that young people face?
- State your opinion by announcing your two choices. Use a clear "opinion" transition, such as:
  If I had to decide, ... / If it were up to me, I would say ...

MAIN BODY (Paragraphs 2 and 3) – Tell them

- Begin with a topic sentence stating your choice and, if you like, the start of your elaboration:
  Paragraph 2: *Probably the most pressing challenge that young people face is ... , which will lead to ...*
  Paragraph 3: *A second major challenge is the fact that ... due to / because of ...*
- Develop the first part of each paragraph with an analysis of the problem, using links such as:
  In other words, ... A case in point is the fact that ... . To make matters worse, ...
  or *It is well known that ... . This is especially true because ... . It also implies that ... .*
- Shift to second part of paragraph with a clear transition statement, using linking phrases such as:
  In order to prepare themselves for this, ...
  or *To overcome this problem, ...*
- Finish with one or more suggestions, elaborated by restatement, reasons, examples and/or results.

CONCLUSION – Tell them what you told them

- Summarize by contrasting the century's exciting potential with the problems it poses. For example:
  To sum up, while the coming century presents ... , it also holds out the challenge of ... .
- Finish with a dramatic restatement of the fact that if steps are taken, the problems can be overcome:
  However, if ... [summary of main solutions] ... , the future should be ... .

Speaking Tests

WHAT TO EXPECT

The ECPE Speaking Test is designed to allow candidates to demonstrate their speaking ability by taking part in a five-stage task between two or three candidates and two examiners. (The three-candidate format is used only if there is an uneven number of candidates present at the testing center on the day of the test.)

The test consists of an introductory phase followed by a four-phase decision-making task. The stages are designed so that the candidates have a chance to speak individually as well as to engage in discussion. During Stages 1 and 5, one of the examiners will participate in the discussion. During Stages 2, 3 and 4, however, the candidates will do all of the talking related to the task. Examiner involvement in Stages 2, 3 and 4 is limited to giving instructions and, if necessary, answering questions that relate to the instructions.

Stage 1: Introduction and Small Talk (3–5 minutes)

This stage of the test is an ice-breaker activity designed to help candidates relax and get used to speaking with each other. When candidates enter the room, Examiner 1 begins with introductions and then initiates a conversation with the candidates on one or more general topics. Candidates are expected to take an active part by providing detailed responses and, if the opportunity arises, to ask each other and Examiner 1 questions. Topics might include:

school	family	hobbies	interest	vacation plans
work	friends	hometown	ambitions	travel

Stage 2: Summarizing and Recommending (5–7 minutes)

After briefly introducing the task, Examiner 1 hands each candidate an information sheet. Candidate A's information sheet contains two options; and Candidate B's information sheet contains two different options, for a total of four options. (In the three-candidate format, there is a total of six options.) Each option has 5–7 bullet points describing the option's strengths and weaknesses. Candidates are then given 2-3 minutes to read over their own information sheet.

Candidate A begins by summarizing his/her two options, while B listens. When A finishes, B offers a recommendation as to which of the two options is better.

Next, Candidate B summarizes his/her two options, while A listens and then makes a recommendation about B's two choices.

Finally, both candidates silently consider the recommendation they have received and decide for themselves which of their two options they prefer and why.

NOTE: During Stages 2 and 3, candidates are NOT permitted to see their partner's information sheet. For this reason, candidates are permitted to take notes, if they wish, to help them remember key points.

Stage 3: Reaching a Consensus (5–7 minutes)

Candidates A and B take turns reporting to each other which of their own two options they think is best. Then, together, they compare and contrast the options they have chosen until they come to an agreement on one single option.

Stage 4: Presenting and Convincing (5–7 minutes)

The goal of Stage 4 is for the candidates to present and justify their choice to Examiner 2, who takes on the role of a person of relatively high status: eg, a school principal or company director.

First, the candidates are given 2–3 minutes to work together and plan a short presentation justifying the option they decided on. Each candidate should present two different reasons in support of their choice. At this point, candidates may look at each other's information sheets if they wish.

Then the candidates present the option and their reasons to Examiner 2.

Stage 5: Justifying and Defending (5–7 minutes)

In this stage, Examiner 2 questions the candidates about the decision they have made. Together, the candidates justify and defend their decision.

HELPFUL HINTS

General

- The examiners are rating you on your ability to take part in an extended conversation. This means that, where possible, you should support your ideas with reasons and not just answer with a word or two. Throughout the task you should try to be as expansive as possible.
- Candidates are expected to contribute equally to the speaking activity, so try not to be either too dominant or too passive. If you sense your partner is hesitant to speak, be sensitive to this and ask his/her opinion after you finish speaking to help the conversation move forward.
- Remember to make eye contact with your partner and the examiners when they are involved in the task. It helps if you don't stare constantly at your information sheet and you keep your hair out of your eyes.
- Don't panic if you make an occasional mistake. Remember that fluency and your ability to make yourself understood are more important than 100% accuracy.

Stage 2

- As you begin the task, remember that there is no set answer; all four options are possible. In the end, the examiners are more concerned about the appropriateness and quality of the language you produce as you and your partner go through the process of narrowing down the choices and justifying your choice to the examiner.
- When you describe the options to your partner, try to summarize the list of features in your own words instead of just reading what is on the information sheet.
- You will not be allowed to look at your partner's information sheet during Stages 2 and 3, so when it's your turn to listen, you may want to take notes to help you recall what was said.

Stages 3–5

- Try to use a variety of strategies when you compare and contrast the options. For example, you could present the strengths of one of the options while focusing on the weaknesses of the other. Or you could begin by pointing out the advantages of both, and then examining the disadvantages. Doing this will allow you to use a wider range of functional language for speech events: eg, considering both sides of an argument, stating opinions and preferences, making generalizations, expressing doubt and certainty, and so on. (For a list of common expressions, see "Fluency Builders" on page 208.)
- After presenting your opinion, it's always a good idea to invite your partner to comment on your ideas with phrases like "What do you think?" or "Do you agree?" This shows that you are making a conscious effort to include your partner and that you are taking an active role in developing the conversation.
- When building on what your partner or Examiner 2 has said, it's also a good idea to begin by acknowledging what was just said with polite phrases of agreement or disagreement. For example, "I totally agree because …" or "That's a good point, but I think we should also consider …" .

PAGE GUIDE TO SPEAKING TESTS

FLUENCY BUILDERS – Common linking expressions to use when speaking

Expressing an opinion
To my mind, ...
As I see it, ...
It seems to me that ...
Personally speaking, ...
In my opinion, ...
If it were up to me, I'd say that ...
I feel strongly that ...

Recommending
I recommend choosing X instead of Y because ...
I'd suggest that you choose X over Y since ...
Perhaps you should/ought to consider ...
I'd advise you to choose X because ...

Stating preferences
I think X is much better qualified than Y.
I prefer ...-ing to ... -ing
There's no comparison. I'd much rather ...
To be honest, I'd prefer to see ...

Giving reasons / justifying
I say this because ...
The main reason for my saying this is that ...
One of the reasons I decided on X is that ...

Sequencing your ideas
Well, for one thing ...
Another thing is that ...
I also believe that ...
What's more, ...
Finally, ... / Last but not least, ...

Considering both sides
On the one hand, ... On the other hand, ...
Some people might say that ... , but others say ....
Although it's true that ... , it could also be argued that ...
One way to look at the situation is to ... But you might also say that ...
It's true that ... , but there's also a downside/a major disadvantage to ...

Making generalizations/conclusions
All in all, ...
On the whole, ...
Finally, ...
To sum up, ...
When all is said and done, we think that ...

Expressing certainty
Without a doubt, I'd say that ...
I'm certain/positive that ...
There's no doubt in my mind that ...

Expressing uncertainty
It's a bit hard to say, but ...
I suppose that ...
My guess is that ...
It's possible that ... , but ...
I'm not sure, but if I had to say one way or the other ...

Asking for clarification
Would you mind repeating that, please?
I'm sorry. What do you mean by ... ?
I'm sorry, I didn't quite catch/get that.
Sorry, I'm not sure I understood. Do you mean ... ?

Adding clarification
What I mean is, ...
What I'm trying to say is that ...
In other words, ...

Agreeing with partner/examiner
I totally agree. To my mind, ...
I'd have to go along with you there because ...
I'm strongly in favor of that as well because ...
You're quite right. That's exactly how I feel.

Politely disagreeing with partner/examiner
I'm not so sure about that because ...
I'm afraid I don't totally agree. I say this because ...
Perhaps there's another way to see it. In my opinion ...
I see it a bit differently. You see, ...

Acknowledging partner's/examiner's input
That's an interesting point. What I think is that ...
Well, it's a bit difficult to say but ...
I've always thought that myself.
Do you really think so? What about ...
Well, I suppose you've got a point, but ...
That's very interesting, but in my opinion ...

Fillers to avoid long awkward gaps
Just a second ... / Hold on a sec ...
Hmm, it's on the tip of my tongue ...
Umm - as I was saying ...
What's the word I wanted ... - oh, yes ...
You know, uh ... ,

SPEAKING TEST 1 Candidate A

Hiring the Director of the Institute of Environmental Studies (IES)

Hillary Carlton

This is a list of points about Ms. Carlton.

- Ph.D. in environmental science
- Taught environmental science at a small college for 10 years
- Published articles in several scientific journals
- Active in Greenpeace protests during college
- Enjoys scuba diving and rock climbing
- Little administrative experience

Barry O'Mara

This is a list of points about Mr. O'Mara.

- Master's degree in ecology
- Environmental director at local nuclear power plant for past 3 years
- 2 years as research coordinator in national park
- Good at getting people to work together
- Enthusiastic organic gardener
- 4 different jobs in past 10 years

SPEAKING TEST 2 Candidate A

Choosing the Best City for New Café Olé Coffee Shop

City 1

This is a list of points about City 1.

- Population: over 8 million
- More than 50 Café Olés in the city
- Location in busy neighborhood with no Café Olé
- Rent: $15,000 per month
- Average income in area: $60,000 per person
- Insurance, taxes and other expenses will be high

City 2

This is a list of points about City 2.

- Population: 30,000
- Home to large university with 20,000 students
- Only 2 coffee shops in area, both family-owned
- Location in downtown area near university
- Rent: $5,000 per month
- Area is economically depressed

SPEAKING TEST 3 Candidate A

Choosing a Proposal for a New Museum of Science and Industry

**PROPOSAL 1:
Museum with Ultramodern Design**

This is a list of points about Proposal 1.

- Design by famous architect Frank Gehry
- Looks like different-sized boxes randomly stacked on top of each other
- Cost: about $70 million
- Exhibit space: 40,000 square feet
- Building site in downtown area surrounded by tall buildings
- Design too "far out" for many in community

**PROPOSAL 2:
Museum Housed in Renovated Factory**

This is a list of points about Proposal 2.

- Renovation will preserve look of old factory building
- Design reflects the historical aspect of the museum
- Cost: about $40 million
- Exhibit space: 50,000 square feet
- Located in old industrial sector near river
- In depressed area 5 miles from city center

SPEAKING TEST 1 Candidate B

Hiring the Director of the Institute of Environmental Studies (IES)

Joseph McCann

This is a list of points about Mr. McCann.

- Master's degree in business administration
- Majored in biology in college
- Fund-raising director/wildlife charity (10 years)
- 3 years as a high-school biology teacher
- Likes to hunt and fish in spare time
- Said to be difficult to work with at times

Suzanne Rich

This is a list of points about Ms. Rich.

- Bachelor's degree in environmental studies
- Assistant director at IES for last 3 years
- Popular with other employees at IES
- Active in clean-up program for local river system
- Leads walks for local birding group
- Only has about 6 years' work experience

SPEAKING TEST 2 Candidate B

Choosing the Best City for New Café Olé Coffee Shop

City 3

This is a list of points about City 3.

- Population: 2 million
- Location in large shopping mall outside city
- Mall popular with people from city and several nearby towns
- One other "big-name" coffee shop in mall
- Rent: $8,000 per month
- Aging population, shortage of workers in the 25-30 age group

City 4

This is a list of points about City 4.

- Population: 50,000
- No Café Olés in this city
- City in southern resort/vacation area
- Waterfront location a popular warm- weather tourist attraction
- Rent: $10,000 per month
- Business falls off during the low season, with few tourists

SPEAKING TEST 3 Candidate B

Choosing a Design for a New Museum of Science and Industry

PROPOSAL 3: Classical-Style Museum

This is a list of points about Proposal 3.

- Traditional Greco-Roman style design
- Easily recognized as a museum
- Cost: about $60 million
- Exhibit space 35,000 square feet
- Building site next to public park
- Too old-fashioned; need something more "21st century"?

PROPOSAL 4: "Green" Museum

This is a list of points about Proposal 4.

- Series of small circular buildings connected to one another
- Energy efficient and built with recycled materials
- Cost: $30 million
- Exhibit space: 25,000 square feet
- Building site near harbor with ocean views
- Design not interesting enough, too small?

SPEAKING TEST 4 Candidate A

Choosing the Best Project for a Local Community Service Club

Thrift Shop

This is a list of points about the thrift shop.

- Would sell used clothing and other articles at reasonable prices
- Town without a thrift shop for 10 years
- Could support itself through sales
- Staffed by volunteers
- Profits would go to local community center (or other project)
- Need to find someone to donate or rent storefront at low price

Children's Library

This is a list of points about the library.

- Donated and new books for kids aged 2-12
- No children's library in community (lack of government funds)
- Local businessman willing to donate a site
- Staffed by volunteers, 3-5 p.m. weekdays and 10 a.m.-3 p.m. Saturdays
- Would offer special programs (eg, story hours, kids' book clubs)
- $5,000 initial investment needed to fix up site

SPEAKING TEST 5 Candidate A

Choosing a Guest Speaker for a Charity Fund-Raising Dinner ($500 a Plate)

Vince Lorenzo

This is a list of points about Vince Lorenzo.

- Popular comedian/musician
- Frequent national TV appearances
- Humorous presentation with serious message and music
- Would attract many people from the community
- Speaking fee: $3,000 (usually $5,000)
- Some guests may take offense at his jokes

Millicent Van Huff

This is a list of points about Millicent Van Huff.

- Professor of anthropology at local university
- Husband a wealthy businessperson
- Contributed $100,000 to this organization last year
- Speech with photo presentation about recent travels to remote area of New Guinea
- Would not charge a speaker's fee
- Topic too boring?

SPEAKING TEST 6 Candidate A

Choosing Which Municipal Project to Cancel Due to Budget Crisis

New Stadium for Soccer Team

This is a list of points about the new stadium.

- Modern stadium with seating capacity of 20,000
- Old stadium unsafe and unsanitary
- Cost of repairing old stadium 2/3 cost of new stadium
- Would bring new business and tax income to city
- Possibility that team may move to another city
- Potential savings: $190 million

New Commuter Train Line to Suburban Towns

This is a list of points about the new train line.

- New line serving two suburban towns
- Need for more public transportation in this area
- Would reduce traffic and need for new roads
- Would stimulate business by bringing more people into city
- Will be more expensive to build in future
- Potential savings: $230 million

SPEAKING TEST 4 Candidate B

Choosing the Best Project for a Local Community Service Club

Soup Kitchen

This is a list of points about the soup kitchen.

- Would offer one free meal (dinner) each day
- Could use kitchen and dining room of local community center
- Food from donations, local food programs, restaurants, etc.
- Staffed by volunteers from community
- Would need one paid part-time administrator
- Requires permits from city in order to serve food

After-School Club for Teens

This is a list of points about the teen club.

- Would offer tutoring services and fun activities
- Would help keep teens off the streets and out of trouble
- Offer of large space for the club from local church
- Staffed by volunteers with knowledge of school subjects
- Would need paid part-time administrator
- Would require constant fundraising

SPEAKING TEST 5 Candidate B

Choosing a Guest Speaker for a Charity Fund-Raising Dinner ($500 a Plate)

Senator Sam Beck

This is a list of points about Senator Beck.

- Currently serving in Washington as senator for state
- Known for his work on human rights issues
- Helped to convince Congress to fund charity
- Speech entitled "Human Rights – A Global View"
- Speaking fee: $1,500
- Topic too political?

Jean Hall

This is a list of points about Jean Hall.

- Champion Paralympic wheelchair racer
- Has been in wheelchair since childhood
- Good reputation as an inspirational speaker
- Speech titled "Work Hard for Your Dreams"
- Speaking fee: $2,000
- Topic too personal?

SPEAKING TEST 6 Candidate B

Choosing Which Municipal Project to Cancel Due to Budget Crisis

New Water Purification Plant

This is a list of points about the water purification plant.

- Good site for plant next to large river
- Area often suffers water shortage in summer
- Would provide healthier, sure water supply
- Needed to accommodate future growth of city
- Would benefit all citizens
- Potential savings: $300 million

New Fine Arts Center

This is a list of points about the new fine arts center.

- Includes art museum and concert hall
- Strong need for more cultural facilities in city
- Would provide good support for city schools
- Magnet for well-known artists and performers
- Building design of lasting architectural value
- Potential savings: $250 million

SPEAKING TEST 7 Candidate A

Deciding on Best Way for Small Hotel to Spend $2,000 Advertising Budget

Launch a Professionally Designed Website

This is a list of points about launching a website.

- Professionally designed with text and photos
- Would allow users to see rooms and book online
- Accessible to large numbers of people around the world
- Easy to update
- Long-lasting form of advertising
- May not reach important business contacts

Create a Brochure

This is a list of points about Mr. O'Mara.

- 1,000 copies, professionally designed and printed
- Offers more control over who receives the information
- Distribute to local tourism agencies
- Mail to relevant people in the area
- Send to publishers of travel and hotel guides
- Need to reprint and update from time to time

SPEAKING TEST 8 Candidate A

Choosing the Winner of a High-School Science Fair

Bob White

This is a list of points about Bob's science project.

Hypothesis: Plants exposed to magnetic field will grow taller.

- Designed own experiment with carrot seeds
- Used proper controls and variables
- Created graphs to show results
- Reported other research on similar experiments
- Found no difference in plants exposed to magnets
- Lacked confidence and clarity in oral presentation

Rita Rose

This is a list of points about Rita's science project.

Hypothesis: Windmill with 45° blade angle generates most electricity.

- Built model windmill with fan as a wind source
- Tested blade angles of 25°, 45°, and 75°
- Used charts and graphs to illustrate results
- Proved hypothesis incorrect; 75° most efficient
- Didn't report on other similar research
- Oral presentation clear and competent

SPEAKING TEST 7 Candidate B

Deciding on Best Way for Small Hotel to Spend $2,000 Advertising Budget

Hire a Freelance Writer

This is a list of points about hiring a freelance writer.

- Would write press releases for local newspapers
- Would write two articles with photos to submit to travel magazines
- Can reach large audience, both local and beyond
- Would provide ample info about hotel and area
- Targets information to appropriate audience
- No guarantee that articles will be published

Place Ads in Local Weekly Newspaper

This is a list of points about placing ads in the local newspaper.

- 4 quarter-page ads, one a week for 4 weeks
- Paper widely read by local business people
- Easy to design and produce
- Can mail copies of ads to contacts outside the area
- Wouldn't provide as much information as other forms of advertising
- Would only run for one month

SPEAKING TEST 8 Candidate B

Choosing Winner of High-School Science Fair

Janet Markham

This is a list of points about Janet's science project.

Hypothesis: Listening to Mozart improves ability to memorize lists

- Designed experiment with 28 classmates as subjects
- Used control groups and a controlled environment
- Reported research on similar experiments
- Found that listening to Mozart improved memory in over 50% of subjects
- Didn't include charts or graphs showing results
- Gave interesting and lively oral presentation

John Bigelow

This is a list of points about John's science project.

Hypothesis: With higher levels of carbon dioxide (CO_2), trees will grow more quickly.

- Used data from experiment at a professional research center
- Analyzed data; confirmed hypothesis is correct
- Created detailed graphs/illustrations for each stage
- Wrote comprehensive report; posed questions for further research
- Student's father a scientist at the research center
- Seemed insecure during oral presentation

Notes